LOVE AND LOVE SICKNESS

ALSO BY JOHN MONEY

The Psychologic Study of Man

Sex Errors of the Body: Dilemmas, Education, Counseling

Man and Woman, Boy and Girl: The Differentiation and Dimorphism of Gender Identity from Conception to Maturity (with Anke A. Ehrhardt)

Sexual Signatures (with P. Tucker)

EDITED BY JOHN MONEY

Reading Disability: Progress and Research Needs in Dyslexia

Sex Research: New Developments

The Disabled Reader: Education of the Dyslexic Child

Transsexualism and Sex Reassignment (with Richard Green)

Contemporary Sexual Behavior: Critical Issues in the 1970s (with Joseph Zubin)

Developmental Human Behavior Genetics (with W. K. Schaie, E. Anderson, G. McLearn)

Handbook of Sexology (with Herman Musaph)

Traumatic Abuse and Neglect of Children at Home (with Gertrude Williams)

LOVE AND LOVE SICKNESS

The Science of Sex, Gender Difference, and Pair-bonding

JOHN MONEY

Professor of Medical Psychology,
Associate Professor of Pediatrics
The Johns Hopkins University

THE JOHNS HOPKINS UNIVERSITY PRESS: BALTIMORE AND LONDON

The Johns Hopkins University Press, Baltimore, Maryland 21218
The Johns Hopkins Press Ltd., London

Originally published, 1980
Second printing, 1981

Johns Hopkins paperback edition, 1981

Library of Congress Cataloging in Publication Data

Money, John William, 1921–
  Love and love sickness.

  Bibliography: pp. 230–42
  Includes index.
  1. Sex differences (Psychology)   2. Sex differences.
3. Sex (Psychology)   I. Title.
BF692.2.M65   155.3   79-3679

ISBN 0-8018-2317-X (hardcover)
ISBN 0-8018-2318-8 (paperback)

TO C.B. AND C.R.
AND TO H.T.

Contents

Preface

There is in my memory a clear image, dated 1972, of waiting for an elevator in a hotel in Stockholm, talking, and having quite unexpectedly in my mind the idea that the final outcome of the discussion Margaret Mead and I were then concluding would have to be a book. I would have to write it, and its title would have to be *Love and Lovesickness.* The discussion that produced this title had to do with a subcommittee report we had worked on for the conference we were attending, one of a series on stress. The published proceedings of the conference constitute the book, edited by Lennart Levi, *Society, Stress, and Disease,* Volume 3, *The Productive and Reproductive Age—Male/Female Roles and Relationships.*

It is fairly obvious that love and lovesickness as phenomena of scientific study belong to the science of sexology. It is perhaps less obvious that they belong also to a science for which the new term, genderology, is needed. Sexology is very much concerned, in the final analysis, with the interconnectedness of what goes on between the groins and between the ears relative to procreation of the species. Procreation, however, though the ultimate or irreducible criterion of sex difference, is not the only one. In addition to sex-irreducible differences, there are sex-derivative and sex-adjunctive differences and, especially in behavior, differences which are sex-arbitrary. These latter are products of historically arbitrary cultural coding of roles on the basis of genital sex. Some of these arbitrary codings apply to work, play, schooling, and legal rights. They are so far removed from genital sex that it is scientifically confusing to designate them as sex-role differences. Confusion is avoided if there are two terms, sex role and gender role. Gender role is the umbrella term. Genital and erotic sex roles are subsumed under it, as are also all nongenital and nonerotic roles that are classified as male or female, as in the wearing of sex-classified clothing.

Herein lies the explanation for the two terms, sexology and gender, in the chapters of this book. They accurately reflect the fact that the book's chapters cover the full range of sex differences from making a baby to learning mathematics. All behavior that is sex-classified or sex-coded, regardless of its genesis, ultimately impinges on pair-bonding and the failure or the success of men and women in their relationships together.

For help in the preparation of this book, I would like to acknowledge the work of Helen Cutler and Mary Kerber.

Introduction

Lovesickness is widely recognized as that condition which ensues when a lover who is separated, however briefly, languishes, mopes, and pines for the beloved. The lovesick mind becomes distracted from its other duties and commitments and is preoccupied instead with an hypertrophy of desire and longing for the beloved. There is no sense of well-being except in the presence of the lover, who thus holds extraordinary responsibility and wields inordinate power over the life of the other. Once you have become part of the mental furnishings of your lover's mind, there you stay forever trapped and unable to engineer your own escape. The consequences can be very profound, either for joy or suffering.

The suffering becomes intense when love becomes so one-sided that one of the partners leaves and rejects the lovesick call for reunion. Then lovesickness becomes a broken heart. Lovelorn suffering is intense. It is like the grief of bereavement. Such melancholy may become laced with rage that escapes in retaliation dreams or nightmares of homicidal and suicidal jealousy. Sometimes the dreams become real-life dramas.

Lovesickness of a second type usually underlies the one-sided breakup of a love affair. This type may also be called sick love. It signifies that the two partners were mismatched to begin with, lacking the correct degree of mutual reciprocity that would keep their love in balanced equilibrium for a long time. They were destined never to establish a durable state of pair-bondedness. Had they known more about pair-bonding, they might never have fooled themselves.

There is every good reason for more people to have more knowledge about pair-bonding. It lies in the fact that a baby becomes bonded to both a father and a mother. Thenceforth, for the remainder of its life, the son or daughter is unable to divorce either parent. Parents may divorce one another, but not their offspring. When they divorce, the children always suffer in some degree the trauma of a broken relationship. Separation and divorce are prevalent among today's families

(Chapter 6). Around 50 percent of each year's marriages end in divorce, and for teen-aged marriages the rate is around 80 percent. The children of divorce are matched by those whose mothers did not divorce because they did not marry in the first place. There are over a million teen-aged pregnancies in the United States each year. More than half the mothers keep their babies, but fewer than half who do so have the baby's father living with them.

The long and short of these statistics is that there are too many millions of children living in one-parent households in too many of which they pay, in consequence, too large a price in psychosocial and psychosexual pathology. No society can afford to meet the bill of so much pathology, to say nothing of the extra cost added by families in which pathological feuding persists without separation or divorce.

Everywhere one hears shibboleths about the sanctity and preservation of the family as the corner-stone of society. Yet the evidence everywhere is that the institution of the nuclear family is flawed—and the children suffer. Here alone lies sufficient justification for a new and serious examination of how people become sexually-erotically pair-bonded, and how this pair-bondedness relates to the formation and continuity of high-caliber family life. Here lies also a justification of the entire new discipline of sexology.

Sexology has a unique qualification in biomedical research and in clinical medicine. It is the specialty in which the patient is not the single individual but the partnership, or couple, even when one of the pair is in absentia or present only in the imagery of fantasy. The closest analogue is in pediatrics, wherein many problems, from child abuse to anorexia nervosa, prove to be problems of family psychopathology for which the treatment is incomplete unless it is family therapy. There is, as yet, no hospital or medical school in the New World or the Old that has its own complete, fully staffed, and autonomous department of sexology. There are a few sexological institutes and an increasing number of sex-therapy clinics, but they do not serve the same function in a medical school or hospital as would a full and administratively independent department of sexology.

Lacking an academic base, sexology has developed haphazardly and in piecemeal fashion as an adjunct of such other specialities as obstetrics and gynecology, population dynamics, endocrinology, urology, psychiatry, and neurosurgery. These are all specialities in which, traditionally, etiology, diagnosis, and treatment are directed toward only one person, the patient. Thus they have no tradition of the etiology, diagnosis, and treatment of the sick partnership, and they have no basic science of pair-bonding.

The therapeutic professions need a science of pair-bonding. So also do population policy planners. But those most in need of a systematic knowledge of pair-bonding and its aberrations are pair-bonders themselves—that is to say, all of us. This is a book for people everywhere who are interested in the perpetuity of romance and the love affair that progresses into marriage and a family life that safeguards the healthy development of their children.

Durable pair-bonding is not a blossom found only on the time-honored tree of a monogamous marriage contract "until death do us part," and it does not depend on rigidly coded and sex-stereotyped conduct for men and for women. In fact, the very rigidity of sex-coded roles becomes anachronistic and can itself prevent durable bonding, given the history of cultural change that is imperative in a dynamic, growing society. Thus it is anachronistic for people to become fanatical about preserving sex stereotypes, asserting that it is the biological difference between men and women that dictates their legal, occupational, and recreational inequality. Pair-bonding can take place perfectly well between a man and a woman who are equal in intellect and in verbal, mathematical, or any other type of achievement—not willy-nilly, between any man and any woman picked at random, for durable pair-bonding is never willy-nilly. It is always a matter of reciprocal matching. A change toward greater equality of the sexes will not be achieved at the sacrifice of love. It will not increase the prevalence of lovesickness and broken homes. Quite the contrary! It will enable more people to become well-matched. In doing so, greater equality of the sexes will require new social formulas whereby parenting and childcare can be shared by both parents, but not at the expense of their being vocationally penalized or obliged to sacrifice career advancement.

Lovesickness that flourishes on mismatching and pits a couple against one another in the power struggle of a chronic adversary relationship, even if they do not break up, is a negative social heritage for children. It does not automatically guarantee that these children will become victims of the same sort of lovesickness themselves, as adults, but it certainly increases the chances. Thus the sickness is perpetuated across the generations. The effect is particularly pernicious when those who have the syndrome achieve positions of social and political power in their adult careers. From the seats of power, they disseminate the disease even more widely by endorsing antisexualism legislatively and in the judicial system. They become the agents of sexual dictatorship, intolerant of sexual dissidence. They are enemies of sexual democracy. Their problem and ours is that we are really a lovesick society, still not recovered from the plague of the Inquisition.

History of Concepts
of Determination
# of Sex

FROM MYTH TO SCIENCE. In all the millennia of humankind's habitation on earth, there was until this century no better explanation of the behavior of the sexes in mammalian mating than in the folk wisdom that it was inherent or innate. Early in the history of animal domestication, castration of the male, since it changed mating behavior, somehow implicated the testes, but there was no knowledge of how the testes exerted their hormonal influence on masculine mating until the mid-nineteenth century.

For only three centuries has there been knowledge of the nature of the male's contribution to fertility in mammalian conception. The year 1977 marked the 300th anniversary of Antoni van Leeuwenhoek's 1677 report to the Royal Society of London, describing the first observation of spermatozoa.

The mammalian egg was first visualized under the microscope even more recently, for it was in 1827 that Carl Ernst von Baer published his report, "De Ovi Mammalium et Hominis Genesi." Only then did humankind dispel the myth of male pregnancy envy, namely, that the female is reproductively no more than an ambulatory womb designed to incubate the miniscule homunculus begat there by the male—a myth that still lingers on in the folk saying that the duty of a wife is to bear her husband's children for him.

Two millennia before Leeuwenhoek, Aristotle proposed that male semen contributed a vital force that shaped and molded the embryo from menstrual blood in the female. Quoting Homer, he also allowed that mares could be made pregnant by the wind (air being one of the four basic elements in early Greek thought, and the one universally shared by all species that breathe). Aristotle also believed in the spontaneous generation of some species, as well as asexual reproduction in others. He stated his ideas on sex determination of the embryo with reference to sheep and goats: that if they submit to the male when north winds were blowing, they were apt to bear males; if when south winds were blowing, females.

Galen, in the second century A.D. accepted the doctrine of Herophilus that women as well as men produce semen, but that it is discharged in the menstrual flow. Galen's explanation for sex determination was that from the right testis of the male is secreted semen from which another male is generated, and from the left testis, a female. Hermaphrodites result from the simultaneous mixing of semen from both testes.

When Avicenna wrote in the eleventh century, he bypassed theories of sex determination that attributed the sex of the embryo to the strength of the seed, or to the relative amounts of male and female semen, and espoused a modification of Galen's right-left theory. Avicenna proposed that male semen put into the right side of the uterus gave a male, the left a female, and the middle a hermaphrodite.

The right-left theory, with females always sinistral and inferior, was not finally disposed of until the mid-eighteenth century when the Swiss physician Albrecht von Haller put it to an empirical test. He reported the case of a man with only one testis who had offspring of both sexes. He reported also male fetuses that had been found on the left side of the uterus and a woman with no right uterine tube who had given birth to both a boy and a girl.

There was no theory of sex determination to take the place of the discredited laterality doctrine until the twentieth century. In 1902, the Philadelphia zoologist, Clarence I. McClung, published in the *Biological Bulletin* his report on "The accessory chromosome: sex determination," in which the chromosomes that would eventually become known as the sex chromosomes, X and Y, were shown to determine whether the egg and sperm, once joined, would differentiate as male or female. The now well-known formula is that the XX genotype differentiates as female, and the XY as male. The way in which the genotype translates itself into embryogenesis still remains largely a mystery, except that it governs whether a testis or an ovary will differentiate from the primordial, un-differentiated anlagen. The newest contribution to the solution of this mystery is the 1976 discovery of H-Y antigen (a Y-chromosome-induced histocompatibility antigen) by the New York immunologist, Stephen B. Wachtel. H-Y antigen is believed to adhere to the surface of all male mammalian cells, including the original Y-bearing sperm of fertilization. In the course of normal embryogenesis, it is held responsible for pro-graming the cells of the undifferentiated gonadal anlage into a testis.

Differentiation of the testis begins at the sixth week of embryogenesis, whereas, in the case of the ovary, the neutral or undifferentiated phase persists for another six weeks.

FETAL ENDOCRINOLOGY. The next phase of the differentiation of the phenotype is masterminded neither by sex chromosomes nor by H-Y antigen, but by hormones. Demonstration of what would eventually become known as the endocrine function of the testes dates from John Hunter's demonstrations at the end of the eighteenth century of the transplantation of a testis from a cock donor into a hen recipient; and from 1849 when Arnold A. Berthold replicated Hunter's experiment by transplanting testicular tissue into capons (Chapter 11). Hunter and Berthold produced the first clearcut experimental evidence of the existence of a substance, internally transmitted, that influenced sexual characteristics, and paved the way for the eventual discovery of the role of sex hormones in the sexual differentiation of the embryo. The vehicle of this discovery was the freemartin, a bovine hermaphrodite long known to farmers. Freemartins were the subject of another study by the eighteenth-century physician, John Hunter. He recognized that the freemartin always has a male twin, and is itself a female maldeveloped as a hermaphrodite. An etiological explanation of this hermaphroditic condition was developed by the Canadian-American, Frank R. Lillie, in 1916, and simultaneously by K. Keller and J. Tandler in Europe. In brief, masculinization of the freemartin's gonads, internal reproductive ducts, and accessory glands were attributable to male hormones secreted by the testes of the co-twin and transmitted to the freemartin through anastomosed blood vessels in the two fused chorions.

There are some aspects of the freemartin phenomenon that remain to be elucidated, but not those that relate to the theory of the hormonal induction of sex differentiation. This theory has been supported by an explosion of empirical research that still has not lost its momentum. The definitive studies elucidating the role of fetal hormones on embryonic and fetal sex differentiation are those of Alfred Jost in Paris. In the 1950s, Jost perfected the extremely delicate technique of surgically castrating embryonic rabbits in utero, without destroying them and without terminating the pregnancy. His experiments demonstrated conclusively that secretions from fetal testes are all-important in programing the differentiation of a male. Without testes, embryos of each genetic sex, XY as well as XX, differentiate a female morphology. An XX embryo without ovaries also differentiates a female morphology as well as it does with them: the primordial wolffian ducts vestigiate instead of proliferating into male internal structures; and the primordial mullerian ducts proliferate and differentiate into uterus and fallopian tubes. It is not yet known whether hormones from the mother or from the placenta may play a role in the differentiation of female morphology, and it is self-evidently impossible to get rid of these hormones without destroying the pregnancy.

There are two secretions from the fetal testis that program the differentiation of a masculine morphology. One is known only as the mullerian-inhibiting substance. Its function is to vestigiate the primordial mullerian ducts. Its failure allows a morphologic and gonadal male to be born with a fully formed uterus and fallopian tubes—a rare but not unknown occurrence in the human species.

The other fetal testicular secretion that regulates masculine differentiation is testosterone, the androgenic hormone that is usually called male hormone, but wrongly so, since it is routinely found in the female as well as the male, though in much lesser quantities. In fetal life, masculinizing proliferation of the wolffian ducts into the internal accessory structures of the male is dependent on androgen. Usually, the androgen is testosterone from the fetal testis; but other physiologically active androgens from other sources are equally effective—for example, from an androgen-secreting tumor in the pregnant mother. Experimentally, in animals, androgen can be injected into the pregnant mother, with consequent masculinization of a daughter fetus. In human beings, the most common spontaneously occurring masculinization of a daughter fetus occurs in the adrenogenital syndrome (Chapter 3). This is a genetically recessive condition in which malfunction of the fetal adrenocortical glands produces a flood of adrenocortical androgen powerful enough to masculinize the genitalia.

This masculinization includes the external genitals. When complete it results in the birth of an XX female with two fertile ovaries internally and a penis and empty scrotum externally. The converse of this spontaneously occurring condition in the XY fetus is known as the androgen-insensitivity syndrome, in which the baby is born as an XY girl with a normally formed female vulva instead of a penis and scrotum. The etiology is a genetically transmitted defect in the cellular usage of androgen. All the cells of the body can use only estrogen, not androgen. Hence the feminization of the genital morphology.

Fetal hormonal masculinization extends beyond the morphology of the reproductive organs to include pathways in the central nervous system. In the 1940s and '50s, Geoffrey W. Harris in England developed the new field of neuroendocrinology, from which has developed the even newer one of psychoneuroendocrinology, pioneered by William C. Young in Kansas, in the 1950s.

In mammalian neuroendocrinology, it is now well established that pathways of the hypothalamus and nearby limbic system of the brain immediately adjacent to the pituitary gland respond to fetal androgen. In the four-legged mammals that have estrous cycles, the effect of androgen is to change the cyclic biological clock of the hypothalamus so that it will forever function in the noncyclic fashion of the male. In the menstruating primates, the cyclic clock is not turned off forever, according to present empirical evidence, but it may be affected so as not to start on time.

FROM HORMONES TO BEHAVIOR. Androgen influences not only the differentiation of the biological clock of the hypothalamus but also other nearby neural pathways that mediate the behavioral dimorphism appropriate to the cyclic phases of fertility. The principle involved, nicknamed the Adam principle, is the same as governs the differentiation of the genital anatomy, namely, that to differentiate a male something must be added. In the present instance, the addition of androgen in fetal life has a threshold effect: it lowers the threshold for the ultimate emergence of sexually dimorphic behavior more commonly observed in males than in females; and, vice versa, elevates the thresholds for behavior more commonly observed in females. To illustrate: parental care of the young is sex-shared behavior, but it is threshold-dimorphic insofar as it is less readily evoked in males than females. Even in the rat, a species in which hormones exert more power than learning in governing sexually dimorphic behavior, repeated exposure of the adult male to the stimulus of a litter of helpless young will finally unlock the parental behavior of nesting, retrieving the pups, and hovering over them. In the mother, by contrast, such behavior is released almost instantaneously (Chapters 9, 10).

In human beings, the Adam principle does not preordain masculinity versus femininity of behavior in a rigid or absolute way. Rather it creates a tendency or disposition that may be incorporated, on the basis of sex or, in the broader sense, of gender, into either a masculine or feminine postnatal phase of the dimorphic differentiation of behavior. In this postnatal phase, social learning is the dominant though not exclusive, mechanism of dimorphism of behavior differentiation, as it is also in the establishment of native language.

The two principles of postnatal differentiation of gender dimorphism of behavior (and its corresponding mental representations or schemas) are identification with persons of the same anatomic and assigned sex; and complementation or reciprocation to those of the other sex.

There is a high degree of neonatal plasticity with respect to gender-dimorphic differentiation of behavior. This accounts, no doubt, for the range, variety, and paradoxes of gender-related behavior in human beings. It also accounts for the degree of freedom that one has in assigning the sex of a baby with a birth defect of the sex organs, as in the various forms of hermaphroditism and in micropenis.

There are two current schools of thought with respect to sex assignment in cases of genital birth defect. One is reductionist and is based on a faulty belief that there is an ultimate, absolute, and irreducible determinant of all sex differences—formerly, this ultimate determinant was the gonadal sex, then the chromosomal sex, and now, no doubt, the H-Y antigen will have its day.

The converse of the reductionist point of view is the constructionist. It is based on the belief that, when there is discordance among the variables of sex, there is no absolute criterion by which to dictate the sex of assignment of a genitally defective baby. Rather, one works to construct the best possible concordance among the discordant variables. Thus, it is useless to assign as a boy a baby whose phallic organ will forever remain too small to function as a copulatory organ, irrespective of hormonal and surgical intervention. The logic of common sense dictates that one should aim to rehabilitate the person in its entirety, and not to rehabilitate the laboratory results or the organ system taken out of the context of whole-person humanism.

Epistemology and Principles

NATURE/NURTURE. In the history of thought about human sex differences, there is a venerable tradition of explaining differences on the basis of dichotomous either/or principles. In the nineteenth century, a favored dichotomy was heredity versus environment, or somewhat more broadly termed, nature versus nurture. For example, in order to explain the paradox of homosexuality, namely erotic pairing with a person of the same genital morphology, nineteenth-century theoreticians resorted to the doctrine that there is a hereditary or inborn form of homosexuality and an acquired or learned form. By implication, if not explicitly, it was assumed that the inborn form could not be changed, whereas the acquired form might be. There is a covert tautology in this assumption, however, for the unchanging form of homosexuality was defined as inborn simply because it did not yield to pressures to change. Correspondingly, the changeable form of homosexuality was defined as acquired, precisely because it did change. To be more precise, this changeable form should have been defined not as homosexuality, but as bisexuality. Homosexuality of the type that is actually one of the alternations of bisexuality is the homosexuality that most of the nineteenth-century doctors who wrote about it would have been familiar with since school days. It is the type of homosexuality that emerges when postpubertal boys and young men are sex-segregated academically or occupationally. They have only other boys with whom to relate erotically and sexually, the only alternative being no erotic partnership at all. Once they become desegregated, they are able to establish a partnership with a female, which typically they do.

The change from a homosexual to a heterosexual partnership is easily attributable to free will or voluntary choice, whereas it is actually no more than an acceptable alternative, usually more acceptable than the prior homosexual pairing. The weighting in bisexuality (Chapter 5) may be 50:50, but it is more likely to be disproportionate, as for example, 60:40 or 80:20. In writings on homosexuality today, the concept of voluntary choice is still resorted to, as in the often repeated claim that the homosexual can be "cured" if he is properly motivated and really wants to be. Of course, one can define motivation deterministically, but most people who use the concept define it not deterministically but teleologically.

MIND/BODY. The teleological doctrine of voluntary choice versus the deterministic doctrine of involuntary imperatives in the etiology and prognosis of homosexuality rests on the bipolarity of mind and body, which is another of the venerable dichotomies to which we have been the philosophical heirs since before Plato and before the Bible. It pervades all thinking about human sex differences—and much else in human behavior as well. To claim the body for science and leave the mind for the Church, Descartes in the seventeenth century invented the myth of the pineal gland as being the seat of the soul. It was a politically useful myth in its time, but it has left us with bipolarity of mind and body which, good intentions notwithstanding, students of human beings and their behavior have not been able to unipolarize. The problem is that a proclamation about the unity of mind and body is not enough. What is needed is a new vocabulary and a new idiom in which to express the unity of mind and body. Then all statements will be made about this unity, and people will not be confronted with the temptation to make one the cause of the other, or to explain each with a different causality.

In today's thinking about sex differences in behavior—or more precisely about sexual dimorphism of gender identity/role (G-I/R)—the old dichotomy of mind and body is very much with us, more often in disguised than open form. Things that belong to the body are likely to be categorized as nature: inherited, genetic, innate, constitutional, biological, organic, physiological, instinctual—and somehow given status as being more scientific and deterministic, more basic, and also more respected. It is more stigmatizing to have a sexual problem that is classified as psychosexual rather than organic, for example. Things that belong to the mind are more likely to be characterized as nurture: environmental, acquired, cultural, and learned, and somehow as less scientific, more trivial, more teleological, and less esteemed. There has always been in psychology in general, and in the specialty of sex differences, a hidden doctrine that if something is acquired or learned, it is easy to shed. Yet, this doctrine is no more true in psychology than in embryology or infectious disease. Everything that is acquired, if it affects behavior and mental life, does so because first of all it affects the brain and its workings. There is a biology of learning and memory. Everything that is learned is encoded in the human brain, if it is learned at all. It is, therefore, as much a part of biology as any workings of the human brain that are programed-in not by learning, but by, say, genetics, or toxins, or experimentally manipulated neurotransmitters.

The politics and the science of sex differences is wide open for reexamination and reformulation today as, in the new age of birth control, the old stereotypes are being attacked as part of the liberation movement. So it is that people everywhere are questioning what it is about masculinity and femininity that is innate versus acquired; what is biological versus what is not (whatever it is that is nonbiological is another issue); what is given or instinctive versus what is learned; and what is organic versus what is cultural.

Most of the time, these questions cannot be given a satisfactory answer, because they are unsatisfactory questions. They are unsatisfactory questions precisely because they are based on the assumption of a split between mind and body and all that this implies.

A 2×2×2 TEMPLATE. It is in order to avoid such unsatisfactory questions, and in the hope of providing more satisfactory answers, that the outmoded dichotomies are left aside in this book and replaced with new ones. The number of new ones is three, and each pair is not independent, but is interdependent with the other two pairs. In tabular presentation, as in Table 2-1, they form a 2×2×2 template juxtaposing the

Table 2-1. Examples of sources of G-I/R dimorphism in a 2×2×2 classification

		Nativistic	Culturistic
Phylographic (Species-shared)	Imperative	Menstruation, gestation, lactation (women) vs. impregnation (men).	Social models for identification and complementation in gender identity differentiation.
	Adventive	Population size. Fertility rate. Sex ratio.	Population birth/death ratio. Diminishing age of puberty.
Idiographic (Individually unique)	Imperative	Chromosome anomalies, e.g., 45,X; 47,XXY; 47,XYY. Vestigial penis. Vestigial uterus. Vaginal atresia.	Sex announcement and rearing as male, female, or ambiguous.
	Adventive	Getting pregnant. Breast feeding. Anorexic amenorrhea. Effects of castration, drugs, infections, toxins.	Gender-divergent legal status, parenting, work, play, ornamentation.

phyletic versus the idiographic; the nativistic versus the cultural; and the imperative versus the adventive or adventitious. It is a template that can be applied to an indefinite number of aspects of human behavior, not only to the dimorphically sexual.

Phylographic determinants of sexually dimorphic behavior are those that are programed into all of us by reason of our being members of the species, homo sapiens. They are species-shared. Idiographic determinants are not programed into all members of the species, but are the product of individual biographies (which begin at conception, and have a nine-month history already at birth). An idiographic determinant may be unique to a single individual, or it may be shared by other individuals who may or may not be related in space and time. Phylographic and idiographic determinants may each be either nativistic or culturistic, and they may be either imperative or adventive.

Nativistic means that a determinant is native to a person; it could be called natalistic, except that it is more broad in scope, insofar as to be native does not necessarily entail being actually present at birth. A nativistic characteristic may be inborn and may not manifest itself until later, and then only if the correct trigger or releasing agent is present. Culturistic means pertaining to culture in the sense defined in cultural anthropology, which in the broadest sense encompasses all of the ecology or environment. Plants, animals, water, and minerals are part of a people's culture, as well as are their artifacts and immaterial customs and habits.

An adventive or adventitious determinant (hereinafter referred to also as an adventitia) is one among two or more possible alternatives, regardless of where or how it originates. An adventitia may be systematic and regularly present, or it may be fortuitous, accidental, and arbitrary. Adventitia include those that are the product of human decisions and those that are not.

Culture itself, contrary to popular misconception, is an imperative—a phyletic imperative or species necessity—and not an adventitia in the differentiation of G-I/R. An individual human being cannot differentiate a G-I/R without exposure to culturally transmitted sexually dimorphic behavioral stimuli. The analogy is with native language. Just as there are many native languages in the world, so also there are many native cultural contents or traditions that will satisfy the phyletic imperative for G-I/R differentiation as masculine or feminine.

In the old way of thinking, which Table 2-1 is designed to replace, culture was always juxtaposed against biology, or even more narrowly against the biologically innate. People still seek for fundamental, irreducible determinants of sexually dimorphic behavior and expect them all to be exclusively biological—given to the organism by some ultracultural endowment, so to speak. This expectation, to reiterate what is written above, masks a completely wrong definition of biology insofar as learning itself qualifies as a biological phenomenon. Whatever an individual learns from his culture and assimilates into his/her own G-I/R, the learning or assimilation takes place only because it becomes part of the biology of memory, that is to say, part of the biology of the brain. The same expectation masks also a completely wrong definition of learning, insofar as learning is not an ephemera, here today and gone tomorrow. There is some learning that becomes so indelible that it maintains the same tenacity, once programed into the functioning of the brain, as do other brain functions that were programed by the genotype, or prenatally by hormones or other brain chemistries.

The other side of the coin of culture as imperative rather than adventive is nativism as adventive rather than imperative. That is, something that is native to the organism may be an adventive and not an imperative and inevitable dictate of biology. From the point of view of the recipient individual, personal choice or planning may be as inapplicable when a nativistic determinant is adventive as when it is imperative.

Used empirically, the $2 \times 2 \times 2$ template requires that people interested in the determinants of sexual dimorphism of behavior approach the issue in an etiological or developmental way. For any given type of sex-different behavior, the greatest likelihood is that there will be no single determinant, but rather that it will prove to be multivariately determined, and the residual product of a developmental sequence contributed to by multiple components or subdeterminants. There is no place here for simple—one almost wants to say simple-minded—and dogmatic, one-on-one causal explanations.

DIMORPHISM, GENDER, AND BEHAVIOR. The three classes of determinants of the $2 \times 2 \times 2$ template are used in this book in the analysis of phenomena which, in much of today's professional literature, are termed sex different or sex-role typed. In this literature, one often has the impression that human beings are constructed like dolls, with nothing between their legs, and that sex exists where sex roles are learned, and only learned, between the ears, like writing on the proverbial blank slate. Here, in this book, the preference is for a different terminology that allows for conjunction of sex between the legs as well as the ears, namely, dimorphism of G-I/R. Gender-dimorphic behavior is an acceptable near-synonym. The erotic/sexual component of G-I/R is more or less synonymous with psychosexual status.

The dual term, identity/role, safeguards the unity of the phenomenon and prompts the user not to slip into the anachronistic habit of splitting mind and body by allocating identity to the mind and role to the body.

One's own personal gender identity is, to all observers except oneself, an inference. It is inferred by the observer from that which one expresses in vocal language and body language. These two behavioral sources of information constitute one's gender behavior (provided behavior is construed broadly enough to include language and such doings or happenings as blushing, or being smelly). Gender behavior, which includes language behavior, and gender role are equivalent. Strictly speaking, each is less inclusive than identity/role, because of the inferential nature of identity, which is more complex than is its manifestation in behavior.

Identity and role are opposite sides of the same coin. Identity is private and subjectively experienced. Others must base their knowledge of your identity on how it manifests itself in what you say or don't say, and what you do or don't do—in other words, on the role you personally live in interaction with others. Your role is not a script that was handed out to you, as a role is given to an actor by a playwright. It is your own personal compilation, put together during the course of your development, from various social and cultural inputs.

G-I/R encompasses anything and everything that has to do with behavioral and psychologic differences between the sexes, no matter whether the differences are intrinsically or extraneously related to the genitalia. Sex-irreducible, sex-derivative, sex-adjunctive, and sex-arbitrary roles (Chapter 7) all are subsumed under the concept of G-I/R.

It is erroneous to follow the example of some writers who juxtapose sex and gender, allocating sex to the body and what they call biology (as if there is no biology of the mind!) and gender to the mind and social learning, apparently unmindful of the biology of learning. In correct usage, gender is a more inclusive term than sex—a kind of umbrella that shelters sex as a manifestation of anatomy and of civil status as well. Sex is a term that needs to be reserved to signify that which pertains to the genitals and their functions, for there is a shortage of vocabulary to accommodate precision and accuracy in communication.

There are various components of G-I/R: erotic, procreational, parental, vocational, recreational, ornamental, legal, and so on.

Using erotic sexuality as a criterion of classification, one can speak of a heterosexual, bisexual, or homosexual G-I/R, each with its own variety of manifestations. It is also possible to speak of a paraphilic G-I/R, specified according to type, as in the expression, sadomasochistic heterosexual G-I/R, and so on.

Dimorphism is a term borrowed from embryogenesis and morphology and applied here to identity/role and to behavior—a usage that is rapidly spreading and being universally accepted. The term is needed because the sexual system, and all that it entails, is the one system of most organisms, the human organism included, that not only develops or matures but also, in so doing, differentiates two forms, male and female (except for special intersexual anomalies), both morphologically and behaviorally.

TELEOLOGY AND PRIMARY DATA. There is an emphasis throughout this book on behavior rather than on thoughts and feelings. The reason is pragmatic: if you can't see, hear, touch, smell, or taste it, then there is nothing about another human being that you can know, the claims of the occult notwithstanding. The primary data of gender dimorphism or sex difference, like the primary data of all the sciences, must be registered through the senses and perception into the cognition and knowledge of the observer. Tastes, smells, and touches are not much utilized in the study of gender dimorphism today, though tomorrow they may be. Today, most of one's raw data can be captured on videotape—what the subject said, and the body language that accompanied the spoken language. The videotape will tell you what the subject disclosed regarding his thought, imagery, fantasy, memory, motivation, feeling, or emotion, but it will not tell you anything about those entities directly. They are inferential constructs, and the inferences one makes about them are on the basis of what the subject said and did. Their value as inferential constructs in organizing one's raw data varies with the task at hand. Their value as causal or explanatory scientific constructs is nil, for which reason they are not so used in this book.

It is not part of the Zeitgeist of our time to repudiate motivations, feelings, and emotions as prime movers and power sources of the doings of humankind. The alternative is alleged to be a mechanistic kind of robotry. But that simply is not so. It is possible to identify dynamics of interaction in the behavior of two (or more) people together and to discover regularities in these dynamics. Within a single individual, one may similarly identify dynamic relationships between prior and present behavior, the prior behavior being in contemporary memory storage, regardless of how easily it can be retrieved. In this case, any other participant is represented in absentia.

Motivations, feelings, and emotions, insofar as one might identify them subjectively and solipsistically, do not exist sui generis. They always have a cognitive component, insofar as they are known at all, as well as being conative and affective. If they do not, then they exist only as inferential postulates, hiding in the unconscious or the biosubstrate, like volcanic steam building up pressure to escape, catalogued into sets or hierarchies of instincts, drives or needs. They can be multiplied at will. All that is needed to make a mockery of motivation theory is to add the suffix -*ivity* to any verb, in order to have a new drive. This exercise reveals a remarkable etymological phenomenon: -*ivity* needs a Greek or

Latin stem on which to graft itself in order to sound correct. Thus it is that in motivation theory one does not invoke, for example, fightivity to explain aggression, but aggressivity can be used to account for fighting. Adjectives that end in *-al* can also serve well by having *-ity* suffixed. Thus, sexuality, orality, anality, genitality can be used to explain play, dreams, and thoughts, but there is no playality or playivity, dreamality or dreamivity, thinkality or thinkivity to explain anything. Anglo-Saxon, Old Norse, and Old French etymological roots do not permit this intellectual game.

Of course, one can modify the language with neologisms, when theory so requires it. It is not obligatory to be trapped by linguistic habit. Yet the truth is that we are so trapped. In consequence, motivation theory is illogically haphazard in its formulations. It's only consistency is that motivation, like vitalism in biology, and like phlogiston in an earlier age of chemistry, is a teleological construct. Phlogiston is a good example of how teleological causes, like self-fulfilling prophecies, are self-proving and tautological. So, in biology, was vitalism. Evolution, in the shibboleth of survival of the fittest, can all too readily be misused in the same way. Motivation, likewise, is too slithery to be pinned down to empirical test. It forever remains, like phlogiston, a dogmatic postulate. It constitutes an embarrassment to psychology and the behavioral sciences, for it gives them special teleological status, thus removing them from the non-teleological universe of discourse used in other biosciences. The penalty of this isolation is intolerable in sexology, where it is imperative to formulate connections between behavior, hormones, neurotransmitters, brain pathways, the vascular system, genetics, anatomy, and the special senses.

It is for this reason that in this book there is no reliance on motivation theory as an organizing principle. There is no sex drive or sex instinct, and there is no need for them, though both terms are accepted as primary data in other people's self-reports. Everything that has to be said scientifically and professionally can be said better without them and without any sacrifice of the dynamics of a person's interaction with others. Motivation has served its term. Like phlogiston, it must be let go.

Gender
Identity/Role
(G-I/R)

G-I/R: DEVELOPMENTAL DIFFERENTIATION. Figure 3-1 is a flow chart that diagrams the developmental sequence of the differentiation of gender I/R, beginning with genetic dimorphism at conception and reaching completion with behavioral dimorphism in adulthood. Behavioral dimorphism, some critics might say, does not include what goes on in the privacy of the mind. Herein lies the issue of solipsism. Oneself, alone, is privy to what goes on in one's own mind. In the absence of its being overtly transmitted to other people behaviorally, that is to say, either in words or in body language, the content of one's mind remains forever covert and unknown to others.

There is no one-on-one correlation between gender-dimorphic behavior in adulthood and the gender-dimorphism of the genetic code transmitted at the moment of conception on the sex chromosomes X and Y. The same applies also to the H-Y antigen, the substance conveyed with the Y-bearing sperm and from it to all cells that carry the Y chromosome. Nonetheless, there is a certain inexorable logic whereby the ending is forecast at the beginning, provided nature's usual developmental routines are unimpaired and uninterrupted. That is to say, it is the person with a Y chromosome, the man, who is preprogramed for fertility as an impregnator; and the person, the woman, without a Y chromosome (having a second X instead), who is preprogramed for fertility as one who menstruates, ovulates, gestates, and lactates after the baby is born.

Every biology student now learns at school that the typical mature male carries in the cells of his body 46 chromosomes one of which is an X and the other a Y. That is, his genotype is 46,XY, and it has been that way since the moment when a Y-bearing sperm and an X-bearing egg

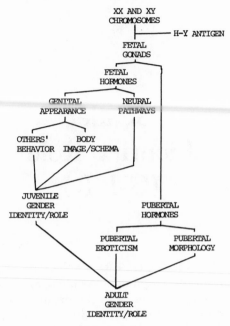

Figure 3-1
*Developmental sequence and differentiation
of gender identity/role (G I/R)*

fertilized each other. The egg provided by the mother is always X-bearing. It must be joined by an X-bearing sperm for the genotype to be 46,XX. This is the genotype of the typical mature female.

Nature exercises her prerogative and produces some atypical genotypes without invariably destroying fertility. A woman with the 47,XXX genotype, for example, may become pregnant; but a woman with 45,X (Turner's syndrome) cannot. Similarly, a man with the 47, XYY genotype may be fertile, though many such men are not. A man with the 47,XXY genotype (Klinefelter's syndrome) is sterile. Sterility in either men or women does not interfere with the behavior of attempting to create a pregnancy. It simply means that when one or both partners is sterile copulation does not result in pregnancy.

Nature exercises her prerogative to break her own rules not only with respect to deviating from the normally expected 46,XX and 46,XY genotypes, but at any phase in the sequence of sexually dimorphic differentiation. She can, and in fact sometimes does, break her own normative rules. Thus one cannot invariably forecast the ending by knowing the beginning. The expected correlations do not always occur. The exceptions are, as is so often the case in science, invaluable for the information they give about normal development.

In the normal development of gender dimorphism, dimorphism at one phase programs dimorphism at the next. The sex chromosomes play center stage for a brief moment of glory as they set the program for the differentiation of the primordial gonadal tissue into either testes or ovaries. The primordial gonads are, in effect hermaphroditic. If the core part differentiates first, under instructions from the H-Y antigen of the XY genotype, then the organ will become a testicle. Testicular differentiation begins at about the sixth week of embryonic life. If the genotype is XX, the primordial gonadal tissue remains undifferentiated for another six weeks, around which time the rind part begins to proliferate and become an ovary.

Once the testicles and the ovaries have come into being as anatomical organs, they hand over to the hormones that they produce the task of programing for sexual dimorphism. More accurately, it is the testis that makes this transfer of power, for at this phase of prenatal development the Eve principle takes precedence over the Adam principle. In other words, nature's first preference is to differentiate a female. Perhaps she utilizes female hormone provided by the mother or the placenta. There is no clear evidence one way or the other at the present time. What is clear is that without any gonadal tissue at all, and thus in the absence of gonadal hormones, a fetus invariably differentiates as a female—minus fertility, of course. To be able to differentiate as a male, a fetus must be supplied with hormones secreted by the fetal testes, or else with a substitute for them. This principle of adding something to differentiate a male has already been referred to aphoristically as the Adam principle.

The something added is actually two substances. The one that exercises the greater influence is androgen, the male sex hormone. The other is of a chemical composition still under investigation. It is known simply as MIS (mullerian inhibiting substance). Its assignment is to suppress, in a male, the growth and development of the mullerian ducts into a uterus and fallopian tubes. This suppression is necessitated because in nature's scheme of things all embryos, XX and XY, develop initially, so far as the internal sexual anatomy is concerned, as potentially hermaphroditic. The future girl and the future boy both have a pair of mullerian ducts and a pair of wolffian ducts (Fig. 3-2). In normal female differentiation, the mullerian ducts proliferate and the wolffian ducts vestigiate. For the male, the reverse holds true, and it is the wolffian ducts that proliferate. In order to do so, they require androgen.

The hermaphroditic potential of the mullerian and wolffian ducts sometimes becomes an actuality. For example, if MIS secretion fails in an

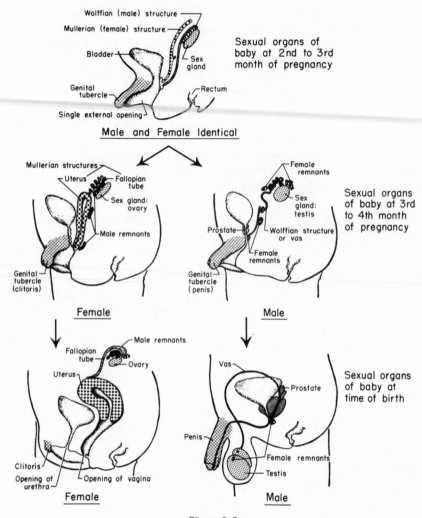

Figure 3-2
Differentiation of the internal
reproductive anatomy

XY embryo, but androgen does not, then the boy that is born has a uterus and fallopian tubes as well as the usual male anatomy. The condition is discovered when a lump or hernia in the groin proves to be produced by the mullerian organs as they follow one of the testicles in its descent into the scrotum. It is rare that the condition occurs without a parallel deficit or partial deficit in androgen production. In consequence, it is rare to find a uterus in an XY baby with a fully formed penis. More often the penis is incompletely formed and so ambigous looking that it cannot be distinguished from an enlarged clitoris.

Sometimes the same ambiguous differentiation of both the external and the internal genital anatomy occurs when the gonads are not testicles but themselves are hermaphroditic. That is to say, both gonads, or possibly only one of them, are constituted of a mixture of both testicular and ovarian tissues, for which reason they are known as ovotestes. In very rare cases, there may be an ovary on one side of the body, and a testis on the other; and among the very rare curiosities of medicine are at least two known cases of a person with two ovaries and two testes. Regardless of where the ovarian and the testicular tissues are situated, any case in which both coexist is, by nosological convention, diagnosed as a case of true hermaphroditism. By contrast, in male hermaphroditism there is testicular tissue only, and in female hermaphroditism, ovarian tissue only. Male and female hermaphroditism used to be known as pseudohermaphroditism, but today the shorter term is preferred. Today it is also recognized that hermaphroditic ambiguity of the sexual anatomy may exist when the gonadal tissue is dysgenetic, so that neither ovarian nor testicular tissue is present.

The counterpart of the 46,XY (male) hermaphrodite with well-developed, internal mullerian anatomy would, by the rules of logic, be the 46,XX (female) hermaphrodite with well-developed wolffian anatomy internally. In actuality, one finds not well-developed wolffian anatomy in female hermaphroditism, though there may be some development of a prostate gland. When the Adam principle prevails in an XX fetus, the external and not the internal sexual anatomy is most profoundly affected. Thus it is actually possible for a 46,XX female to be born with a penis and an empty scrotum externally, and two ovaries and a fully differentiated mullerian anatomy internally. There is no exact converse of this condition when the Adam principle fails in a 46,XY male, apparently because coexistent total failure of both MIS and androgen does not happen in the 46,XY embryo. When MIS fails and androgen does not, then a boy is born with a uterus and fallopian tubes (see above). When MIS does its work and androgen fails, then the baby is born with a vestigial or cord-like uterus, as well as vestigial wolffian structures internally, and with normal-appearing female external genitals. The gonads are testicular in structure but aspermatogenic and sterile. They may be undescended, or may appear as lumps in the groin. The vagina may be too short, for the innermost part, like the uterus, fails to differentiate. In teenage it can be lengthened by dilation. Etiologically, this condition is produced not by the absence of androgen, but by failure of the body's cells to use androgen. Hence the diagnosis:

androgen-insensitivity syndrome (formerly known as testicular feminizing syndrome) in 46,XY women or girls.

In the chronology of fetal sexual differentiation, the external organs are finished last. Here nature changes her earlier ambisexual or hermaphroditic plan of laying down the male and female anlagen together and then proliferating one set while vestigiating the other. For the external organs, the plan is to produce first a sex-neutral set of structures and then to differentiate them as either male or female (Fig. 3-3). The

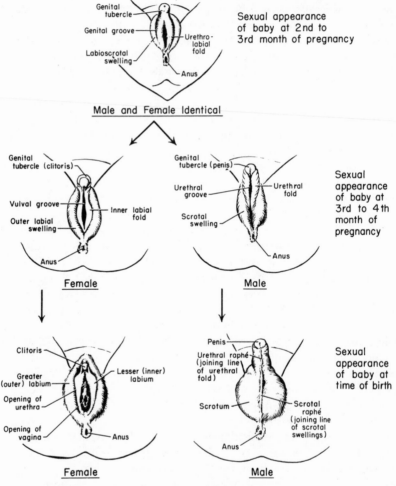

Figure 3-3
*Differentiation of the external
reproductive anatomy*

genital tubercle becomes either the clitoris or the penis. The flaps of skin, the urethrolabial folds that lie, one on each side of the open genital groove, in the female remain unfused as the hood of the clitoris and the labia minora. In the male they become the foreskin of the penis and, fused along the midline, the skin covering of the penis and its urethra. The labioscrotal swellings lateral to the urethrolabial folds remain separated as the labia majora in the female. In the male they fuse along the midline and, hanging down, form the scrotum.

The program for masculinizing the undifferentiated anlagen of the external genital anatomy is under the control of androgen. Under ordinary circumstances, the necessary amount of androgen exists only in an XY fetus. Nonetheless, if sufficient in quantity and properly timed, androgen can bring about the same degree of masculinization of the external genitalia of an XX, female fetus.

Experimentally, this masculinizing effect can be demonstrated in animals by injecting the pregnant mother with male hormone at the time the sex organs of the fetus are differentiating. The daughter will then be born with a penis instead of a clitoris. In human beings a similar effect has been reported, albeit rarely, when a pregnant woman happened to have an androgen-secreting tumor of the ovary or adrenal cortex. Cases of a daughter born with a penis and empty scrotum have also been known as a result of treating a pregnant mother with synthetic progestinic hormone in order to prevent a threatened miscarriage. The offending hormones, now no longer used, in rare and unexplained instances had a paradoxical androgenizing effect.

A daughter may be born with a penis also as a result of hormones produced by the fetus itself. This is what happens in the adrenogenital syndrome of female hermaphroditism, the commonest syndrome of masculinization of an XX baby. Usually the masculinization does not result in a normal-looking penis with a urethral tube, but in an organ that lacks a urethral tube, having instead an open gutter on its underside, with the urethral opening in more or less the female position (Figs. 3-4, 3-5, 3-6). Because of its great size, the organ may be called either an unfinished (hypospadiac) penis or a giant (hypertrophied) clitoris. In either case surgical feminization, if the baby is sex-assigned as a girl, is both feasible and successful. When the penis is anatomically normal, the baby's sex assignment may be that of a boy. There are also known cases in which a very large hypospadiac organ was successfully masculinized surgically.

The adrenogenital syndrome is a genetically transmitted condition. It is transmitted as a genetic recessive. That is to say, both parents must be "hidden carriers." Then there is a one-in-four chance at each conception that the baby will be an "open carrier." If so, then in fetal life the adre-

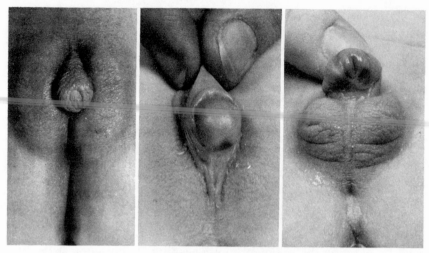

Figures 3-4, 3-5, 3-6
*Three cases of ambiguity of the external genitalia. In all three cases
the internal reproductive anatomy is female (adrenogenital syndrome).
However, the same external anomalies occur also in association with male
or mixed internal anatomy.*

nocortical glands erroneously produce not their proper product, cortisol, but a close biochemical relative that is sufficiently androgenic in physiologic action as to masculinize the external genitalia of the developing daughter-fetus.

PRENATAL HORMONES AND THE BRAIN. The Adam principle in prenatal life applies not only to the differentiation of the anatomy of the sexual organs, as already mentioned, but also to the programing of certain pathways in the brain. Had this statement been written before 1950 it would have qualified as scientific heresy. In those days, there was no accepted scientific knowledge, not even a well-acknowledged hypothesis, that sex hormones might have a direct influence on the masculinity or femininity of the developing brain. However, the basis for a good hypothesis had, in fact, turned up serendipitously as a spin-off from experiments by Steinach early in the century (Chapter 11) on producing hermaphroditic female guinea pigs by injecting the pregnant mother with the male sex hormone, testosterone. Shortly before World War II, another experimenter, Vera Dantchakoff, had noted in passing that her treatments of the same type had changed not only the anatomy but also the behavior of the hermaphroditic offspring. The destruction coincident with the war terminated these studies. The idea of a prenatal influence of sex hormones on the brain and hence on subsequent behavior lay dormant until the late 1950s, when it was pursued once again by William C. Young, then in Kansas.

Young and his coworkers embarked on replicating their predecessors' hermaphroditic experiments for the purpose of studying the outcome of prenatal hormonal manipulations on subsequent sexual dimorphism of behavior. The conclusion they drew from their investigation was that prenatal androgenization, even when it does not masculinize the external genitalia of the chromosomal female, does indeed affect mating behavior, namely, by metamorphosing it in the masculinizing direction. That is to say, whereas ordinary females show some mounting behavior, androgenized females show more of it, though not to the extent of ordinary males.

Speculating on their findings, Young and his group formulated the hypothesis that the changed behavior of their animals was secondary to a prenatal "organizing effect" of androgen on brain pathways that would subsequently mediate sexually dimorphic behavior. This hypothesis linked Young's hormone/brain/behavior ideas with the neurohormonal ideas released in the early 1950s as a result of the experiments of the neuroendocrinologist, Geoffrey Harris, in London. Harris and his coworkers had shown that there is a sex difference in the brain of adult male and female rats, specifically in the hypothalamus, immediately adjacent to the pituitary gland. An adult male's hypothalamus will forever function acyclically to program its pituitary gland to release a steady flow of gonadotropins—the hormones that stimulate the gonads—even if the pituitary gland is replaced by a transplant grafted in from a female donor. By contrast, an adult female's hypothalamus will forever function in cycles, to program even a transplanted male pituitary gland to release gonadotropins in cyclic surges. In this way, the ovaries also function in cyclic hormonal surges, producing the cycle of estrus in lower mammals, or the menstrual cycle in primates.

A subsequent experimental advance demonstrated it to be the brain cells of the hypothalamus that program the pituitary, insofar as they themselves secrete hormones—the releasing factors, as they are now called. Still another experimental advance demonstrated it to be during fetal life that the hypothalamus itself is sex-differently programed according to the Adam principle. That is to say, when the fetal hypothalamus is flooded with male hormone at the critical phase of development, it becomes masculinized and will remain so with respect to regulation of the pituitary's release of gonadotropin. In the absence of fetal androgen, the Eve principle takes over, and the hypothalamus forever works cyclically in its regulation of pituitary gonadotropin release.

With today's neuroendocrine technology, it is possible to begin to identify the hypothalamic cells, nuclei, and pathways involved in the release of neurotransmitters and releasing factors that program the pituitary's gonadotropins; it is also possible to begin to distinguish them from nearby nuclei and pathways through which the programing of associated sexually dimorphic behavior is routed. These behavioral pathways, like their pituitary counterparts, are subject to the Adam principle while they are being differentiated prenatally. Thus, if a chromosomal female is flooded with androgen at the critical prenatal phase, the subsequent sexual behavior as well as the pituitary function will be to some degree masculinized.

The experimental evidence from which the foregoing principles have been formulated has been obtained from rodents more than primates, and it is more detailed and complete with respect to hypothalamic/pituitary function than to hypothalamic/behavioral function. In primate sexuality, the precise way in which the hypothalamus affects behavior has not been directly demonstrated experimentally, and the same applies to any other regions and pathways of sexuality in the primate brain. For monkeys and human beings, the prenatal hormonal/brain/behavioral story is one in which the observed correlations are between prenatal hormones and postnatal behavior. The observations in both monkeys and humans parallel one another, and they both follow the Adam principle. That is to say, feminization takes priority, and something—androgen—must be added to induce masculinization of behavioral thresholds. The chromosomal sex of the baby is irrelevant. Because masculinization of behavior is not specifically correlated with the XY chromosome pattern, nor feminization with XX, a sex-chromosomal test by itself will not predict the extent to which the behavioral development of a boy or girl will be predisposed toward being stereotypically masculine or feminine, respectively.

Among the determinants (Fig. 3–1) that exercise their influence before birth, prenatal sex hormones hold what can be defined, on the basis of today's knowledge, as the key position. Prenatal sex hormones do not preordain the details of what will happen postnatally, but they do lay down a predisposition or threshold that feeds into postnatal programing of G-I/R and its differentiation as masculine, feminine, or mixed.

Prenatal sex-hormonal predispositioning takes place in the brain itself, particularly though not exclusively in the region of the hypothalamus. In experiments on rodents, the methods used are those of neurosurgical ablation of selected brain nuclei and pathways; brain stimulation with implanted microelectrodes and implanted microcannulae through which electrical current or hormones, respectively, are applied directly to brain cells, and measurement of the uptake by brain cells of radioactively labeled hormones injected into the bloodstream or directly into the ventricles of the brain. In prenatal studies, hormones injected into the pregnant mother cross the placenta and enter the fetus. The newborn baby may be given additional injections. The effects of prenatal and/or neonatal hormonal injections are ultimately evaluated in terms of what they do to brain structures; of how they influence pituitary-gonadal hormonal output at puberty; and of how they influence sexual functioning and mating behavior.

In monkeys, the effects of prenatal hormone injections on brain structures have not yet been evaluated, as the animals are scientifically more valuable alive than dead. Their long-term influence on delaying pubertal onset has been observed, as has their influence on sexually dimorphic behavior both before and after puberty. The effects on behavior come close to replicating those observed in human clinical studies, so that the monkey qualifies as an "animal model" for the study of some aspects of dimorphic human behavior.

If the monkey studies were repeated on human beings, the experiments would represent a complete abrogation of ethical responsibility. Experiments of nature, in the form of spontaneously occurring inborn syndromes are, therefore, utilized instead.

PRENATAL HORMONAL EFFECTS IN PRIMATES. Boys whose behavioral development does not conform to the traditional stereotype of boyishness may have been subject to a relative insufficiency of the Adam principle, prenatally—though it is also possible that their nonconformity is of postnatal onset only. The converse holds true for girls.

Boys who do not conform developmentally to the masculine stereotype are likely to be stigmatized as sissy, or as artistic, or sensitive. All these epithets are pejorative. By contrast, girls who do not conform developmentally to the feminine stereotype, but manifest instead some effects of the Adam principle, are not so stigmatized. They are called tomboys. Such is the sexism of our society that this term is not pejorative. Rather, it is congratulatory and carries less an implication that it is a fortuitous asset or talent than a product of androgynous intent or achievement.

Any time that an audience is told that tomboyism in girls who are known to have been prenatally exposed to an excess of androgen may be a delayed action effect of that prenatal androgenization on the central nervous system, there is certain to be a question that reopens the nature/nurture controversy. "If a baby is born with a genital organ that, even though ambiguous, looks like a penis," the questioner asks, "then won't the parents always expect their child to be boyish, and so condone boyish behavior, even though ostensibly rearing the child as a daughter?" The answer is that they may, but that there is an equal probability that they will react the other way, disciplining all manifestations of tomboyism and demanding conformity to the stereotype of orthodox girlish behavior. The issue probably never can be settled by empirical observations of family behavior alone, for one cannot hold constant all the other intertwining and interfering variables. In human beings, it is not possible to hold constant or even ascertain the amount of androgen to which the fetus has been exposed.

The issue need not, however, stay hanging in midair, forever unresolved, for there is a convergence of evidence pointing in the same direction regarding the effect of the Adam principle on the subsequent sexual dimorphism of behavior: the effect holds across species; the effect on monkeys and human beings is recognizably similar; and the effect is remarkably predictable, even in human beings, who are usually notoriously difficult to predict. In addition, there is a growing body of evidence that the reverse effect, namely, failure of the Adam principle, applies jointly to prenatal hormones and behavior. Here the necessary experiments on subhuman primates still have not been performed, and the human clinical population against which to test the hypothesis is sparse.

Experiments to test for the effect of the Adam principle on subsequent sexually dimorphic behavioral development in monkeys were first undertaken by William C. Young, Charles Phoenix, Robert Goy and their colleagues. At the outset, the pregnant mother is injected with testosterone, the male sex hormone, for several weeks, beginning early in the pregnancy, before the external genitals are differentiated. If the fetus is a daughter, and if the treatment does not produce a miscarriage, then the daughter will be born as a female hermaphrodite, that is, with a penis instead of a clitoris.

It is now generally agreed, on the basis of fieldwork studies, that monkey mothers inspect the genitalia of their babies with interest, and also they treat their sons differently than their daughters. Thus, there is in monkeys, even as there is in human beings, the same causal quandary as to which came first, the mother's or the baby's sex-differential behavior. No one has yet taken the step of fooling the monkey mothers by operating on the androgenized, hermaphroditic daughters, so as to feminize their genitalia immediately after birth. One may, however, take heart in the fact that even if the mothers do mistake their penis-bearing hermaphroditic daughters for sons, the baby grows up to behave not exactly like boy monkeys, but more like them than do ordinary, untreated daughters.

Experimental monkeys almost always live in cages like prison cells, so the varieties of behavior they manifest are more limited than if they were free-ranging in the wild. Within the constraints of this limitation the sexually dimorphic behavior of prenatally androgenized hermaphroditic female (46,XX) monkeys has been judged to be tomboyish, according to the criteria of an increased prevalence (for a daughter) of initiating play, and of engaging in rough-and-tumble play, chasing play, threatening play, and sexual-rehearsal play involving not only mounting but mounting with foot-clasping the partner's legs. Except for mounting, the manifestation of tomboyism in the play of infancy and early childhood faded with the approach of puberty. Mounting led to intromission and the appearance of ejaculation (but with no ejaculatory fluid) on at least one occasion.

ADRENOGENITAL SYNDROME IN GIRLS. Among human beings, the key group of people for obtaining information about the prenatal workings of the Adam principle with respect to postnatal sexually dimorphic behavior are chromosomal (46,XX) females with the adrenogenital syndrome (see above).

Before 1950, there was no known treatment for the adrenogenital syndrome. Girls with the condition were, therefore, foredoomed postnatally as well as prenatally to inhabit a body that virilized like that of the ordinary adolescent boy—except that it did so prematurely, with signs of virilizing puberty in evidence from even as early as age three. Thus, in earlier generations of adrenogenital women, it was not possible to sift out the effects of prenatal from postnatal hormonal masculinization.

The cortisol (or cortisone, to use the term favored earlier) era of treatment began in December 1949, when at both the Massachusetts General Hospital in Boston, and The Johns Hopkins Hospital in Baltimore, the first adrenogenital patients were given this newly synthesized adrenocortical hormone. Cortisol proved to be the hormone that their own adrenocortical glands could not make. Given in replacement doses, cortisol did the work that the adrenocortical glands could not do. It induced the glands to cease laboring in vain to make cortisol and thus to cease producing the faulty androgenizing hormone that they had been secreting in its place. Thus, since 1950, there has grown up a generation of adrenogenital girls who were hormonally masculinized before birth, but who from infancy onward grew up with further masculinization held under control by cortisone substitution therapy. Early corrective, feminizing surgery ensured that their genital morphology, as they grew up, did not look abnormal.

The girls of this first generation of early-treated adrenogenitalism shared in common, as they grew up, the features of behavior that go by the name of tomboyism. They regarded themselves with pride as tomboys and were recognized as tomboyish by their friends and family. They engaged in play activities that involved a prevalence of outdoor, athletic energy expenditure. They gravitated toward competitive team sports of the type that are traditionally considered the prerogative of boys. They liked boys to permit them to play on their baseball, football, and other teams, but they did not become dominant or assertive to an extent that would not be tolerated by boys. Though they were not timid in self-defense, they were not assaultive or violent, nor aggressive in the sense of picking a fight in order to improve position in the dominance hierarchy of either girls or boys. In keeping with their energetic outdoor interests, they preferred utilitarian grooming and functional clothing, particularly jeans or shorts, rather than dresses or skirts and fashionable feminine accessories and fashions. They were not, however, compulsive cross-dressers, as is frequently the case in the childhood histories reported by transvestites or transexuals in adolescence and adulthood. They did not grow up to become people requesting sex reassignment, though they might quite frankly have admitted that, had they been given a choice, they would have elected to have been a boy. In addition to liking boys' games, they also preferred boys' toys of the type that are part of the paraphernalia of energetic games. They neglected the dolls they possessed, or else gave them away. They were either indifferent to rehearsing parentalism in doll play and playing house with friends, or else actively avoided such play, and when they became older, baby sitting. They were not averse to learning how to cook, but they had no enthusiasm for other stereotypic feminine domestic skills, such as embroidery. They envisaged themselves as growing up to have a primary interest in a nondomestic, professional career concordant with their school achievement, which was in most cases above average. They were not averse to the idea of ultimate romance and marriage combined with an independent career, but to be a wife was secondary and distant in their image of the future. So also was motherhood. The projected family size was one or two children at most. In childhood they did not, so far as could be ascertained, engage in sexual rehearsal play. If they had sexual rehearsal fantasies, they kept the information private. Likewise with masturbation. In teenage they reached the dating and romantic stage three to nine years later than their age mates. In young adulthood they disclosed, in about one-third of cases, bisexual content of erotic imagery, and exclusively homosexual imagery in one-tenth (in a sample of thirty). The others either reported exclusive heterosexual imagery and practice, or else, perhaps were reticent to disclose too much.

It sometimes has happened that a 46,XX baby with the adrenogenital syndrome has been assigned, reared, and habilitated as a boy, with appropriately masculinizing hormonal and surgical treatment, as needed. In such cases, the child's behavioral development has the same characteristics as those denoted as tomboyish in the foregoing, except that there was no psychosexual delay in teenage, when there developed a typical boy's romantic and erotic interest in a girlfriend.

SEX-SHARED/THRESHOLD-DIMORPHIC BEHAVIOR. One cannot describe a boy as tomboyish. There is no sex-shared word to apply to such sex-shared behavior. The very idiom of our language forces us to dichotomize male and female. Thereby we maximize the differences rather than the similarities. One does not dichotomize breathing as either masculine or feminine in type. It should be self-evident that masculine and feminine, if they are to have any precision of meaning, should be used as mutually exclusive only as in the saying that it is masculine to impregnate, and feminine to menstruate, gestate, and lactate.

Applying this strict criterion then, it appears that, whether in monkeys or in human beings, all the above-listed examples of tomboyish behavior are neither masculine nor feminine. They are sex-shared. It is not in any absolute sense that they are sexually dimorphic, but only in a relative sense, insofar as there is a sex difference in their prevalence, incidence, intensity, ease, duration, or span of occurrence. Parentalism is an example: regardless of species, males or females can be parental, but the threshold for the release of parental-care when the helpless young demand it is different, the mother being more immediately responsive.

Since there has not yet been a Linnaeus to rationalize a classification of human behavior, all students of behavior are largely at sea with respect to what the basic criteria of analysis should be when attempting to analyze the complexity of sex-shared, threshold-different behavior. Influenced by ethologists, one may engage in a search for what may be called basic phyletic mechanisms—which can be identified by cross-species comparisons and by experimental and clinical comparisons within species. The behavioral outcome of prenatal androgenization in both monkeys and human beings has thus led to the differentiation of a tentative list of nine variables or parameters of sex-shared/threshold-dimorphic behavior (Table 3-1).

Table 3-1. Nine parameters of sex-shared/threshold-dimorphic behavior

General kinesis—activity and the expenditure of energy, especially in outdoor, athletic, and team-sport activities
Competitive rivalry and assertiveness for higher rank in the dominance hierarchy of childhood
Roaming and territory or boundary mapping or marking
Defense against intruders and predators
Guarding and defense of the young
Nesting or homemaking
Parental care of the young, including doll play
Sexual mounting and thrusting versus spreading and containing
Erotic dependence on visual stimulus versus tactual stimulus arousal

First is kinetic energy expenditure, which, in its more vigorous, outdoor, athletic manifestations is typically more readily elicited and prevalent in males than females, even before males reach the postpubertal stage of being, on the average, taller, heavier, and more muscular than females.

Second is roaming and becoming familiar with or marking the boundaries of the roaming range. Whereas pheromonal (odoriferous) marking is characteristic of some small animals, in primates and man vision takes the place of smell. The secretion of marker pheromones is largely under the regulation of the male sex hormone and thus is more readily elicited in males than females. The extent of a sex difference in the threshold for visual marking in primates is still conjectural.

Third is competitive rivalry and assertiveness for a position in the dominance hierarchy of childhood, which is more readily elicited in boys than girls. A position of dominance may be accorded an individual without fighting, or after a victory. Whereas fighting and aggressiveness per se are not sexually dimorphic, despite a widespread scientific assumption that they are, sensitivity to eliciting stimuli may or may not be. An example of the latter is retaliation against a deserter or rival in love or friendship, which is not sex-specific.

Fourth is fighting off predators in defense of the troop and its territory, which, among primates, is typically more readily elicited in males than females.

Fifth is fighting in defense of the young, which is more readily elicited in females than males. Females are more fiercely alert and responsive to threats to their infants than, in general, are males.

Sixth is a provision of a nest or safe place for the delivery, care, carrying, and suckling of the young. It is possible that this variable is associated with a greater prevalence of domestic neatness in girls than boys, as compared with the disarray that is the product of, among other things, vigorous kinetic energy expenditure.

Seventh is parentalism, exclusive of delivery and suckling. Retrieving, protecting, cuddling, rocking, and clinging to the young is more prevalent in girls' rehearsal play with dolls and/or playmates.

Eighth is sexual rehearsal play in which evidence from monkeys is that juvenile males elicit presentation responses from females, and juvenile females elicit mounting responses from males, more readily than vice versa. The taboo on human juvenile sexual rehearsal play and on its scientific investigation prohibits generalization regarding boys and girls.

Ninth is the possibility that the visual erotic image more readily elicits an initiating erotic response in males than in females, whereas the tactile stimulus more readily elicits a response in females. Here again no generalization can yet be made with confidence, because of the effects of the erotic taboo and erotic stereotyping in our society.

Sexual mounting and thrusting as a predominantly male behavior, even in the sexual rehearsal play of prepuberty, is not well documented in human beings, whereas it is in monkeys, for the obvious reason that sexual play in children is a taboo and a punishable offense. For the same reason, there is no documentation of a possible sex difference in visual stimulation relative to erotic arousal in childhood. Until this gap in knowledge of visual stimulation is filled it will not be possible to settle the issue of whether there is or is not a prenatal hormonal determinant that renders certain individuals in some degree more vulnerable than others to the differentiation of a juvenile G-I/R that incorporates a postnatally acquired error of visual erotic arousal, that is to say, a paraphilia.

One further point needs mention. In subprimates like the dog and sheep, prenatal androgen programs the male urinary posture, as can be demonstrated in androgen-induced hermaphroditic bitches and ewes. The significance of this finding for primate and, specifically, human G-I/R remains to be ascertained.

Behavior that is threshold-dimorphic but sex-shared is, by definition, neither masculine nor feminine. Only its prevalence or the ease with which it is elicited can be labeled masculine or feminine. Each type of behavior can be integrated into either a masculine or a feminine G-I/R. On the basis of individual variation within each sex, it can be expected that, for any given type of behavior, some men will show more of it than do most other men, or less of it—or even less of it than do most other women, despite its lesser degree and/or prevalence in women than in men. To illustrate with the converse: a tomboyish girl may not only differ from her female age mates, but may also surpass many boys on their own grounds.

In the population at large, whereas the phenomenon of tomboyism is extremely prevalent, its origin cannot be specified. There is no presently known way of ascertaining the prenatal hormonal history in retrospect of a person selected at random; and there is no logical justification to generalize from tomboyism in the adrenogenital syndrome, and to assume that all tomboyish girls were to some extent prenatally more androgenized than their nontomboyish age-mates. However, the story of the adrenogenital syndrome does serve to remind us all that we dare not attribute all shades of difference in gender-related behavior to postnatal social and cultural determinants. Indeed, the adrenogenital syndrome can be used to teach everyone the lesson of respect for individual differences when neither the etiology of their development nor the formula for their change is known. Rather than attempting to force children to conform to rigid gender stereotypes, let us respect their individual differences and idiosyncracies. Some will assimilate the gender stereotypes readily. For others, it is imperative that the old gender-dimorphic traditions be revised. With greater flexibility of the stereotypes, all children will be better served in differentiating the postnatal phase of their G-I/R—the phase that is greatly subject to social learning by way of identification and reciprocation—and in attaining their full human potential.

There is a possibility that, heterosexualism, bisexualism, and homosexualism—maybe transexualism and transvestism also—are to some degree determined in a rather direct way by the amount of androgenic influence on the brain in prenatal life. If so, then there is no known way of specifying this degree, and the hypothesis itself, though scientifically legitimate, is still largely science-fictional with respect to proof. It is equally feasible to hypothesize that all people are potentially bisexual when born, and that some become postnatally differentiated to become exclusively heterosexual or homosexual, whereas others always retain their original bisexuality as a sex-shared/threshold-dimorphic trait.

IDENTIFICATION AND RECIPROCATION. In its postnatal phase, G-I/R differentiation follows the two principles of identification and reciprocation, the former well known, the latter not. Identification signifies imitating or copying a role model, a person of the same sex. The most important role model is the person of the same sex to whom the infant became pair-bonded in neonatal life. This person is typically the same-sexed parent, though another may substitute. As development proceeds auxilliary identification figures, for example, a slightly older playmate or sibling, or a television folk hero, may augment the role of the primary identification figure.

The primary reciprocation figure is typically, though not imperatively, the opposite-sexed parent with whom the infant pair-bonded neonatally. As in identification, this person may be replaced by a surrogate and supplemented with additional reciprocation models. Reciprocation signifies that a child uses and practices behavior that has been acquired by identification to reciprocate the behavior of the reciprocation figure— just as a small daughter dances with her father, and her brother with his mother.

Reciprocation is irrelevant when behavior is not dually coded, as it is in sex-stereotyping. Even though much of the stereotyping is arbitrary, a child learns it nonetheless, as inevitably as he learns to speak his native language with the accent of his region; and as inevitably as he learns what to eat and not to eat according to the customs of his native regional diet.

The two schemas of behavior representing identification and reciprocation become separately coded as two schemas in the brain. The identification schema is labeled "for direct personal use," so to speak, whereas the corresponding label for the reciprocation schema is "for predicting responses of the other sex." Since everyone has both schemas, we are all, in a literal sense, bisexual. Only a few, however, have a 50:50 capacity to transpose the two schemas. Others who play at transposition as a charade, at a party say, are awkward, uncomfortable, clumsy, and laughter-provoking as they impersonate the other sex.

The differentiation of the schemas of identification and reciprocation is facilitated when an infant is healthily pair-bonded to each parent (or substitute) neonatally and remains so. It is also facilitated when the parents together give a unified message as to what constitutes masculinity and femininity, instead of a garbled and contradictory one. It is further facilitated if the child's development is not disrupted by events which he is too immature to cope with, such as illness, death or threat of imminent death within the family; or excessive sibling competition; or excessive poverty and economic disaster in the family, and so on.

The proper differentiation of the schemas of identification and reciprocation in the development of G-I/R is also facilitated if the specific genital component is not evaded and not subjected to punishment. Childhood sexual rehearsal play, beginning with bodily self-stimulation and masturbation and advancing to play in pairs or groups, is a species characteristic of many, if not all, the primates, human beings included (see above). Though still insufficiently systematic, there is a beginning body of animal, clinical, and cross-cultural evidence to indicate that impairment and disorder of the erotic/sexual component of G-I/R in adolescence and adulthood has its genesis in deprivation and/or prohibition of sexual rehearsal play in infancy and childhood.

In this respect, the years of early childhood appear to be more crucial than those of later childhood and prepuberty. For G-I/R as a whole, the period from 18 months to 4½ or 5 years of age is the crucial period of differentiation, as judged from the evidence of attempts to impose a sex reassignment on hermaphroditic children by edict. This is the same period during which native language becomes established and after which, though it may fall into disuse, it cannot be eradicated from the brain except by surgery or trauma. After age 5, G-I/R is not totally unmalleable, but its main contours are already fixed, with or without impairments or errors, and will remain so regardless of what may be subsequently added or inhibited with respect to both its erotic and nonerotic components.

The schema of reciprocation or complementation can be rewarded and reinforced by people of either sex. This is possible even when there is no primary identification figure present in a child's household. Thus, when the father is absent, the mother can reinforce her young son's manliness, whether he assimilates it from a father surrogate, from his

own age mates, or from entertainment heroes. The representation of a
father or any other identification figure in absentia means that missing
or inadequate models can be compensated for. Such compensation is of
significance for children in one-parent households. It is also significant
with respect to current debate about children with one or both parents
involved in a homosexual relationship: they do not automatically identify with every aspect of a homosexual parent's behavior when to do so
would be dissonant with the reciprocation schema simultaneously being
built up and rewarded by the responses of others, including peers.

HORMONAL ONSET OF PUBERTY. The biological clock that regulates the timing of puberty still has not been discovered. It is something
of a mystery that the age of puberty has been decreasing by an average
of four months every ten years for the last century and a half. No
explanation, including improved nutrition, or change in the dark/light
ratio after candles and firelight were replaced by kerosene lamps, gas,
and electricity amounts to more than a speculative hypothesis.

Though it does not always hold up in cases of extreme precocity or
delay in the onset of puberty, there is a correlation between body size
and the ratio of fat to lean body weight and the onset of puberty. The
correlation itself does not clarify which is cause and which effect. In cases
of child abuse dwarfism (also known as reversible hyposomatotropic
dwarfism, and as psychosocial dwarfism), not only growth hormone but
also, at the age of puberty, gonadotropic secretion from the pituitary
may be suppressed. In one extreme case, a boy aged sixteen had the
stature and nonpubertal development of an eight-year-old. Rescued
from the home of abuse, he grew rapidly and became pubertal in less
than a year.

The most likely localization of the biological clock of puberty is in the
central nervous system. There is some clinical and experimental evidence to implicate the brain's pineal gland, especially in cases of early
puberty occurring in conjunction with a pineal tumor. Today's evidence,
however, points primarily to the hypothalamus and its nearby connections in the limbic system of the brain. The hypothalamus secretes its
own neurohormones or neurotransmitters that signal the endocrine system via the pituitary gland. The pituitary, in turn, signals the gonads to
secrete their own sex hormones.

Today's favored endocrine hypothesis of pubertal onset is formulated
in terms of gonadal-pituitary-hypothalamic feedback, but without an
explanation of how the "gonadostat" is changed at puberty. From a
purely logical viewpoint, this pubertal change of the gonadostat could be
formulated in terms of either the activation of a previously dormant
biological clock, or, in terms of the deactivation of a biological clock,

phyletically programed to inhibit puberty, perhaps by way of a juvenile hormone or neurotransmitter substance. The existence of a juvenile hormone has been demonstrated in the endocrinology of insect metamorphosis. It is not fashionable, however, to entertain the analogous hypothesis of a juvenile hormone in vertebrates, nor to search for one. The most parsimonious explanation of the anomalies of pubertal onset, either precocious or delayed, would be in terms of the disappearance or persistence, respectively, of an as yet unidentified juvenile hormone or hormone substance. Hence the possibility cannot be discarded a priori.

The hormonal change from prepuberty to puberty begins earlier than the visible body signs of the onset of puberty, and it correlates with physiologic age (physique age) rather than chronologic age. In the female, the change begins at least a year, and at most two years, earlier than in the male, at some time between ages seven to eleven years versus eight to twelve years, respectively. In the female, the first measurable hormonal change is an elevation of FSH (follicle stimulating hormone), which eventually stimulates the ovarian follicle to produce estrogen. In the male, the first measurable increase is in LH (luteinizing hormone), which stimulates testicular growth and, eventually, the secretion of testicular androgen. In both sexes, FSH and LH secretion from the pituitary greatly increase as puberty progresses. In the female, those two hormones are secreted cyclically to regulate the menstrual cycle, whereas in the male their secretion is acyclic.

As the gonads respond to FSH and LH by secreting their own puberty-inducing hormones, the body undergoes its familiar, progressive pubertal changes. Without these body changes, the psychosocial maturation of puberty is severely restricted, for the juvenile-looking person, regardless of chronological age, is treated as juvenile by other people. Conversely, the child with somatically precocious puberty is expected by others to be socially and psychosexually more mature than his/her chronologic age permits.

The sex difference in the timing of the onset of puberty as gauged by the rise in gonadotropin release, with eventual change in testicular size, in boys, and breast budding in girls, is approximately a year, not the two years conventionally cited. The earlier onset of puberty gives the typical girl a temporary statural advantage over her typical male counterpart, the implications of which are speculative, since there have been no studies that attempt to correlate behavior with physique age rather than chronologic age. The same applies to the somewhat earlier advent in girls of the sexual maturity of the body. In human beings, the heightened eroticism of puberty is not automatically expressed in sexual behavior as it is in lower mammals, being regulated also by cultural norms. Cases of precocious somatic puberty illustrate this point well, for affected children may be able to procreate by age eight or nine, but they do not establish procreative relationships nor fall in love with older teenagers for whom they are socially too inexperienced and immature. In content, the erotic behavior and imagery of the somatically precocious child parallels social age, which in turn parallels chronologic age more closely than hormonal age.

In our own culture, it is widely taken for granted that the female will be shorter and younger than her male partner. Not only at the time of the onset of puberty, but throughout the life cycle, there is a strong bias in favor of disparity in the ages of heterosexual partners until, in the geriatric age group, there are not enough surviving older men to be partners for the somewhat younger women who, because of their greater longevity, will be forced to live a second spinsterhood.

The sex difference in the onset of the somatic maturation of puberty has generated some speculation regarding a parallel difference in mental maturation, to which is added the further speculation that a relative delay in boys may have permanent sequelae on cerebral lateralization and the greater prevalence of praxic and mathematical achievement in boys than in girls. Such speculation has not yet been substantiated. It could be pure science fiction, for there is currently no way of disproving that the sex disparity in praxic and mathematical reasoning is anything more than an educational artifact derived from an earlier era of history in which it was considered unladylike for a female to receive any education except in the domestic and decorative arts (Chapter 10).

HORMONAL AND EROTIC/SEXUAL PUBERTY. It is still a part of the popular mythology of child development that something called sexual instinct or sexual drive arrives on the scene, de novo, contemporaneously with the body changes of puberty. As mythically characterized, sex drive is caused by hormones, and it in turn causes adolescence to be a period of emotional turmoil and unpredictable moods, made worse by a body that becomes increasingly unfamiliar and awkward to coordinate. According to the myth, sex drive is dangerously wild and morally undisciplined when it first appears and is easily inflamed by bad example and influence. Thus, the centerfolds of *Playboy*, to say nothing of coital picture books, lead to masturbation, fornication, and illegitimate pregnancy, it is falsely claimed, and they have even been blamed, in all seriousness, for teenage sexual crimes. Further, it is falsely proclaimed as a political issue that meeting or knowing a homosexual leads to recruitment to a life of homosexuality, or with a pimp or prostitute, to a life of prostitution, and so on.

Contrary to this popular mythology, the correct conception of hormonal puberty is that it puts gas in the metaphorical tank and upgrades the model of the vehicle, but it does not build the engine nor program the itinerary of the journey. The hormones of puberty mature the body and activate in the mind the erotic sexualism that is already programed therein. The content of that erotic/sexual program will present itself partly in the spontaneous release of precoded erotic/sexual imagery, in fantasy, dreams, and daydreams; partly in the stimulus-response release of precoded imagery when a precoded response is matched by an eliciting stimulus, either in living example or, derivatively, in narrative or pictorial form; and partly in reciprocal interaction and exploration of possibilities with a partner. Pubertal adolescents do not choose their erotic sexualism. They encounter it, as preformed in the mind. That does not preclude the possibility of one's having the personal, subjective experience (or illusion) of choosing or selecting among options, for there are different weightings to the different preprogramed components of each newly pubertal individual's erotic sexualism. The protruding shape of girl's nipples, for example, may be heavily weighted as an erotic turn-on in a particular boy, so that it enters imperatively into his erotic fantasies, whereas the shape of the buttocks is relatively insignificant and lightly weighted by comparison. This boy will classify himself as a "tit man," rather than an "ass man." He will probably say that he prefers or selects breast imagery as an erotic turn-on, and even persuade himself that his preference is a voluntary choice, whereas in point of fact it is an option that was preprogramed into him without his informed consent, perhaps as early as the age of three, when he was still unweaned and suckling at his mother's nipples.

The profile of one's erotic turn-on imagery is as personally idiosyncratic as one's signature, one's face, or finger prints. It is a worthwhile experiment in personal growth, development, and pair-bonding to discover one's own profile and to know it explicitly and in full, rather than haphazardly and piecemeal. There are seven parts to this profile as listed in Table 3-2.

Table 3-2. Profile
of erotic/sexual imagery

Images of sight
Images of haptic sensuality received
Images of haptic sensuality given
Images of sound
Images of taste
Images of smell
Composite images or fantasies

The number of items in each of the seven parts is not infinite, but the finite number of them has never been ascertained. That is a task for future research. In personal discovery, one may begin one's personal check-list of erotic/sexual imagery at the top of the head, and end at the tip of the toes (which also are erotic!). Include all the organs, regions, and cavities of the body in between.

This head-to-toe imagery may be exclusively of self-reference, that is, of oneself masturbating. It may also be of other-reference, that is, including a partner, and is almost certainly so for most people most of the time, even if they have self-referent imagery some of the time. When a partner is included, the check-list of imagery includes all the possible juxtapositions of the organs, regions, and cavities of the two.

In imagery of other reference, the partner may vary according to age, sex, and kinship. There may be not one partner, but two or more, serially or together. The partnership may be consensual or imposed; it may or may not be augmented with supplementary erotic/sexual toys or other artifacts, which also may be used alone. Obviously, the number of permutations and combinations of items of erotic/sexual imagery on the basis of the foregoing classifications is of great magnitude, even without consideration of their composition and sequential arrangement into fantasies or dramatic enactments.

No one has yet undertaken the task of classifying erotic/sexual fantasies that are religiously, morally, and legally defined as acceptable and ideologically defined as normal. The law, unliberated from anachronistic canonical doctrine, may be so restrictive, as it is in some states, that the only acceptable fantasy (and actuality) is that of a man and a woman, married, concealed in a room, covered with a sheet, and in the "missionary position" of him on top of her, doing nothing more than penovaginal thrusting, only as frequently as is necessary for the conception of offspring.

Today, the public morality is far less restrictive than the church and the law in what it accepts as ideologically normal in erotic/sexual imagery and practice. Oral sex is an example. Nonetheless, the most liberal ideological norm is still so narrow that it is dangerous for a pubertal adolescent to reveal any part of his/her erotic/sexual imagery and fantasy that does not conform. Secrecy, suffering, and solitude are the penalties to which the nonconformist is condemned in order to avoid stigmatization, ridicule, or punishment.

On a more positive note, there are nowadays some enlightened families, blue-collar as well as middle class, that do not require erotic/sexual secrecy of their teenagers. These families have worked out a modus vivendi whereby their adolescent members may bring their lovers to their own beds and conduct their sex lives safely in the privacy of their own homes. The agreed contract is for no illegitimate grandchildren. This arrangement does not incite the younger siblings in the household to a premature onset of their own sex lives any more than does a visit from a married sibling and spouse who sleep together in the same bed. What it does do is reduce domestic tension and dispute and make the family a more hospitable and pleasant unit of affiliation, and adolescence a more tranquil and pleasant phase of the life cycle.

MENSTRUAL AND MOOD CYCLES. Like the onset of puberty, the menstrual cycle is programed by a biological clock situated in the hypothalamus but with connections elsewhere to the brain. By inference, it is the existence of these connections that allows, at least in some women, personal life experiences to interfere with the hormonal rhythms that govern menstrual regularity and to suppress ovulation for various periods of time. Releasing hormones (RH) from the hypothalamus program the cyclicity of pituitary gonadotropic hormones which, in turn, program the cyclic hormonal functioning of the ovaries, which program the endometrial cyclicity of the uterus.

There are different starting points for counting the days of the menstrual cycle. One convention is to begin with the first day of bleeding as day one. At the conclusion of the menstrual flow, the preovulatory or follicular phase begins and culminates in mid-cycle with the day of ovulation. Then ensues the postovulatory or luteal phase, lasting about two weeks, though variable according to whether the total cycle is longer or shorter than twenty-eight days. The premenstrual phase that terminates the luteal phase is loosely defined and has no fixed duration. It ends abruptly with the onset of the next menstrual flow. Apart from the beginning and ending of the menstrual flow, the only other fixed point in the menstrual cycle is ovulation, the occurrence of which can be determined by a rise in body temperature, if a daily temperature chart is kept or if, according to a new method, the viscosity of the cervical mucosa is tested.

Figure 3-7 shows the fluctuations of estrogen and progesterone during the course of the menstrual cycle (androgen is not represented). Estrogen and progesterone are low at the beginning of the follicular phase. Then estrogen and androgen both rise in the preovulatory phase. Ovulation is precipitated by a dramatic rise in luteinizing hormone and a lesser rise of follicle stimulating hormone. Then follows a rapid decline in estrogen level as progesterone elevates, soon to be joined by a mid-luteal increase in both estrogen and androgen. Before estrogen reaches the same high level that heralds ovulation, it begins to decline, along with the levels of progesterone and androgen, to the low levels that precede the onset of the next menstrual flow. The level of ovarian androgen is

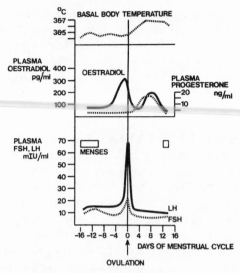

Figure 3-7
Schematic representation of hormonal and temperature
fluctuations of the menstrual cycle.
Courtesy H. K. A. Visser (1973)

highest during the luteal phase; it is mostly androstenedione, which is also secreted by the adrenal cortices. About 10 percent of androstenedione is converted to testosterone intracellularly and the remainder secreted in the urine.

Knowledge of the sex-hormonal concomitants of the menstrual cycle, still not complete, dates from the 1920s, when the gonadal steroids were first isolated, and from the 1930s, when they were first synthesized. One of the earliest attempts to establish a behavioral endocrinology of the menstrual cycle is the 1931 paper, "The Hormonal Causes of Pre-menstrual Tension," by Robert T. Frank. "It is well known," Frank wrote, "that normal women suffer varying degrees of discomfort preceding the onset of menstruation. Employers of labor take cognizance of this fact and make provision for the temporary care of their employees. These minor disturbances include increased fatigability, irritability, lack of concentration, and attacks of pain."

It was not these normal women with whom Frank was concerned, however, but with a group of patients in whom pain played a predominant role, requiring a day or two of bed rest; and another group in whom grave systemic disorders, including epilepsy, were exascerbated during the premenstrual period. These latter were so disabled that Frank put to use the new ovarian hormonal knowledge of his day and by "applying a sterilizing dose of roentgen rays to the ovaries," so as to suppress their endocrine output, prevented menstruation, and successfully dispelled the symptoms that had become premenstrually exaggerated. Today, such an overdose of x-rays would be prohibited.

Since 1931, progress toward understanding the etiology and phenomena of premenstrual tension was slow until the physiologic functions of potent chemicals, the prostaglandins, produced by many body tissues, became better understood in recent years. Prostaglandins are many and varied in function in men and women. In women, they have an important part to play in triggering uterine contractions associated with menstruation and also with labor pains and delivery. It is now known that women who have excessive menstrual cramping do so in response to an excessive release of prostaglandin from the uterus (Marx 1979). This excess can be rapidly controlled by medications that inhibit prostaglandin synthesis, for example, naproxen, the use of which is still under clinical investigation. The medication controls not only menstrual cramping and pain but also the prostaglandin-related symptoms of nausea, vomiting, diarrhea, and headache, if they occur.

Experimental proof of how the menstrual surge of prostaglandin release relates to premenstrual tension as well as to menstrual cramping remains to be worked out in detail. Until that is done, the most effective method of ameliorating premenstrual tension is by altering the hormonal fluctuations of the menstrual cycle. The principle is the same as that on which the contraceptive pill is based. The progestinic content of the pill interrupts the ovulatory hormonal cycle and also has a direct inhibiting effect on prostaglandin release.

The diagnosis of premenstrual tension has become fashionable since the 1930s, even to the point of achieving syndrome status. As in the case of other fashionable diagnoses, dyslexia for example, or minimal brain damage, the medical popularity of the syndrome has outstripped the capacity of research to define it. Thus the premenstrual syndrome has become something of a medical grab-bag, its meaning stretched to include the ills of menstruation itself, of the week preceding it, and even of the days surrounding ovulation. The behavioral correlates of the syndrome have been extended to include not only subjectively experienced mood changes but also an increased prevalence of poor judgment, delinquency, violence, accidents, hospital clinic visits for self and children, acute psychiatric illness, suicides, and calls to a suicide prevention center.

Correlations intrinsically fail to tell anything about etiology. Sampling bias distorts the truth about the population at large. Faulty research design or method masks the complexity of multivariate determinism. Established maxims become enshrined as dogma. Nonetheless, the premenstrual syndrome does exist in some women. It is variable in degree of severity; some women have it not at all. It occurs across cultures and classes and so almost certainly is not simply an artifact of cultural taboo. Nonetheless, it is not culture free. Even in its mildest manifestation, better known simply as premenstrual tension, it is multidetermined.

From the point of view of sexual politics, there is no doubt that the concept of the premenstrual syndrome has been misused, and the adverse effects of premenstrual tension on both work efficiency and mood have been exaggerated. It is time to call a halt to the misrepresentation of premenstrual behavioral endocrinology and to study groups of men as well as women. In a 1976 study of 24 couples, Dan found that mood variations of women and their husbands were comparable, over a given period of time, regardless of menstrual cycling. In women, fluctuating mood change may coincide with the premenstruum, but the percentage who report such a fluctuation changes if the information is ascertained retrospectively, instead of contemporaneously, according to a 1976 study by May.

In 1977, Rossi and Rossi published the findings of a very important study in which they correlated mood changes with not only the body time of the menstrual cycle but also the social time of work days versus weekend days. They found that if either menstruation or ovulation took place on a weekend there was significant increment in positive mood scores, whereas, there was a lessening of such positive scores if either of the two phases of the cycle took place during the working days of the week. In the luteal phase of the menstrual cycle (which includes the premenstrual phase), there was no parallel correlation of mood with days of the week. Instead, there was an overall increase in negative moods and decrease in positive moods during the luteal phase. This lessening of positive mood during the luteal phase, together with no particular exaggeration of negative mood during the premenstrual days, contradicts earlier and statistically less rigorous studies. By contrast, the Rossis' findings confirmed those of earlier studies in which positive mood increase is associated with the ovulatory phase and negative mood increase with the early part of the bleeding phase. The pattern of cyclic ebb and flow of mood was not found in women on the contraceptive pill, which abolishes the cyclic ebb and flow of endogenous hormones, namely, estrogen and progesterone (Chapter 6).

The weekend mood effect in women showed itself as an elevation of positive mood related to somatic well-being (e.g., healthy or sick) as well as to psychosocial well-being (e.g., happy or depressed). In men, by contrast, the parallel positive mood-enhancement effect on weekends applied primarily to somatic well-being (e.g., sexual arousal).

4

Sexosophy: The Principles of Erotic Sexuality

SEXOSOPHY: DEFINITION. Sexosophy is a new term, coined to fill a lexigraphical gap and provide the word we all need to refer to the principles and knowledge people have about their own personal experience of sexual erotic functioning within themselves. Whereas sexology refers to the science of sex and eroticism in human and other species, sexosophy refers to the philosophy of sex and eroticism that people have with reference to themselves, either personally or collectively. It includes values, personal and shared. It encompasses a culturally shared system of values. Thus one may refer to the sexosophy of the Middle Ages, or of the Protestant Church, or of the Sexual Revolution of the 1960s. Developmentally, one may refer to the sexosophy of childhood, adolescence, or any other period of life. There is as yet no well-organized discipline or body of knowledge that comprises sexosophy, as such, though a good deal of what might well be subsumed under sexosophy currently passes as sexology.

ORIGINAL INNOCENCE, ORIGINAL SIN. Love, sex, eroticism, coitus, copulation, sexual intercourse, "making love," "going to bed," "sleeping with," kissing, fellatio, cunnilingus—this is the meager polite vocabulary we adult human beings have with which to talk about the diversified experiences and nuances of our own erotic sexualism, our own sexosophy. Impolite colloquial and street language adds additional terminological precision, but not enough. The intrusive sense of shame and guilt that historically and culturally permeates and contaminates our own sexosophy, despoiling our birthright, is so pervasive that even the colloquial language of the people itself is incomplete to deal with all the subtleties of human erotic/sexual experience.

43

It scarcely needs to be said that if we lack an adequate vocabulary for the nuances of adult sexosophy, then we lack also a vocabulary for the nuances of infantile and childhood sexosophy. Worse still, we lack full empirical knowledge of the erotic/sexual manifestations of infancy and childhood, let alone the terminology for expressing them.

Our cultural tradition is at odds with itself regarding the erotic sexualism of infancy and childhood. It declares that childhood is the age of erotic and sexual innocence and that the innocence must be guarded from being contaminated or destroyed by the serpent that brought about the downfall of Adam and Eve. Contradicting itself, our cultural tradition also declares that children, all having been born in original sin, have a disposition to wickedness, especially wickedness in the guise of sexual pleasure. To ensure righteousness, signs of sexual wickedness must be watched for, prohibited, and punished.

The unanimous verdict of the two doctrines, original innocence and original sin, is that sex is wicked in childhood, whether the wickedness is a transmitted pollution from without, or a self-generated pollution from within. Since the institutions of our society strongly support this verdict, the opportunities to gather empirical evidence on childhood erotic sexualism are greatly limited. That is to say, the hard, plain facts are few. There are none at all pertaining to male/female differences in erotic sexualism as subjectively experienced and reported in childhood.

The range of erotic sexualism as experienced in childhood is variable, dependent partly, no doubt, on the sociosexual folkways of childhood, and partly on idiosyncratic regulation of the balance between erotic sexual inhibition and expression.

The following story, reproduced by courtesy of Professor Brian Sutton-Smith, exhibits a rather wide range of sexual information in a six-year-old. The boy, white and middle class, narrated it spontaneously on tape as a contribution to a project on children's creativity. The theme was self-selected.

This kid, his name was Zeke, walks down the street one day and he sees this girl. And then he goes into a little corner and they both take off their clothes. And they go home and they get into bed [snicker]. And they take off her bra and their clothes and their underwear [snicker, again]. And they're all naked.

[The story teller is playing with a toy eggbeater.] And they started cooking naked, with a blender. And they had supper. And they started FUCKING [spelled out].

And they went out on the street naked. And then a man walks by and laughs and says: "Ha, ha, ha, you can't win them all." And then Zeke and his girlfriend go get married.

There's another girl that walks by that's even prettier than Zeke's girlfriend. And then Zeke falls in love with that girl, and the first girl says: "I'm getting out of here."

And then they go and they say: "Let's get married." They get married. And he says: "Let's go to the drive-in and FUCK there. And go home and get married again, and go to bed, and take off your clothes. I'll help. Okay, let's start FUCK-ING, FUCK, again. And let's go to Martha's Vineyard and we will FUCK a lot there, and we'll come back and start again."

AGE-AVOIDANCY. The sexual and erotic explicitness incorporated into this story is usually not entrusted to the ears of adults. Even this storyteller had, at age six, learned the convention of prudery that prescribed the spelling out of stigmatized words. It is, of course, during the developing years of childhood that boys and girls assimilate the taboos, stigmas, and avoidancies of our society's mores and folkways. Thus, all children learn the overall forbiddenness of sex in the community at large, even if there is a more open-minded policy at home. They are obliged to assimilate a set of social rules that are not explicitly formulated and transmitted as such to children. They concern time, place, and person with respect to sexual talk or participation. Nonconformity to these rules may be utilized as an expression of rebellion, as, for example, in some manifestations of delinquency.

One rule, to use the parlance of cultural anthropology, is the rule of age-avoidancy. One of its constraints is verbal, namely, on the range of conversation on erotic/sexual matters that may take place between individuals of different age groups. For example, children of prepubertal age may be very open-minded in talking with age-mates, whereas they apply rather stringent rules and restrictions on how much information they would make available to children of, say, eight or nine years of age. They may apply these restrictions even to the formal sex education curriculum for younger ages, whereas they regard all information as quite suitable and morally safe for themselves—and correctly so. Younger teenagers might wrongly be deprived of the right to full information by their teenaged seniors, who had no restrictions on its accessibility when they themselves were younger.

The age-avoidancy rule dictates constraints not only on talk about sex but also on erotic/sexual participation. Though children of similar age who play genitally together may be punished severely enough, more severe punishment is likely when an older child plays with a younger one. When the older person is postpubertal, such play is rated legally as an offense—child-molesting or statutory rape—and the punishment is severe, indeed, in many jurisdictions. When the age discrepancy involves gerontophilia and an actual genital relationship between two adults, one young and one much older, there is no legal sanction against it. However, the fact that such a relationship offends the folkways is attested to by the jokes, smirks, and jealousy it meets with.

INTIMACY-AVOIDANCY. The rule of age-avoidancy partially over-laps with the rule of intimacy-avoidancy. The rule against intimacy dic-tates that one be circumspect in disclosing details of one's own biography and feelings, not only to younger people but also even to one's intimate erotic partner. A pint of blood from a donor is used up in a transfusion and nothing is heard of it ever again, whereas a donated item of bio-graphical information can travel indefinitely and endanger the person who released it. Within families today, the rule of intimacy regarding the erotic/sexualism of their children in adulthood is widely respected by parents. Reciprocally, grown children obey the intimacy rule and do not pry, uninvited, into their parents' erotic/sexualism. It is in the childhood years that the intimacy rule is nonreciprocal and lopsided, for parents usually expect to be privy to everything in the erotic/sexual development of their children, while being completely unable to disclose anything personal about themselves. The ensuing onesidedness of dialogue effec-tively prohibits complete frankness in sex education at home, not so much with respect to the physiology of procreation as to the psychology of the partnership in love, pair-bonding, and coital reciprocity. Erotic sexualism is the one part of human experience that we fail to transmit to our children directly and visually, relying instead on oral traditions, customary folkways among age-mates, books, and maybe designated other people, instead. We have been singularly successful, however, in applying the taboo of intimacy-avoidance to radio and television. Thus, their immense power to transmit healthy sexual knowledge simultane-ously not only to thousands but millions of needy children remains dor-mant.

The rule of avoiding intimacy creates for parents two problems in particular regarding their children's sex education: the parents' own nudity and their own copulation. For millions of the world's population, notably those millions who live in single-room dwellings, parental nudity and copulation are matters of decorum, though not necessarily of pri-vacy and secrecy. It is otherwise in our own society, except that in recent years there has been some relaxation of the prohibition against nudity in the home. The new, relaxed rule is that parents do not conceal their nudity on the ordinary occasions when people dress and undress, as when bathing or, possibly, nude swimming, but that they do not appear nude as if they were at a nudist colony. Unorthodoxy, whether in reli-gion or life style, imposes on children two alternatives: either to be ashamed of it and defensive among their age mates, or to flaunt it and be grand. Today there are so many families following the custom of occa-sional nudity within the home that mention of it outside the home poses no special problem for children among their peers.

Such is not the case with respect to parental copulation, which is still governed by the rule of avoiding intimacy. Copulation is something to be done in private, secretly. Visual privacy is easier to maintain than is auditory privacy in modern dwellings. Consequently, many parents find that their sex lives are curtailed and almost furtively relegated to times when the children are away or asleep. It is possible to have more open understanding, however, as some parents have done, by defining coitus as a "mommy-and-daddy game," and a game that is played preferably in private. A seven-year-old girl in the clinic called it "push-ups." If a child does happen to encounter his parents copulating, they need only request privacy until their game is completed. In a fair trade-off, the privacy that they claim for themselves is accorded also to the child, who may request privacy for some of his/her own activities, sexual or otherwise. A bonus of such a trade-off is that parents are not excluded from knowing about and guiding their child's emergent sexuality, while at the same time they realistically adhere to community mores. Then children are obliged neither to be ashamed of their knowledge of copulation, nor to flaunt it. For them it is literally one of the facts of life, and one for which, in their own lives, they will be prepared with a sense of healthy well-being. For them there is no trauma of the primal scene, so called.

The custom of copulatory privacy in the mores of our society applies not only to the sex lives of parents but also to the individual sex lives of other members of the household, including brothers and sisters. Siblings in some instances do get into body-contact play, as in playing doctor, or in genital inspection play, or in explicit coital play. They learn that such play is negatively sanctioned in our society and that punishment is the usual outcome for failure to keep it private. The older the siblings, the more likely that discovery will involve the legal sanction against sibling incest.

Despite the stringency of the law against incest, and despite the fascination of social theorists to prove the universality of the incest taboo, parents in the average grown family do not and do not need to make incest an issue: in adolescence and later, it is only when relationships are psychopathological that incest is likely to be an actuality. According to the research of Shepher, pair-bonding in love, sex, and eroticism routinely does not occur among adolescents and adults who share a common history of having been reared together and of having shared their nudity and playful sexuality together from infancy until age five or six. Shepher came to this conclusion after completing a study of the marriages, and also of the nonmarital love affairs, of the first generation of young adults who had been reared in close proximity from infancy onward, in children's houses in the Israeli kibbutzim. These children were reared together as intimately as if they were siblings, whereas in fact they had been assigned together because of the proximity of their

birth dates, regardless of genealogy. Thus, the fact of early living together outweighs in significance an actual genealogical relationship in
establishing the so-called incest taboo.

ALLOSEX-AVOIDANCY: TALK. The foregoing two avoidancy rules
of erotic sexualism, namely, age-avoidancy and intimacy-avoidancy, are
not sex disparate, but are applied equally to boys and girls in the course
of their development. A third rule, allosex-avoidancy is, by contrast, sex
disparate. This rule puts constraints on what males may do or say erotically and sexually in the presence of females, and vice versa. Though it is
more rigidly enforced after puberty than in childhood, children are acculturated to obey the rule of allosex-avoidancy from infancy onward.

The rule of allosex-avoidancy regulates how much of one's body may
be exposed to members of the other sex. In infancy, it is acceptable for
boys and girls to appear naked before one another and other people,
under such circumstances as bathing or showering. By school age, genital exposure is forbidden, except maybe at home, and girls are already
required to keep their nipples covered when boys are not. The conven-
tions of modesty, clothed or unclothed, commonly are adhered to in the
presence of one's own sex as well as in mixed company; but with one's
own sex, it is allowable to be more relaxed. Even so, a sex divergency
prevails. Boys, for example, are by convention permitted to swim naked
and shower in communal shower rooms, whereas girls are trained to
wear swim suits and shower alone in cubicles. All told, more constraints
are imposed on girls than on boys to hide their bodies. A parallel is the
partial incapacitation of locomotion by wearing high-heeled shoes—or,
in pre-1949 China, of having the feet deformed by binding.

In conservative Moslem culture, women are forbidden to show their
mouths naked in the presence of adult males, other than their husbands.
Elsewhere on earth, for example, in aboriginal Australia, men and
women used to wear no clothing. They saw each other's nudity in toto.
For the Australians, the unclad appearance of any part of the body was
not, per se, an erotic signal. Eye talk and finger talk, to use the translation of their own terms, and not the uncovering of the body, were the
medium of erotic communication.

The rule of allosex-avoidancy regulates not only bodily exposure, but
applies also to conversation between the sexes. The language of sex that
is stigmatized as crude, vulgar, and impolite (and to a large extent
Anglo-Saxon rather than Latin in origin) is actually the erotic/sexual
language of males among themselves. When small boys use this language
in the hearing of females, with or without other males present, they are
punished. They are not actually instructed that such talk is acceptable in
exclusively male company, but they soon learn this lesson for themselves.

There is no counterpart of an erotic/sexual language exclusively for females, but there is a tradition among some females to use the forbidden language of males, but only when no males are listening. Thus, whether or not they endorse the doctrine of the double standard, men and women are trapped in it conversationally.

The social institution of an erotic/sexual language for men only is linked to the institutionalization of another rule, namely, the rule of the joking relationship. According to this rule, it is permissible to talk about sex, but only in a joking way. Among boys and men, the institutionalized erotic/sexual joking relationship may be quite personalized, as in personalized gibes about masturbation, which mock the individual for what he is assumed to do without requiring that he admit to doing it. Such mockery is not limited to men only, but as a social institution it is stronger among men only than among women only, or than among men and women together.

The other manifestation of the joking relationship is less personalized and is not sex disparate. It is the institution of the dirty joke in verse or prose recited by a man or woman. By telling a joke, one may initiate communication on an erotic/sexual topic with a listener without committing oneself to an explicit overture or expecting an explicit response. Erotic/sexual joking is the most effective way of circumventing the sexual taboo in our society, while still obeying it. It attacks the taboo while simultaneously endorsing it; and it sounds out the listener's point of view.

Erotic/sexual jokes and the joking relationship are the most important medium of sex education in our culture, apart from frank and direct information. When the latter is absent, as it still is for some children, sex joking and sex education are synonymous. This is true for boys and for girls, and it has the great disadvantage of equating sex with dirt. A sex joke is, in the vernacular, a dirty joke.

SEX AND DIRT. Turn to the *Oxford English Dictionary* and its 1972 *Supplement* for a goldmine of information on the Middle English and Old Norse noun, *drit,* meaning excrement, and the transmogrification of its meaning, metaphorically, to be synonymous with filth, that which makes unclean or soils the body and, by extension, the morals and the mind.

By the fourteenth century, the upper layer of the earth in which plants grow was on its way to becoming the dirt that made the gardener's hands dirty. One is tempted to fill in the missing documentation with the speculation that earth first became dirt only if it had animal excrement mixed with it in the barnyard, or spread on it in the field, as a fertilizer. It is not difficult, then, to speculate further that the barnyard serves as a link between dirt and sex. That speculation must be dismissed as too egregious, for the written record shows only that between the fourteenth and the seventeenth century dirt became established as a synonym for the unclean, the impure, the defiled, the degraded, the worthless, the scorned, the undesired, the corrupt, the despicable, and, more recently, the treacherous and the scandalous.

Despite its excremental origins and the negative connotations derived therefrom, dirt, as a substantive, had by the seventeenth century become a respectable synonym for soil, earth, dust, mud, and various left-overs of mining. There was no corresponding respectable usage for the adjective, dirty. Dirty has a negative connotation. To be dirty is to be avoided. It is disapproved of, perhaps mildly, or at the extreme of loathing and opprobrium.

There is no systematic history of how or when dirtiness became attributed to particular types of action or speech as a synonym for moral impurity or uncleanness. Thus, there is no systematic history of the usage of dirty as a qualifier of sex and as a vernacular synonym for the adjectives, pornographic and obscene. It is only in its 1972 *Supplement* that the *Oxford English Dictionary* gives this usage, listing as examples dirty book or bookshop, dirty joke or story, and dirty weekend. The first quoted example is dated 1912, from Rupert Brooke's letters: "I shall repeat poetry to you; you will repeat dirty stories to me." When such dirty expressions are used in contemporary formal and scientific English, they are used as colloquialisms, which is presumptive evidence that the adjective, dirty, does not have as long a history as a qualifier of sex as do its more ornate classical counterparts, obscene (etymologically, a prohibited scene) and pornographic (etymologically, harlot books or writings).

In the terminology of sex, there are clean words as well as dirty words. The clean ones are chiefly of Latin or Greek derivation and were originally of aristocratic usage, a heritage of the Norman Conquest. The dirty ones, many of them playful euphemisms, are chiefly of Anglo-Saxon and Old Norse derivation and were originally plebian in origin.

The cultural relativism of dirty versus clean sexual terminology is well illustrated by the complete reversal of the categories in English usage in Nigeria. In the history of acculturation, the moral taboos of sex were taught by missionaries and administrators who used only clean words. These were the words that became taboo. The dirty words used as part of the vernacular of sailors, traders, and the like, became part of Nigerian vernacular English, with no taboo attached. In consequence, today it is as forbidden to say sexual intercourse, penis, and vagina on Nigerian television as it is to say fuck, cock, and cunt on the national networks in the United States. In Nigeria, the latter terms are considered normal and respectable. In individual conversation, the same holds true. To say that a young woman has a vagina or that she has sexual intercourse is an affront to her modesty that is not tolerated. The correct and expected reference is to her cunt and to fucking.

The taboo on the word, fuck, has left generations of people whose native language is English without a publicly usable verb or noun that fits into everyday usage as colloquially as does eat, sleep, think, talk, and dream. That is not fortuitous, for it is in the very nature of a taboo to proscribe an activity in which human beings otherwise might ordinarily engage (Chapter 6).

Though it encompasses all manifestations of sexuality, our sexual taboo is above all a taboo against nudity and the visual depiction of the sex organs and their use. Moslem culture has a taboo on the graven image of the face; ours is a taboo on the graven image of the groin. Thus, in the courts today, there is more prosecution of dirty picture books and dirty movies than of dirty stories.

If the sexual taboo was not strong in Europe before the advent of Christian sexual doctrine, with its antisexual penitentials or manuals of penance, then it was so subsequently. Yet, the fragmentary records available indicate that the suppressive injunctions of the penitentials were never totally successful in eradicating all dissidents. There was an undercurrent of earthy, if not dirty, bawdiness in Elizabethan England, which surfaced in force during the Restoration and then went underground in the Victorian era. Today, Victorianism is much maligned, but it was, in fact, a period of the reconciliation of opposites—of empire that coexisted with the growth of social equality, of religious revivalism that coexisted with the growth of modern science, of academic prudery that coexisted with the growth of modern sexology, and so on (Chapter 6).

One may add that the Victorian era was one in which sexual taboo coexisted not only with the discovery of modern birth control but also the new morality of sexual freedom thereby made possible. The beneficiaries of this new morality began to talk in their own vernacular, illustrated with its pictorial counterpart, that was more idiomatic and down-to-earth than the stilted terminology of medicine and the law.

For down-to-earth, substitute dirty. Then calling sex dirty becomes yet another manifestation of the Victorian genius for the reconciliation of opposites. Though officially tabooed, in art, literature, and behavior, sex was returned to the people, but under the label of dirty. Now it is time to clean up the dirt and to equate the dirty with the earthy, for the earth is clean and regenerative. The age at which to begin is childhood.

SEXUAL REHEARSAL PLAY. For both boys and girls, erotic/sexual development does not begin at puberty, as one folk dogma would have us believe. It begins, in fact, in earliest infancy, in the relationship of clinging, hugging, and cuddling. The now famous Wisconsin studies demonstrate that, if baby monkeys are deprived of these haptic or tactual experiences by being separated from their mothers and reared in total social isolation, then the entirety of their social behavior with other monkeys is impaired for life. The impairment affects adult sexual behavior. Males are even more susceptible than are females to impairment of the ultimate ability to perform coitus. In females, the impairment additionally affects parental behavior. If pregnancy is induced in an isolation-reared female, she becomes a mother unable to care for her baby. She is so neglectful and abusive, in fact, that the young one, especially the first-born, may not survive.

When not reared in isolation, but with others of their troop, monkey infants typically engage in play that is a form of sexual rehearsal. Developmentally, this sexual rehearsal play is absolutely imperative insofar as baby monkeys deprived of adequate opportunities to engage in it grow up unable to mate and reproduce their species.

Under naturalistic conditions of troop life, baby monkeys may begin mounting each other, and even displaying the mature foot-clasp mount, by two or three months of age (Goldfoot 1977). At first they climb on each other from all directions and are indiscriminate as to which sex does the presenting or the mounting and as to the sex of the partner. Eventually, their moves become sorted out so that males mount females, predominantly, and do so with their own feet off the ground, clasping the shanks of the female who presents in the four-legged position.

Rearing conditions pervasively influence the manifestations of sexual rehearsal play, and the age of its appearance. In an all-female group of juveniles, for example, there develops a hierarchy in which some females are dominant and others subordinant, and in which some mount others more often than they present and are mounted. Conversely, in an all-male group, there develops a hierarchy in which some males are subordinant and others dominant, and in which some present and are mounted more than they mount. In a mixed-sex group, males occupy the top of the dominance-subordinance hierarchy and establish a prevalence of mounting females who, reciprocally, become subordinant and present to be mounted.

To ensure sexual proficiency in adulthood, juvenile monkeys require not only sexual rehearsal play but also playmates of their own age with whom to engage in sexual rehearsals. A monkey male reared in isolation with an artificial, dummy mother may actually be observed going through the motor performance of mounting an appropriately positioned dummy, yet he remains forever incapable of mounting another live monkey. A baby reared in isolation not with a dummy, but with its real mother, also is not able to be a breeding partner as an adult.

Less severe conditions of socially restricted rearing produce less severe and sometimes partially reversible sexual defects. For example, when male infants were permanently separated from their mothers at 3 to 6 months of age, and allowed half an hour of peer-group play daily, about 30 percent of them developed foot-clasp mounting, but its appearance was delayed until they were 18 to 24 months of age. The remaining 70 percent tried to mount and were either wrongly oriented or, if correctly oriented, without success at foot-clasping, and their failures persisted as they were observed longitudinally over three years.

The absence of foot-clasp mounting in the yearling or juvenile male monkey is predictive of deficient sexual behavior in adulthood. Delayed development of foot-clasp mounting, as in the 30 percent above, is followed in adulthood by copulatory and breeding proficiency that is defective by comparison with animals reared in the wild. Males who do not ever develop foot-clasp mounting as infants or juveniles are incapable of copulating as adults.

The number of studies of the effects of depriving human infants and juveniles of sexual rehearsal play is exactly and precisely zero. Moreover, anyone who tried to conduct such a study would risk imprisonment for contributing to the delinquency of minors or for being obscene. Just imagine the headlines and the fate of a research grant application requesting funds to watch children play fucking games! Imagine, by contrast, headlines accusing parents, priests, and teachers of criminal neglect and abuse of children for depriving them of sexual rehearsal play or punishing them for it.

Deprivation and punishment notwithstanding, young children do sometimes engage in sexual rehearsal play, even in our own culture. There are other cultures in which the sexual rehearsal play of childhood is not outlawed or punished. It is in these cultures that the existence of such play has been most fully documented.

In the absence of the necessary evidence, it is not yet possible to argue in favor of an exclusively cultural hypothesis to explain the erotic/sexual rehearsal play of childhood. It is more likely that such play represents yet another of those aspects of human development for which the way is prepared in prenatal programing, but which cannot be completed without postnatal input from the social environment at an appropriate critical phase of development. The exact nature of the prenatal phyletic program or mechanism has not yet been ascertained. It may be a mechanism that has to do with close body contact in romping play. It may more specifically have to do with pelvic thrusting movements and genital presentation. Whether the prenatal program is different for each sex cannot be specified confidently on the basis of present knowledge. The sum total of animal observations suggest that the familiar principle of sex-shared but threshold-dimorphic behavior applies yet once again:

that is to say, in its earliest manifestations, erotic/sexual play is not sex-specific, but it gradually becomes consolidated to be so under the influence of social reinforcement.

Children may learn, more or less by trial and error, from one another or from their slightly older age mates, or the learning may be from much older people. In our society, erotic/sexual play and knowledge are transmitted in all three ways. Thus, at the kindergarten age, one may observe daughters being socially rewarded for being coquettishly flirtatious with their fathers, and sons for being manly little escorts with their mothers. At the same age, kindergarten boys and girls rehearse romantic pair-bonding, complete with glamorous plans for a wedding in Baltimore, a honeymoon in the Caribbean, and a cowboy ranch in Texas. The same children, accepted into the play of older children, are ready learners of more grown-up information on how-to-do-it sexuality. As they become older, their erotic/sexual rehearsal play becomes more guarded, as they assimilate the mores of prohibition and taboo and the self-regulation of behavior that ensues. The middle childhood years are not years of sexual latency, as a still popular doctrine asserts. They are years of sexual prudery in which sexual rehearsal play goes underground. Copulatory play is engaged in from time to time, as privacy permits, and the pair-bonding of a genuine love affair is occasionally encountered.

The adverse outcome of deprivation of sexual rehearsal play in rhesus monkeys has been documented, and there is no corresponding information regarding the effects of deprivation or, as is more usual, partial deprivation, moral prohibition, and punishment of sexual rehearsal play in children. However, according to a hypothesis published in 1978 by K. E. Money of Ontario, the period of several years of enforced postpubertal sexual deprivation in girls, which includes anorgasmia if a girl does not masturbate, may produce lasting damage. He draws an analogy with the permanent neural degeneration found in the visual regions of the brains of animals experimentally deprived of light and sight for a prolonged period after birth. There is support for this analogy in the 1953 Kinsey report on women, as in the conclusion: "While there are many females who appear to get along without such an outlet during their teens, the chances that a female can adjust sexually after marriage seem to be materially improved if she has experienced orgasm at an early age." Kinsey and associates also found an association between degree of religious devoutness and orgasmic response, devoutness being presumably related to antisexual moral injunctions in childhood, at least in the religion quoted, namely, Catholicism: "There were 21% of the devoutly Catholic females who had not reached orgasm by thirty-five years of age ... though most of them were then married and regularly having coitus in their marriages. It was not more than 2% of the nominal, nonreligious Catholics who had not reached orgasm by that age." Of course, the figures themselves do not guarantee cause and effect, but they certainly suggest a causal hypothesis.

The possible effects of deprivation are not restricted to females. In fact, deprivation of infantile sexual rehearsal play may have more widespread and long-term damaging effects of delayed onset than anyone has yet suspected in either men or women. There is, hypothetically, a very good probability that in the absence of rehearsing ordinary male-female sexual interaction, and the imagery of it in mental representation, children establish instead various improvisations and substitutes that become the basis of full-blown paraphilias in later life. The bonding of exclusive homosexuality may also be facilitated in this way. A child's parents, of course, have no cognizance of what is going on. Themselves victims of the sexual taboo in our society, they are culturally required to leave their child's psychosexual development to chance, instead of being able to shape its normalcy. It is possible that all the anomalies of eroticism and psychosexuality in adolescence and adulthood, not only the paraphilias but also the hypophilias and hyperphilias, share the same source, namely, deprivation of normal sexual rehearsals in infancy and childhood.

Just as errors and idiosyncracies of speech and language may be postnatally programed, so also may errors and idiosyncracies of erotic/sexual imagery and arousal. Though it cannot be categorically stated that such errors and idiosyncracies can be programed into the person at puberty or later, the weight of today's evidence is that they are programed-in much earlier in childhood. It is highly likely that this aspect of development is contemporaneous with the manifestation of erotic/sexual rehearsal play in the early years. Deprivation of such play, or punishment of it, may well have adverse effects on erotic/sexual development far greater than most people conventionally believe.

Conventional beliefs have been able to survive challenge because early errors of erotic/sexual development may remain relatively covert or dormant until puberty. It is with the hormonal changes of puberty that the thresholds for erotic/sexual expression and for the manifestation of erotic/sexual imagery are lowered—behavior and imagery both appear with greater ease and frequency than in childhood.

At puberty, the sex disparity in imagery shows itself rather dramatically in the erotic dreams of boys, so-called wet dreams that culminate in orgasm. There is no corresponding phenomenon in girls. In fact, according to present evidence, even the frequency of erotic dreaming without orgasm is less in adolescent girls than boys. For females, the frequency of erotic dreaming peaks in young adulthood, at which time it is already lessening in frequency in males.

Of course, it is easy to point out that the sex disparity in erotic/sexual dreaming faithfully reflects the greater stringency with which our society's sexual taboo is applied to girls than boys, in the developing years. Anthropological studies in sexually open-minded societies have not addressed themselves to sexual imagery and dreaming, so that there are no data on what happens to women who are not taboo-ridden. In our own society, there may soon be a small population of women sufficiently emancipated from the taboo in childhood who will be able to supply the information currently lacking. Meantime, it is reasonable not to assume an exclusively cultural origin for the sex disparity in visual/erotic imagery, but to view it as the joint product of both prenatal-hormonal and postnatal-social determinants. Here is yet another example of sex-shared, threshold-dimorphic behavior in child development.

In other species, especially subprimates, the nose is the organ of erotic/sexual arousal at a distance. In the case of the dog, for example, the male smells from a distance the pheromonal odor secreted from the vagina of the ovulating bitch and pursues her in order to copulate. Pheromonal attraction has been experimentally demonstrated in primates, but in humankind the sense of smell is subordinate to vision as the medium of erotic/sexual arousal at a distance. It is quite possible that some people, male and female, are more responsive than others to erotic odors. Thus it is possible that some men and women surpass others in their enthusiasm for oral sex.

CULTURAL LEGACIES OF EROTIC/SEXUAL CODING. Adolescents among the various indigenous ethnic peoples in America have their own indigenous erotic/sexual legacies or codes, more or less modified by contact with the now dominant imported culture of mainstream America. The Eskimo tradition, for instance, differs from, say, the Hopi or the Navaho, and each differs from the tradition of the kinship family and open sexuality in adolescence that characterizes the Polynesian erotic/sexual tradition of American Samoa.

The erotic/sexual script for adolescents of the mainstream of both American and European culture is derived not from a single tradition, historically, but from three. They may be termed Mediterranean, Nordic, and Amerafrican. Each has a different formula for the relationship of men and women. Though the remote history of each of these component traditions is lost in the mists of time, a few features can be reconstructed, conjecturally, on the basis of present evidence.

The Mediterranean Legacy. In a somewhat pejorative way, it is currently fashionable to call this Eastern Mediterranean legacy Judeo-Christian, but its origins are undoubtedly older than the Bible, putatively in or east of the region of the fertile crescent. Its regional representation still extends far beyond the Biblical realm of Judah, through India to China and Japan. It is the tradition of the virgin bride and the double standard of inequality between the sexes. One may conjecture that this tradition was historically related in origin to the development of urbanization. Urbanization itself was related to the institution of hierarchical power and wealth. Historically, the first cities may possibly have evolved as hypertrophied villages, that is as an egalitarian collection of huts, all uniform in design, and each one constructed by its own occupants. The record of archeology shows, however, that a very long time ago cities featured elitism: a hierarchy of residential grandeur, including palaces, temples, and monuments, dependent on wealth. Elitism requires that the poor or enslaved labor for the wealthy and powerful. From occupational enslavement, it is an easy step to sexual enslavement. In a patriarchal tradition, sexual enslavement means that men own women by paying a bride price to the woman's parents, irrespective of her own consent. The greater the wealth and power, the greater the number of polygamous wives or of concubines in the harem.

According to the binary logic of sex, the greater the proportion of sequestered women in a society, the greater the proportion of unpaired males for whom the society must provide an alternative—wars and feuds in which they die, enforced celibacy, homosexual pairing, or shared pairing with harlots. The whorehouse, the public harem, is the counterpart of the seraglio, the private harem. The polyandry of the one matches the polygyny of the other, and the institution of the double standard is complete. Women are either whores or madonnas. Only the whores of society are entitled to more than one male partner. Their children are their own responsibility. Madonnas are bound by the rule of chastity and fidelity. They bear children for their master or husband, and he owns them until, if daughters, he gives them away in marriage or, if sons, they reach legal adulthood.

Whereas legal polygamy has long since disappeared in our society, the institution of the whorehouse has preserved itself since ancient times, and the concubine or mistress, the kept woman, still exists. The doctrine of the virgin bride and the double standard is still the official one, and still honored in many articles of the law, though otherwise increasingly honored in the breach rather than the observance.

The Nordic Legacy. Today's adolescents who establish their sex lives by breaching the doctrine of the virgin bride and the double standard are, whether they know it or not, adopting a modern counterpart of another very ancient tradition, one which undoubtedly covered a region more vast than the term Nordic or Scandinavian would imply. This is the tradition of betrothal and sexual egalitarianism. It is called Nordic because it survived longest in Scandinavia. There it resisted the incursion of the Mediterranean system, which spread into Northern Europe as an adjunct of Christianity. There, especially in remote rural areas, it may still be traced. As recently as the last century, it could also be traced southward through Eastern Europe to the Alps. In the seventeenth century, it crossed the Atlantic from northern Britain and Scotland to New England, where it was known as bundling. In Denmark, it is known as night courting, and the translation of the Finnish term is taking your night legs for a walk.

As its name implies, the betrothal system is one in which not the marriage but the betrothal of a young couple is the ceremony that marks the highpoint of their beginning as a breeding partnership. As recorded in nineteenth-century Finland, the season for betrothal began with the advent of spring, for in the winter a typical farm family and its hired hands survived the subzero nights by sleeping in the big kitchen around a great fireplace or heating stove. In spring, the loft of the night-foot house became the sleeping quarters of the young unmarried women. From the lower floor, used for storage, they reached the loft by a ladder let down through a trap door that closed behind them. To admit visitors, they either unlatched the inside trap door, or hung a rope outside from their upstairs window. The visitors were young men from the local region who banded together to serenade the girls. The girls decided whether or not to invite the boys to join them, and also whether to invite them to return. When it happened that a boy and a girl became romantically interested in one another, it was proper for their friends to allow them to meet together alone. Thereafter they followed a prescribed routine whereby the boy would stay the night with his girlfriend, but sleeping with his clothes on and above the covers. Step by step, visit by visit, he got under the covers, and then under the covers with his clothes off, at which point the couple announced to the family their intent to be betrothed. The betrothal would lead eventually to marriage, but only if a pregnancy had ensued. Marriage itself was a confirmation of parenthood rather than of coition. The ability to create a family was socially and economically more important than the right to have sexual intercourse. In this farming and fishing culture, the family was historically the vocational and economic unit. In such a family unit, the woman's role was as important as the man's. There was a high degree of erotic egalitarianism between the sexes, even though the society was a patriarchal one in which men dominated in political and military leadership.

The ancient betrothal system left its mark on contemporary Scandinavian mores even when it no longer survived intact, for there has always been in Scandinavian urban culture an easier acceptance of adolescent and young-adult sexuality leading to marriage, in place of the Mediterranean custom of marrying first and testing sexuality and fertility afterward.

The Scandinavian system was ready made for the age of birth control, an age in which adolescents and young adults can live together in an erotic/sexual relationship not for the purpose of finding out whether they can become parents, but because they know that with birth control they can avoid becoming parents until they are financially, vocationally, and personally ready to take on the responsibilities of parenthood. The reborrowing of the time-honored system of betrothal has been made possible by reason of cultural diffusion in print, in film, and in the direct international travel of students. Betrothal represents not a loss of moral standards, but the reinstatement of a time-tested morality that happens to be uniquely appropriate to the age of birth control, and an age of a newly discovered erotic/sexual egalitarianism. The old morality of betrothal fills our society's need for a new ethic of recreational sex prior to taking on the responsibilities of procreational sex.

The Amerafrican Legacy. The morality of both the betrothal system and the virgin-bride system in our society today is based on the assumption of a two-person pair-bond and, when children are born, of a nuclear family rather than an extended kinship family. The tradition of Black Amerafrican adolescents in the era of slavery in the New World was different. The aftermath of this tradition is still a powerful cultural influence not only in the New World. It is present also in Europe by reason of cultural borrowing from America, and by reason of the influx of citizens from former colonial countries into the European homelands.

Because African slaves were haphazardly distributed in the New World without consideration of their cultural or linguistic origins, there is no way of linking the erotic/sexual mores of slavery to the mores of respective tribal origin, some of which were patriarchal and some matriarchal, some sexually restrictive and some not. The erotic/sexual mores of slavery can, however, be linked to the institution of slavery itself in America. American slaves legally had the status of animals insofar as they had no legal rights whatsoever. Marriage is a legal right, and so American slaves had no legal right to claim to be married. Lovers and parents had no legal right to remain together, nor to have their children remain with them. To stay together as lovers or as a family unit was a privilege bestowed by the master. There was no guarantee that it would be bestowed. There is no historical record of how often families were allowed to remain together, nor of how often they were sold and permanently separated. Such statistics were not kept by slave owners whose own morality was officially Biblical and Christian. It is known, however, that there were slave breeding customs analogous to animal husbandry, and that it was common for slave-owning males, their sons, and their male relatives and friends to exercise their sexual rights of ownership with female slaves, though if a white woman did the same, then by definition she had been raped by a slave who paid the penalty, usually with his life.

A young slave mother had no right to stay at home with her offspring. While she went to her assigned work, the baby stayed in the yard under the care of yard slaves, who were the elderly and the infirm. Regardless of genealogical relationship, these older people constituted, in fact, the grandparental generation. It was in this generation that couples lived together in a relationship, an actuality made possible partly because they were less saleable in old age, and partly because, in some cases, of a master's sense of loyalty to his slaves. Thus the culture pattern of slavery was that infants and juveniles would be looked after by the aged, while the young, parental generation did the daily work of the plantation. Whatever was supplied to juveniles by way of food, shelter, and clothing was decided by the plantation manager. His place today has been taken by the local Department of Welfare in black urban ghettos, and likewise, but to a lesser degree, in rural ghettos. Thus is perpetuated a culture of poverty in which young mothers are obliged to live on welfare, or else to work for inadequate wages while their young children are left by day in the care of someone else. The someone else is typically the grandmother, with or without the man to whom in middle life she may have become married. The day nursery today may replace the grandmother. The young father of the young children may or may not contribute to the children's financial support. He may or may not be in close contact with his children. Even if he does not bother to see them, he does not repudiate paternity, but rather is proud of it. It is rare that a child does not know who its father is, for even though a woman may not be ensured of a long-term relationship with her child's father, only occasionally is pregnancy one product of multiple concurrent sexual liaisons.

There is much that is positive in the Amerafrican system of pair-bonding and erotic/sexual relationships—the system of grandmaternal responsibility and of rotating the care of children across three generations. It is a system that potentially recognizes the erotic sexuality of adolescence and early adulthood. Its great defect is specific to the society in which it exists, the United States society of the mainstream, namely, that there is no effective, institutionalized economic support for the rotational system of child care (every breeding system is interlocked with the economic system of its society). Thus, young parents cannot provide economically for their own offspring, and they remain so impoverished that, as grandparents, they still do not have an adequate budget for the care of grandchildren. And so poverty perpetuates itself. As a by-product of such a system, women are given an excess of independence and responsibility in comparison with men, but not the necessary economic support and authority with which to exercise their responsibility. They have the domestic autonomy that would be denied to them in the Mediterranean system, but it is an autonomy that does not mean much in the absence of vocational and economic autonomy.

As transmitted to adolescents, each of the three legacies, Mediterranean, Nordic, and Amerafrican, explicitly prescribes how to begin, establish, and pursue a breeding-partner relationship. That is to say, they are prescriptions for the three erotic/sexual phases, proception, acception, and conception that are taken up in Chapter 5.

BETROTHAL TODAY. Historically, reinstatement of the Nordic system of becoming betrothed in order to mark the onset of a sex life together began innocuously enough among college students at around the time of World War I. This was the generation of students who interpolated a new ceremony, pinning, into the established ritual of courtship and romance. When a student pinned his girlfriend by attaching his fraternity pin to her sweater, his fraternity brothers greeted the news by organizing a serenade. With lighted candles, they assembled beneath the girl's window. When she and the other girls of her dormitory appeared at their windows with their own lighted candles, the men sang to her. Subsequently, the event was chronicled in the college newspaper. By wearing her pin, a girl signaled hands-off to all potential suitors. She already belonged to her own special boyfriend, and dated only him. Their relationship could be terminated by giving back the pin, or it could progress through the traditional ritual of engagement with a diamond ring, to marriage and a wedding band.

Being pinned meant being faithful as a dating companion, but it did not mean having sexual intercourse—or at least not openly and frankly admitting it. Methods of contraception were available in that early part of the century, but they were not widely acceptable nor easily obtainable, especially for young unmarried partners. It was in the jazz age of the '20s that contraception became more acceptable to the unmarried who were ready to begin their sex lives, but not yet ready to become parents. This was the era of the flappers. Young women were more emancipated than ever before, and there was a new style of dating among the sophisticated—"playing the field" before going steady and having only one boyfriend. Then, perhaps, they began their sex life.

At the end of the '20s, the thin latex condom was on the market for the first time. It enabled the male partner to take the initiative and the responsibility in contraception, and it was thin enough for men to find it acceptable.

Despite the social disruptions of World War II, going steady became an increasingly prevalent custom in the '50s. The fraternity pin gave way to the high school class ring as the token of attachment, or the girlfriend wore the boy's letter-man sweater or jacket, or his neck chain with a St. Christopher medal on it. Sometimes friendship rings were exchanged, and the boy wore his girlfriend's ring not on his own finger, but on his neck chain.

In the '50s, going steady was in vogue among the high-school age group. In all age groups, going steady usually gave a positive sanction to heavy petting, but not to going "all the way" to include penovaginal penetration. Couples varied as to how complete their heavy petting would be. For some it included orgasm induced digitally or orally. Oral sex was more likely to be fellatio (a blow job, or giving head) than cunnilingus (eating out). Finger and manual stimulation were more likely to proceed to the climax of orgasm for the boy rather than the girl. A few couples even adapted themselves to sleeping naked together without actually enclosing the penis in the vagina. Those who did include penovaginal intromission were for the most part obliged to keep quiet about it in order to avoid social disapprobation and stigmatization, especially of the girl. The double standard gave more protection to the reputation of the boy than the girl.

The college-age group of the '60s dispensed with pin, ring, or other token as a declaration of going steady. Sex that included penovaginal copulation gradually gained acceptability for those who were going steady, provided the girl accepted and the boy obeyed the formula of declaring that he loved her. The greatest impediment to establishing a sex life, except on the proverbial back seat of a car, was lack of a comfortable and private place to rest. Motels with private individual entrances solved the problem for those with spending money. They led the way for hotels to become indifferent as to whether couples who registered together were married or not.

The '60s were the "hippie" era in which many traditions were challenged and values reformulated. Sexual cohabitation and a couple's shared living quarters were taken for granted by hippie movement people. Hippies gained for their generation the right of betrothal—the right not simply to go steady, but to live together sexually, openly, and for an indefinite period of time, with or without an eventual commitment to marriage or childbearing.

This right of betrothal has, in the '70s, become more widely accepted, even for daughters, and by fathers who, only a decade ago, would have gone berserk, according to the precepts of the double standard and the virgin bride, had they found one of their own daughters in bed with a man.

The new morality of betrothal makes it possible for some parents to permit their betrothed teenagers to sleep in one bed at home (Chapter 3). For these people marriage is an economic and a procreational contract, as well as an erotic/sexual one. It guarantees the welfare of offspring. Thus it is possible to envisage that the new morality of betrothal will allow couples to better match themselves for marriage, thereby allowing a marriage to be more long-lasting, once it is contracted. Thus, living together in betrothal may be the new generation's answer to the decline of the nuclear family, to use a hackneyed phrase. It may ensure that, once procreation is embarked upon, the children will have the continuously unbroken bond with each parent that is needed in the juvenile and adolescent years to guarantee sexual and behavioral healthiness in adulthood.

SOURCES AND CONTENT OF ADOLESCENT INFORMATION ON SEX AND LOVE. Adolescents grow up in our society today with a prior history of having received a patchwork of messages, derived from all three of the legacies. These messages pertain to the male and the female roles in all three phases of erotic sexuality. The sources of these messages, for the most part haphazardly uncoordinated, are the home, the church, the school, the peer-group crowd one runs with, and the media. The most conservative sources are the home, church, and school, and the publications that they endorse or sponsor. From these sources emanates a well-formulated moral or sociological education, but one that is marked by what social anthropologists would call cultural lag, for it was originally formulated in the precontraceptive era and has not been updated. It embraces the official morality of modesty, virginity, marriage, monogamy, and chastity.

Though equivocal about it, these same sources are, between them, capable of formulating an elementary procreational sex education comprising the physiology of pubertal body changes, menstruation, fertilization, pregnancy, and venereal disease, plus or minus warnings about masturbation and copulation, and usually minus explicit information about delivery. What these conservative sources are not well able to formulate, or are evasive about, is love education and the erotic aspects of pair-bonding: infatuation, falling in love, dating, going steady, breaking up, disobeying the double standard, techniques of eroticism, contraceptive procedure, timing the onset of one's sex life, and atypical practices and partnerships, like sex parties and homosexuality.

The gap in love education left by the conservative sources is filled by the more liberal sources of the peer group and the media, especially the entertainment media that the peer group supports. Much of the peer group tradition is handed on by word of mouth, and occasional graffiti. There is still a persistence of two oral traditions, girls' talk for girls only, and boys' talk for boys only. The two traditions are themselves part of the double standard that they help to reinforce and maintain. The extent to which adolescent boys and girls cross the boundaries of each other's sex talk is increasing, especially in older adolescents, but the actual amount of increase remains to be ascertained. The greater amount of shared information comes not from shared talk, but from the media. Reading material is sex-segregated more than it is sex-shared. Love stories and true confessions are girls' domain. In their own way, they are girls' pornography, though quite legal. The counterpart for boys is visual erotica, around which they can spin their own erotic fantasies. Erotography for pubertal boys may be as legal as the female negligée pages of the Sears, Roebuck catalogue; or as illegal as hardcore, stigmatized pornography.

The prime source of sex-shared love education is music—the lyrics of popular songs. They are a virtual barometer of where adolescents are at, in love and sex. For those who understand the argot and the idiom, popular songs have recently become increasingly raunchy in making reference to erotic sensation, genital arousal, intercourse, and orgasm. But always the rationale is love, the irresistible tidal force that carries one, powerless, away. Love is prodigal. Love is profligate. There is no place in this romantic philosophy for pragmatism and the practicalities of contracting to live together, and of resolving the stresses of living together and of having offspring. Love conquers all, devours all, and justifies all. Love spurned and love unfaithful bring intolerable anguish to the loser. But that cannot be helped. When new love beckons, that also cannot be helped. It must be obeyed. Then euphoria reigns forever.

FALLING IN LOVE: PAIR-BONDING. Love means pair-bondedness, and falling in love is the experience of establishing a pair-bond. Like the charismatic religious experience of being saved or born again, falling in love may be sudden and dramatic—love at first sight—or it may be a slow and gradual realization. For the human species, nature did not design a pair-bond between the sexes that is brief, as it is in those species in which mating is timed by the female's period of heat, or estrus. Nor did nature design us to be seasonal pair-bonders. Rather, we pair-bond with no fixed time limit, in some instances until the proverbial "death do us part." It is possible, though probably infrequent, for a lasting pair-bond involving sexual eroticism to be first established in prepuberty. For the majority of people, however, puberty predates the forming of the first erotic pair-bond, sometimes by many years. Multiple pair-bonds may be simultaneous, though they are more likely to be serial. If they are simultaneous, they are likely to differ in intensity at any given period. Advanced age is not a barrier to establishing a new pair-bond. After separation or death of the partner, bereavement precludes the establishment of a new pair-bond, usually for at least two years.

The experience of falling in love resembles what, among ethologists, is called imprinting. That is to say, there is within the organism a developmental condition of readiness, the timing of which is governed phyletically, to encounter a particular type of perceptual stimulus. The configuration and dimensions of this stimulus are variable, but there are limits or boundaries which, like timing, also are governed phyletically. When the external percept becomes imprinted into the perceiving organism, it becomes personal property, so to speak. Personal ownership then becomes projected onto the source of the percept, in the present instance, the love-mate or partner. If the partner has been undergoing a parallel and complementary experience of becoming love-imprinted, then a reciprocal feedback is established and the love affair or pair-bond is very intense and durable, even though each partner may be judged abnormal by social or legal criteria. The more one-sided or skewed this feedback, the more unstable the pair-bond and the more likely the chances that it will pull asunder. A strong pair-bond maintains itself at its level of highest passion typically for a maximum of two or three years. It may be construed as nature's guarantee that a pregnancy will ensue. When it wanes, it also metamorphoses to encompass the possibility of extension to incorporate mother-infant and father-infant bonding. Parent-child pair-bonds are usually exceptionally durable. Once established they are virtually unbreakable, though in certain instances they fail to become established.

There is a rather sophisticated riddle about what a boyfriend (or girlfriend) and a Rorschach inkblot have in common. The answer is that you project an image of your own onto each. In many instances, a person does not fall in love with a partner, per se, but with a partner as a Rorschach love-blot. That is to say, the person projects onto the partner an idealized and highly idiosyncratic image that diverges from the image of that partner as perceived by other people. Hence the popular idiom that love is blind, for a lover projects onto a partner, or love-blot, his/her unique love image, as unique as his/her own face or finger print. The lover cannot tolerate or absorb criticism of this love-blot partner.

For example, a young man secretly obsessed with transvestism projects onto his younger girl friend an image of compliance and positive happiness in his cross-dressing, without telling her about it. She projects onto him an image of a savior who will deliver her from the bonds of an alcoholic father, into a life of idyllic happiness, despite the fact that she has a secret phobia of vaginal penetration. Each has a hidden agenda for the other that neither can live up to, any more than an ink-blot can become a butterfly. Revealing the hidden agenda may not help. Under the pressure of disillusionment, if it ensues, the pair-bond weakens, disputes proliferate, and love turns to hate and destructive violence.

When the partner is cast in the role of a love-blot, his or her existence is, so to speak, metaphorical. Conceptual or metaphorical existence of any partner is an identifying characteristic of sacred as compared with profane love. This is true even if the partner should be apostrophized as a deity, mother nature, the fatherland, or whatever.

Profane or secular love may be either affectional or erotic. Affectional love may be filiative, neighborly, or comradely. Erotic love may be either recreational or procreational, regardless of whether it is connubial or companionate. The separation of recreational from procreational love formerly was a function of the age of fertility of the female, which is why the very concept of recreational sex conjures up in people's minds an image of the philandering male, exploiting women and taking no responsibility for paternity. In the age of birth control all that has changed. Any couple, married or unmarried, may now plan most of their copulation as recreational.

Procreation may take place without love-bonding, as in donor insemination, to take an extreme case. Recreational sex may take place with only the most perfunctory and transient bonding. Even in a one-night stand, however, there may be a passionate onset of what could become long-term bonding. Popular idiom notwithstanding, there really is no such thing as a purely physical relationship. The meaning of that saying is that one partner, usually the male, does not guarantee a continuing and economically supported relationship. As exemplified by the institution of the bride price, marriage is an economic as well as a sexual bond—a sort of guarantee that where the sex organs go the checkbook will follow. So it is that many people, especially young people, adhere to a ritual formula for being in love, with the presumption of a long-term economic commitment guaranteed, in order to justify engaging in coitus, even though reluctantly and without erotic enthusiasm and abandon. In such a relationship, the imagery and expectancy that each has of the other seldom match reciprocally. Inchoately and inarticulately trying to find words to express the mismatch, each senses the self to be a kind of mannequin for the other's fantasy, and not an authentic and sufficient stimulus for the other's erotic arousal. Each is on the periphery of the other's eroticism, and there is no mutual erotic feedback, no abandon, between them. The woman often falls back on the platitude of being wanted only for her body. Her dilemma of erotic loneliness and isolation is not female-specific. It affects men too. In both sexes, it is quite likely to set one on the path of searching for better love elsewhere.

The difficulty that people have in matching themselves for a lasting pair-bond is evidenced by the fact that today's divorce rate is approximately 40 percent of all marriages (Chapter 6). That figure would be tolerable if all divorces were childless. The children of divorce pay too great a psychological price for their parents' mismatching—a price that society at large must eventually absorb and can ill-afford to do. The problem of failed pair-bonds is one that needs more serious investigation than divorce courts alone can give it.

Pair-bonding is a growth experience, somewhat akin to a religious conversion, in which each partner accedes to being made over in the image of the other, at least to some degree. The extent to which this accedence is exclusively a product of pair-bonding, and the extent to which the couple gave complementary cues and collusional signals to one another ahead of time is still a matter of conjecture and guesswork. The transvestite, to use that example again, discloses nothing about his transvestism to the girl he courts. She a teenager, ten years his junior, seeking to escape the vicissitudes of submitting to the impositions of her alcoholic father, fails to disclose the existence of her problem of penovaginal phobia. Her transvestite lover perhaps recognizes that she is habituated to being imposed upon and adapting herself to someone else's foibles or pathology. Conversely, she perhaps realizes he is somehow odd. With uncanny frequency, regardless of the explanation, men and women do, in fact, habituate themselves to a partner's erotic imagery, even when it is quite pathological.

Sometimes coincidence may dictate one's biography of pair-bonding. Thus, under the deprivation of living sex-segregated in prison, a man may discover in himself a bisexual versatility formerly hidden. Then he may impose a homosexual encounter on a nonconsenting partner. But he may also match up with a consenting partner, a so called joy boy. Thereby he demonstrates rather nicely the dependence of a person on his environment to provide him with a partner for an erotic pair-bond. The gender-transposed and the paraphilic person are in a similar position, for there is no guaranteed system of reciprocal partner-finding for those, including the physically handicapped, whose requirements are atypical. By contrast, under ordinary circumstances, age-matched men and women are attracted erotically with sufficient prevalence to ensure a society that is predominantly heterosexually pair-bonded.

A long-lasting reciprocal love-match between two partners is one in which there is reciprocally a very close love-blot match. That means there is a very close fit between the actuality of each partner and the love-blot image projected on to him or her by the other partner, and this is a two-way fit. For this high degree of fit to take place, it is irrelevant whether the two partners are replicas or polar opposites of one another in temperament, interests, achievements, or whatever. What counts is that they fulfill each the other's ideal in imagery and expectancy, even though neither may be able to spell out this expectancy in words. Over the years, what also counts is that change of imagery and expectancy, if it takes place, is mutual and not one-sided. A couple can grow together as they change, or they can grow apart. There are, as yet, no foolproof rules for determining which dynamic will prevail. However, it seems likely that the closer the love-blot match at the outset, the more will the relationship change and grow in mutual harmony, and the more durably will their pair-bondedness become fused.

Fusion into mutual harmony may be either helped or hindered by the legal contract of marriage. The very idea that marriage may hinder harmonious pair-bondedness is a sacrilege, according to the folk belief that wedded couples live happily ever after. The marriage contract, however, is a public declaration of a change not only of status but also of role. Assimilation into the new role, even for a couple who have lived together for some time, is synonymous with a corresponding change in identity. With uncanny frequency, identity/role change and change in name or nickname parallel one another. Name change is, by tradition, imposed on the woman at marriage. The wedding ceremony does not impose a name change on the man, but husband and wife, especially after the first baby is born, may both address one another no longer by first name as lovers, nor even as friends, but as poppa and momma, or dad and mum, respectively. Insidiously, they change their mutual identity/roles.

With or without the dramatization of a name change, marriage drama-tizes a change of role from that of courtship and betrothal to that of spouse. Some couples retain a high degree of reciprocal matching when they make this transition, whereas others do not. Whether the transition results in reciprocal matching or mismatching hinges with great fre-quency on the fact that newlyweds inchoately fall back on the husband-wife role model that they lived with and assimilated in their own child-hood. They do so, even though they may have subsequently become alienated from their parents and from everything that they despised in their parents' marriages. There are no guaranteed prophesies as to who will become durably pair-bonded with whom, but a likely combination is that of a couple each of whom had, as models, parents who themselves had a durable and harmonious pair-bond as spouses.

For many people it may sound rather preposterous on first hearing, but it is in fact true that animals, at least of some species, experience the equivalent of what human beings rejoice in as falling in love. That is to say, one partner is more attractive than others that are available, and the bond established between the pair is more durable. Some years ago, Frank Beach discovered this preferential attractiveness and attracted-ness in beagle dogs. When young, these dogs had participated in an artificial lekking experiment. That is to say, several males were tethered to posts, widely separated around the edge of a field. Bitches in heat one by one were then set loose in the field, so that they were free to visit with all the males without being pursued, and then to copulate with one of them. Different bitches mated with different males. The basis of their individual attraction remained unknown, and it could have been transient. But it was not transient. The animals did not meet together again for seven full years, at which time Beach serendipitously hit on the idea of repeating the experiment. Lo and behold, the bitches showed an extraordinary tendency to return to exactly the same mate.

This same kind of preferential partner attraction and bonding has been observed also in subhuman primates—monkeys and apes—under experimental conditions and in the wild. Among chimpanzees in the wild, there is, indeed, something that resembles a honeymoon, insofar as a dominant male and a favored female, when she is ovulating, may take off from the troop and spend two or three days alone together in the bush.

The favoring of one partner over another may even cross the boundary of species. There is a true story of a female rhesus monkey in one lab who fell in love with her keeper. She paid no erotic attention to male monkeys and rebuffed their approaches, but demonstrated her interest in her keeper quite unequivocally. Once, after he had been on leave for several months, she went wild with excitement when he returned and she saw him for the first time.

The converse of favoring one mate over others is what may be termed the novelty effect with an unfamiliar mate. In laboratory experiments, the novelty effect in species like the rat is easily evident in males, for, after they have quit copulating with a familiar female in estrus, if a new female is put into the cage, copulation will resume. Monkeys show the same novelty effect. Michael and Zumpe kept laboratory records over a three-and-a-half-year period on the copulations of male rhesus monkeys paired regularly with the same females. Year by year, the scores gradually decreased. Then a novel female was introduced, and up went the scores dramatically. They stayed up for several weeks until the new partners were relocated and the old ones returned. Down went the scores to the same low level as they had been when the pairs were together at the end of the three-and-a-half-year period of familiarity, prior to the arrival of the new females.

LOVE DISPOSSESSED. Michael's experiment was not designed to demonstrate whether the novelty effect applies to females as well as males. Among human beings, it has long been one of the sex stereotypes that men are more promiscuous than women, and more afflicted with the roving eye, whereas women are alleged to be more given to monogamy and long-term romanticism. There is no way of obtaining statistics with which to argue the point, for people like actors assimilate so well the roles in which they are type-cast that there is no way of differentiating either the role or the type-casting as either the cause or the effect of the assimilation. The situation is rather like that of trying to prove that only Chinese can speak Chinese perfectly without being able to rear non-Chinese babies to have Chinese as their mother tongue. Statistics notwithstanding, it is a matter of everyday observation that some women as well as some men do encounter the novelty effect. Either a man or a woman may be jolted out of a sagging relationship by the unexpected onset of a new love affair.

In the Mediterranean system of monogamy that officially prevails in our society, it formerly was partially sanctioned for the husband to have a mistress or concubine, as well as a wife. There was no corresponding custom for the wife to have a paramour.

Today's wife is as likely to be intolerant of her husband's new paramour as he is expected to be of hers, if she has one. The Mediterranean system offers no prescription for adultery except either to relinquish the paramour, or to divorce the spouse, or to be killed in a crime of passion. In Islam, adultery is punishable by death. No alternative does justice to one of the primary realities of pair-bonding, namely, that each partner in a pair-bond becomes the personal psychic property of the other, owned and possessed in his/her imagery, thoughts, and fantasies while awake and in dreams while asleep. The person can depart, bodily, but the imagery, thoughts, fantasies, and dreams leave far less promptly. To be dispossessed by a lover is, in the vernacular, to have a broken heart. It is a state of despair, grief, and bereavement, as in loss by death; but, since the partner is not dead, it may also be a state of enraged hatred.

Despair and rage when a love relationship is unilaterally broken are intensifications of similar reactions that are experienced when only one partner in a beginning relationship has the complete experience of falling in love and the other responds companionably, even erotically and sexually, but without the special frenzy of being love-smitten. The partner smitten with love is, to use a new term coined by Dorothy Tennov, in a state of limerence. He/she wavers between euphoric bliss, when the signs of the other partner's reciprocity are deciphered as positive, and melancholic jealousy, when they are not. The kind of disequilibrium that ensues fairly readily leads to the possibility of self-injurious or self-sabotaging maneuvers or, even more readily, to injurious or sabotaging maneuvers aimed at the partner, or sometimes another person. Whichever way, the two partners enter, in effect, into an adversary relationship, the proverbial lovers' quarrel. Typically, the quarrel ends in a reconciliation. For a while, the limerent lover walks on air, and the other lover makes concessions until, eventually, the cycle repeats itself. Some couples go on in this way indefinitely. Others finally quarrel for the last time. Usually, they are able to make a permanent break only if the relationship is completely severed for a prolonged period, despite the suffering that a complete break engenders, especially in the partner who continues to be love-smitten. The love-smitten one can be expected to recover when sufficient time has passed to permit the onset of a new love affair with a new partner. It is much the same as when a lover or spouse is lost by death or divorce.

In some cases of lopsided love, in which only one partner is truly smitten, the couple will attempt to resolve their disequilibrium by getting legally married. When this relationship as adversaries continues, they may then resort to the formula of having a baby. In effect, the baby is assigned the task of reconciliator, a responsibility which, of course, is too great a demand on any baby.

People do not have voluntary control over whether they will become love-smitten or not. Nor do they have voluntary control over the special love-blot characteristics, typically highly idiosyncratic, of the person who will trigger their reaction. Neither science nor society have, as yet, a coherent tradition to transmit to young people to help them spare themselves the lovelorn agony of love unrequited or love dispossessed. In particular, there is no tradition of how to fight fair. Rather the tradition is that true love, by definition, excludes conflict and disagreement. But that is not true of any long-term human relationship.

In our folkways regarding pair-bonding, there is no preparation of partners for an open relationship based on a primary allegiance that will not be threatened or destroyed by the involvement of either or both in a supplemental relationship. On the contrary, preparation from childhood onward is for sexual jealousy and exclusivity. Ironically, the generation of elders that upholds the system while transmitting it to their children are blinded by their self-righteousness so that they fail to foresee the suffering that they may be saving up for themselves. They may be scheduled for a second time around, either because of break-up or divorce, or because of death of one of the partners. Then they may find that jealousy and exclusivity don't work so well on the second time around. The system was not designed for the pairing of older partners. In fact, it was designed at a time when very few people lived long enough to need a second partner in middle or old age. This defect in the system is particularly acute for the older women today, because men die younger. Thus there is a surplus of lonely, still active older ladies for whom no single, exclusive male partner can be found. In addition, some older couples who are well suited to live together are reluctant to become legally remarried because their combined incomes are greater if they remain unmarried. Some also are restrained from marriage by their children, either for moralistic reasons, or to protect their expected inheritance.

Older people have good reason to reexamine the popular linkage of love and sex with commitment. Commitment to what? Commitment to raising a family was completed the first time around. It could be commitment to nursing care, or to paying the bills, or to being companionable and sharing activities, or to being dominating or dominated and exclusively possessed. There should be no hidden agenda of commitments, expectancies, and responsibilities not specified. Likewise, there should be no fixed agenda of commitments that must be signed into all contracts. There may be one commitment only, namely, commitment to giving one another an optimum of sensuous, sensual, and erotic recreation. There's no age limit on that!

The changes of age impede fertility and in women terminate childbearing. In neither sex do they automatically abolish enjoyment of copulation nor of the preliminaries of arousal that precede it. The frequency of opportunity may become more limited. The biological clock may slow down so that the interval increases between one erotosexual encounter and the next. There is at any age great individual variation in the health and functional well-being of the genitalia themselves.

One way of assessing the latter is by means of measuring the phasic changes of genital physiology, especially blood flow, that synchronize with REM (rapid eye movement), sleep, and dreaming. These changes occur in both males and females. In males they are more evident, as the penis erects. The degree of tumescence can be recorded instrumentally by means of a gauge on the penis more easily than can the parallel bloodflow changes in the vulva and vagina. Nocturnal penile tumescence occurs across the life span from infancy to old age. Normative age changes in prevalence, frequency, quantity, and duration of nocturnal tumescence remain to be ascertained, as do the corresponding norms for phasic changes of the female genitalia in sleep.

Three
Phases of Sexual
Eroticism

PROCEPTION/ACCEPTION/CONCEPTION. In 1976, Frank Beach, the dean of American animal sexologists, proposed that the term proception, also used by Rosenzweig in 1973, be adapted to refer to the beginning phase of a sexual pairing. The term applies across species. It includes human beings. It refers to all the stimulus and response interactions between both members of a sexualizing pair and avoids the oversimplification inherent in attributing pairing only to the receptivity of the female. In the ordinary course of events, proception leads to acception, a two-way interaction of the penis and vulva, which receive one another. Acception, in the ordinary course of events, leads sooner or later to conception and parenthood.

In human sexology, the conceptive phase is the one that so far has received the majority of scientific and medical attention. Problems of fertility and sterility, conception and contraception, pregnancy and childbirth, can be, and historically have been, isolated from the more taboo-ridden sensual and erotic part of reproduction and from the act of copulation itself. It is a cop-out, of course, to have permitted this isolation, but one that was historically inevitable as a first step in breaching the ramparts of the sexual taboo on behalf of medicine and science. In some Moslem and Hindu cultural regions, it is still taboo for a physician who is usually a man to give a woman a medical examination undressed, even if she has cancer of the pelvic organs.

The work of Kinsey, and subsequently of Masters and Johnson, constitutes the thin edge of the wedge that will split the log of the acceptive phase of human sexuality for science and medicine. The day still has not arrived, however, when a couple with copulatory impairment or failure expect to have their problem diagnosed by direct observation—only by talking about it. In every other branch of medicine, experts go to extraordinary lengths to probe, palpate, cannulate, radiograph, electrograph, photograph, and surgically explore in order to get first-hand evidence of the source of malfunction. Only in sexology is direct observation verboten—for which the patient ultimately pays the price in prolonged or unrelieved suffering.

The proceptive phase of human sexuality still is subject to enormous scientific and medical neglect. In part, this neglect is rationalized as a respect for the poetry and the mystery of love and romance. "Isn't anything sacred, any more?" the critics of science ask, implying that to investigate is to destroy. Their question circumvents the evidence of the pathology of love and romance, which is not even recognized for what it is, since such pathology is typically given the label not of paraphilia but of perversion and criminality. So labeled, it is for the most part dispossessed by science and medicine and relegated to the police, the courts, and the penal system. Even under the labels of love-sickness or brokenheartedness, the disorders of proception are not taken too seriously by science and medicine, though they are of major importance to the individuals affected by them.

In many four-legged mammals, the nose is the primary organ of proception. When a bitch is in heat at the time of ovulation, an odoriferous substance, a pheromone, chemically identified as methyl p-hydroxybenzoate, is produced in the vagina. Even at a distance, the nose of the male is sensitive to this odor. Hence, the familiar picture of a bitch being followed by a pack of males, each sex engaging in highly stereotyped mating behavior. By a process that is not yet known, the bitch selects one of them as more attractive to her than the others and they copulate.

The pheromone that is a sexual attractant in primates is known biochemically as a series of short-chain aliphatic acids. This pheromone is not species-specific, though cross-species testing has not yet been very extensive. As of the present writing, it is known that the pheromone released in the vagina of an ovulating woman replicates the pheromone from the ovulating rhesus monkey's vagina, so that the wipings from a human vagina smeared on a virgin female monkey are a "turn-on" for a male monkey, under laboratory conditions.

The role of the vaginal pheromone as a sexual turn-on for the human male remains uncertain. The same applies with respect to odoriferous stimulation of the female. One possibility is that, just as human beings vary in hair color, perspiration odor, and ear wax (orientals have grey, flaky ear wax, and no underarm exocrine odor; westerners and blacks have yellow, oily ear wax and strong underarm odor), so also do they vary in responsivity to genital odor. If this hypothesis is correct, then it would help to explain why, above and beyond the effects of cultural conditioning, some human beings go wild over oral sex, whereas others are repulsed by it. Neither response need be considered abnormal.

Table 5-1 shows the three phases—proception, acception, and conception—and features associated with them.

In human mating, proception goes under the name of courtship when it lasts over a long period of time prior to the acceptive phase. When of short duration antecedent to penovulval acceptance, proception may be defined as flirting. It also may include necking, petting, and foreplay.

Proception is the phase of invitation, of solicitation and seduction, and of attraction—of being both attracted and attractive. The communications that constitute proception may be vocal, or they may be expressed in body language. The cues may be very direct, or they may be covert and almost subliminal, as in the glint of the eye, tone of the voice, or pressure of the touch by which a lover indicates that this is the occasion, or that tonight is the night. There is an elaborate body language of human proception that Madison Avenue knows very well how to capture on videotape and use in advertising. Most people use it without analyzing what they are doing, and they do not have a systematized knowledge of either its vocabulary or its syntax.

The possibility of olfactory arousal notwithstanding, for us human beings it appears that nature shifted from the nose to the eyes as the primary organs of sexual arousal at a distance, leading to the initiation of partner-pairing in tactual proximity.

It is likely (Table 3-1), though not conclusively proved, that males are more dependent than females on visual arousal, women being more dependent on haptic or tactual arousal. The difference is not an absolute but only a relative one. One piece of evidence that may be adduced in support of this hypothesis (Chapter 4) is that visual erotic imagery ac-

Table 5-1. Three phases of eroticism and sexuality

	Activities	Organs	Disorders
Proception	solicitation	eyes	inertia and ultraertia
	attraction	nose	gender transpositions
	courtship	skin	paraphilias
Acception	erection	mouth	hypophilias
	lubrication	genitals	hyperphilias
	copulation	anus	
Conception	pregnancy	wolffian	infertility
	delivery	mullerian	miscarriage
	childcare	mammary	nonlactation

companied by orgasm in the wet dreams of pubertal and adolescent males has no dream counterpart in females of the same age. Another piece of evidence is that the paraphilias, as presently recorded, are more varied and more prevalent in males than females.

The paraphilias are a reminder that imagery in the proceptive phase of erotic/sexual arousal is not only perceptual but also fictive, that is a fantasy product of the imagination. The paraphiliac's ideal is to be able to stage his/her erotic fantasy so as to perceive it as an actual experience. This being not always possible, the shadowy substitute is to restage it from memory in the mind's eye or the mind's story-book. People who are not paraphiliacs may do the same thing. For them, a feature of the proceptive phase is to imagine something different than what is actually happening with the partner, or someone different than the actual partner. Thus, a woman may fantasy that she is being possessed by her rock-and-roll hero; a man may fantasy himself in adultery with a nymphet; a gay husband may in fantasy replace his wife with his boyfriend, and so on. In some cases, continuation of the fantasy of the proceptive phase into the acceptive phase may be imperative to the acceptive performance of the genitalia. The fantasy then becomes a barrier between the two partners for, under ordinary circumstances, imagery of the proceptive phase, whether perceptual or fictive, yields as acceptive excitement builds up. The two partners then become totally immersed in the tide of erotic sensations until its waves crash into the resplendent surf of orgasm.

GROOMING. What the eyes do for arousal at a distance, the skin and its senses do for arousal in intimate proximity. In subhuman primates, stroking, smoothing, combing and scratching of the fur and skin is known as grooming. Grooming occurs as a manifestation of infant care, of social friendliness, of sexual proception, and of postcoital relaxation.

Among human beings, the term, grooming, conventionally pertains to personal neatness, especially of the hair. It is not yet idiomatic to use the term in its erotic connotation, but to substitute instead such terms as hug, hold, press, cuddle, touch, tickle, squeeze, massage, pet, rub, pleasure and sensate focus. The unifying concept encompassing all of these terms is grooming. It is a concept much needed to fill a gap in the language of our sex lives.

Whatever the activity in which we manifest it, grooming has managed to remain surprisingly uncontaminated by the taboo on sex. It is a morally sanctioned and unexpurgated activity. The secret of its success is that it can take place entirely above the belt. The belt is the dividing line between romance and carnal knowledge. Above the belt, sex and eroticism belong in the realm of lyricism and love, poetry and dawn mists.

Above-the-belt sex, breasts excepted, may be displayed in public, on television, and in the movies—in the Christian cultures of the West, that is, where passionate kissing scenes in movies are taken for granted, whereas they are attacked with the scissors of censorship in Islam, in Hindu India, and in communist Asia.

Below the belt, sex and eroticism belong in the realm of animalistic passion and lust, dirty jokes, and shadowy stealth. Below-the-belt sex is culturally classified as too lewd and lascivious to be permitted in public, and in the media it is censored as obscene and pornographic.

What a difference the belt makes! Yet it is not as straightforward and dogmatic a difference as convention dictates it to be. It conceals within itself the terms of a paradox: sex below the belt is dirty, carnal, and lustful; therefore, save it for the one you love! It is small wonder that, when the timetable says go, many couples experience extraordinary difficulty in taking off the belts of their chastity. For these couples, the wedding night holds no ecstasy. It is a nightmare.

With remarkable tenacity, the nightmare perpetuates a split between grooming and copulating. "You want me only for my body" is some women's nightmare complaint. In this saying, body is only a euphemism for another four-letter word. "You want me only for my cunt (Latin: *cunna*)" is the real meaning. What this desperate woman would say, had she had available the diagnostic terminology, is that she suffered a phobia of penetration. "Marauders keep out," is the notice that would be posted on the temple gates of her vagina. Sexuality for her is divorced from the genitalia and is equated with romance, that is, with the grooming preliminaries of the proceptive phase.

According to our cultural stereotypes, there is no corresponding complaint for men. Men have long been cast in the quite different mold of perpetual and insatiable Priapus, indiscriminately driven to couple anonymously with a female—any female. Men do not, of course, fit this mold of promiscuity any more often than do women. Men fall in love, and they too become pair-bonded. They are as much likely to be victims of the split between grooming and copulation as women are. They also may believe that they are used only for their bodies. They also, like women, may become erotically inert and anorgasmic. Or they may have the penis fail to erect, as in women the vagina may fail to lubricate.

The solution to the metaphorical problem of the chastity belt for many people becomes, inchoately, a split between the saint and the sinner, the madonna and the whore, the progenitor and the paramour. A man may be forever trapped, insofar as he can cast his wife only in the madonna role of an immaculate virgin who does not need a man in order to conceive, whereas a partner on birth control who can abandon herself to the wantonness of mutual sexual delight must, by his customary definition, be a whore, adulteress, or mistress. The converse may hold true for a woman: the progenitor of her children must be cast in the role of little more than a donor inseminator, whereas a partner in the wantonness and abandon of sexual delight must by her customary definition be a paramour, adulterer, or gigolo.

The split between saint and sinner may be self-established and not generated by the partner. A woman may herself be a madonna whose eroticism cannot advance beyond grooming; and a man may himself be a near celibate whose love-making becomes arrested at the grooming stage. In either instance, the inhibition may be specifically related to the sanctity of marriage. There are some couples whose sex life began rather well before they were married, only to become desiccated after they became legally wed. In a proportion of such marriages, the affected partner may be able to undergo an erotic revitalization, but only in an extramarital affair that dispenses with the inhibitions of saintliness in favor of the recklessness of sin.

The counterpart of a fixation on grooming is an evasion or avoidance of it. Under the name of foreplay, lack of grooming received marked attention in the marriage manuals of one and two generations ago, and engaging in it came close to being the antidote for all copulatory problems. Redefined as pleasuring and sensate focus in contemporary sex therapy, grooming still is overworked as an antidote for sexual problems. Yet the fact of the matter is that a person who says: "I can't stand to have him/her so much as touch me" sometimes means exactly that. Such a phobic withdrawal from touch is not uncommon when the relationship between a couple has gone sour on some other count. "I pray to God," one woman said, "to spare me to survive him (my husband) if only for twenty-four hours, so that I can have the satisfaction of knowing what it's like to live at least one day without him near me." He survived for twenty-five years and more, during all of which time they lived together and did not touch each other—and, of course, had no sex.

Deprivation of grooming when a partner dies or departs sometimes is experienced by the survivor as a devastating loss of perhaps even greater magnitude than the loss of genital stimulation and orgasm. The loneliness of having no one to cuddle close to has its roots far back in infancy in the grooming of mother-infant care and breast feeding. No one has yet collected the statistical evidence for human babies, but it is clear from monkey studies that infants deprived of grooming suffer from psychosocial and psychosexual pathology for the entirety of their lives. Those not so deprived develop normally.

APATHY OR INERTIA OF EROTIC/SEXUAL AROUSAL. Contradicting the myth of the male as the sexual stud, ever ready to give service, there are, in fact, some men for whom the onset of proception is blocked by an invisible barrier, the nature of which is not presently understood. The same barrier may affect women also, in which cases its existence may pass unnoticed, or be wrongly interpreted as confirmation of the myth of the female as the sleeping princess waiting to be awakened by her knight in shining armor. In both sexes, the affected person appears to be erotically and sexually apathetic or inert. The degree of inertia is variable. So also is the etiology.

In some instances, erotic/sexual inertia is associated with a syndrome of known etiology. For example, a cytogenetic factor is implicated in men with the supernumerary X chromosome (47,XXY) of Klinefelter's syndrome. The mechanism of inertia of erotic/sexual arousal in this syndrome is not a simple deficiency of testosterone circulating in the blood stream. However, high-dose treatment with testosterone may help to surmount it. Thus, one may implicate the intracellular uptake and usage of testosterone as the basic defect, but this explanation is purely speculative at the present time.

Inertia of erotic/sexual arousal is prevalent in both males and females with a history of hypopituitarism, with or without statural dwarfism. The pituitary deficit may be developmental (idiopathic), or may occur as a sequel to neurosurgery for removal of a pituitary tumor, most commonly a craniopharyngioma. Such surgery encroaches on the nearby hypothalamus and limbic system and may adversely affect it. Inertia of arousal is not corrected by endocrine replacement therapy with sex hormones. This failure may signify that sex-hormone replacement by itself in hypopituitarism is insufficient, and that some other unknown synergistic hormonal substance is missing and is not being replaced. In support of this hypothesis, is the fact that testosterone replacement in hypopituitary males does not bring about the same satisfactory degree of virilization, for example, beard growth, as it does in the treatment of castrates, or even of female-to-male transexuals. There is an alternative hypothesis, a dualistic one. It implicates not only malfunction or destruction of hypothalamic nuclei and pathways responsible for the secretion of the releaser hormones that govern the release of the pituitary's own hormones, somatotropin (growth hormone) and gonadotropin (LH, luteinizing hormone, and FSH, follicle stimulating hormone) being of particular relevance in the present instance. It also implicates concurrent malfunction or destruction of other hypothalamic nuclei and pathways responsible for the mediation of the erotic/sexual behavior and, in particular, the pair-bonding, that matches or parallels the pituitary-gonadal hormonal secretions. Thus, it well may be that inertia of erotic/sexual arousal in hypopituitarism is secondary to impairment of brain pathways that mediate pair-bonding or falling in love.

Undoubtedly there are other syndromes, like the 47,XXY and the hypopituitary syndromes, in which erotic/sexual inertia is a characteristic primary symptom, but they have not yet been catalogued. Degenerative neurological syndromes are among them, for example, the Shy–Drager syndrome (which involves also orthostatic hypotension and impotence secondary thereto).

In the absence of evidence to the contrary, it is widely assumed that the majority of cases of inertia of erotic/sexual arousal are developmental and psychogenic and thus subject to remission, perhaps under the influence of psychotherapy. It is wise not to be too dogmatic about psychogenesis, whatever that may mean, at the present time, since there is an insufficiency of either developmental or clinical data. Some males with the condition develop through puberty without discovering masturbation, and without learning about it from others, and a few report a total absence of wet dreams postpubertally. A partial degree of erotic/sexual inertia may be primary and associated with more time for overachievement academically, or at least with high achievement in a highly competitive system, such as entrance into medical school or other professional training. Alternatively, overachievement may be primary, and a function of time spent on achieving at the expense of sexualizing. Or the hyposexual-overachievement equation may be far more complex and associated perhaps with obsessionalism and an episodic depressive tendency.

Erotic/sexual inertia is a primary symptom of severe depression. Depression is a brain-biochemical dysfunction as well as being a subjectively experienced dysphoria. Thus, one may infer that the accompanying depressive disturbance of appetite, sleep, and erotic sexuality are brain-biochemical dysfunctions also, and that the responsible neurochemistries will be understood when the neurochemistry of depression becomes progressively elucidated.

ULTRAERTIA OF EROTIC/SEXUAL AROUSAL. The opposite of inertia is ultraertia, meaning exceeding the common or ordinary in erotosexual arousal. Ultraertia may lead beyond proceptive arousal to further involvement of the genitalia, whether alone in masturbation or in participation with a partner. That is to say, ultraertia, which is proceptive, may carry over to hyperphilia which is acceptive. Ultraertia may be heterosexual, bisexual, or homosexual.

In popular belief, it is usual to regard the adolescent years as the most hot-blooded—the years of sowing one's wild oats—more specifically for boys than girls, according to the dictates of our culture. For most people, it is probably true that ultraertia is a developmental characteristic of adolescence as compared with subsequent years, but there are no statistics by which to gauge either the prevalence or speed of such a development from more to less.

There are also no statistics or measurements against which to compare the strength of ultraertia from one adolescent to another. The frequency of wet dreams, to use one criterion, has a wide range of variability from none at all to one or more a night, and there may be a parallel variability in masturbation fantasies, and in fantasies triggered by erotic perceptions. Some boys are preoccupied with erotosexual fantasies and many erections on a daily basis. They may be scarcely able to walk along the street without paying attention to a stimulus, usually the sight of a particular type of female, that triggers an erotosexual fantasy and genital response. The same may happen, correspondingly for girls, some of whom have quite explicit fantasies with a vaginal lubrication response. Others, in conformity with the mores of the culture in which they have been reared, have fantasies that are conventionally defined as romantic and do not include explicit imagery of the sex organs in action.

Males and females, in teenage or later, both may have fantasies of which the imagery itself portrays an ultraertial erotosexual life. For males, these fantasies may be classified under the titles: harem, orgy, playboy, gigolo, and hustler. For females the corresponding titles are: gang-bang, orgy, playgirl, call-girl, and whore. These ultraertial fantasies figure prominently in commercial erotography or pornography—narratives, comics, graphics, photographs, and movies. In the lives of some people, their fantasies become translated into their daily existence and their way of earning a living. For the majority, however, ultraertial fantasies exist only as masturbation or copulation fantasies that promote genital performance, or simply as dormant images of what might have been. Sometimes these dormant images may not be quite so dormant, but may express themselves as inflated claims. It is very common, for example, when a husband and wife are separately questioned about their sex life, for the husband to rate it better than his wife does, and to estimate a higher coital frequency.

PARAPHILIAS. Para- means beyond, alongside of, aside from, modified from, subsidiary to, and faulty, and -philia means love.

It is a feature of all the paraphilias that they involve a fantasy drama or ritual that is either rehearsed in imagery—predominantly visual imagery—or enacted with a supporting cast of one or more partners, plus or minus stage properties. A paraphilia involves an inclusion image or a displacement image that intrudes itself into each erotic/sexual episode, with or without a partner present. The inclusion image bears a peripheral relationship to ordinary two-person eroticism, even though in a quite idiosyncratic way. In the paraphilia it becomes central. For example, in klismaphilia, getting an enema becomes not simply erotically arousing, but essential to getting an erection, maintaining it, and ejaculating; and penovaginal activity is either irrelevant or achieved only while recalling the enema in imagery. The displacement image is sequentially or temporally peripheral under ordinary circumstances, but becomes central in the paraphilia. For example, the exhibitionist does not display his penis to a consenting partner as a preliminary to penovaginal coitus, but to an unsuspecting stranger as an essential maneuver to getting an erection and reaching orgasm, either by masturbation or when he returns to his regular partner and relives the episode in imagery.

Some paraphilias are always noxious and totally unacceptable to society, for example, lust murderism, violently assaultive rapism, and violently assaultive pedophilia (Chapter 12). Others range in degree from playfully harmless to noxious, for example, sadomasochism, which at the noxious extreme may become the masochistic stage-management of one's own murder. There are no fixed rules as to the dividing line between the harmless and the noxious in paraphilia. The noxious paraphilia always invades or trespasses upon the inviolacy of the partner and brings nonconsensual sequelae. This is the criterion of noxiousness in paraphilia.

Table 5-2 is a listing of currently known paraphilias. By convention, they are socially and legally, more than scientifically, defined. They are not universally stigmatized. Thus, exhibitionism applies only where people wear clothes, and ephebophilia only where there are laws prohi-

Table 5 -2. Inclusion and displacement paraphilias

Acrotomophilia (amputee partner)	Kleptophilia (stealing)	Rapism or raptophilia (violent assault)
Apotemnophilia (self-amputee)	Klismaphilia (enema)	Sadism
Asphyxiophilia (self-strangulation)	Lust Murderism	Scoptophilia (watching coitus)
Autoassassinatophilia	Masochism	Somnophilia (sleeper)
Coprophilia (feces)	Mysophilia (filth)	Telephone scatophilia (lewdness)
Ephebophilia (youth)	Narratophilia (erotic talk)	Troilism (couple + one)
Exhibitionism	Necrophilia (corpse)	Urophilia or undinism (urine)
Fetishism	Pedophilia (child)	Voyeurism or peeping-Tomism
Frotteurism (rubbing)	Pictophilia (pictures)	Zoophilia (animal)
Gerontophilia (elder)		

See glossary for definitions of each of the paraphilias.

biting sex between youths and older people. Zoophilia does not apply in cultures, as on the Caribbean coast of Colombia, where teenaged boys are expected to have sex with donkeys in order to reach manhood—and, incidentally, not get unmarried girls pregnant. In military history, rape has often been embodied in the mores of war.

An example of the harmlessness in paraphilia can be found in fetishism for undergarments worn by women. This particular fetishism may be rated as statistically normal for males reared in our sex-covered society. It is extremely widespread; witness the circulation of magazines that display pictures not of nude women, but of women wearing garter-belts and hose.

Idiosyncratic variations occur within each type of paraphilia, especially the fetishes. Idiosyncracies also occur as transitional or combination types, for example, masochistic rubber fetishism. It is rare that an individual with one paraphilia manifests also another, as postulated in the faulty theory of moral degeneracy. Degeneracy theory would claim, for example, that a peeping Tom (voyeur) eventually becomes a sex murderer, or that a homosexual becomes a child-molesting pedophiliac. Such is not the case. The paraphilias tend to be extraordinarily specific and unchanging. One apparent exception to this rule may occur when a paraphilia is partially held in abeyance in teenage and comes into full flower later. In teenage, for example, a boy who manifests a fetish for female underclothes, with which he masturbates, may in adulthood undergo a metamorphosis from which he emerges to declare himself a transexual.

The list of Table 5-2 does not include transvestism and transexualism, both of which qualify doubly as paraphilias and as gender-identity transpositions (Table 5-3), with which they are listed. The other transpositions are bisexualism and homosexualism, which do not, per se, qualify as paraphilias.

The rationale for not including bisexualism and homosexualism with the paraphilias is that, like heterosexualism, they do not, of and by themselves alone, interfere with or intrude restrictions or limitations on falling in love. Intrinsically, they do not possess the essential features of a paraphilia. These essential features are that the imagery prerequisite to the paraphiliac's erotic arousal and genital/sexual performance is insistently and autonomously reiterative, as is usually the case in proceptive imagery regardless of content, but it is sufficiently atypical or bizarre that there is no partner, or none readily available, whose own imagery reciprocates it. Thus the paraphiliac is prone to type-cast a partner nonconsensually into the erotic ritual prescribed by his paraphilic imagery, which, by analogy with a psychomotor epileptic seizure, propels its own expression and fails to be contained. In many paraphilic patients, there is evidence of dissociation, a so-called altered state of consciousness, and, rarely, there may be an actual amnesia for the paraphilic episode.

The variety and the prevalence of paraphilias is greater in males than in females. There is, as yet, no explanation of this disparity between the sexes that is entirely satisfactory. It may have to do with a greater dependence of the male on visual imagery for erotic arousal (see above); and with vulnerability of the male in early childhood to anomalies of visual erotic imagery that become fixed and permanent. Excessive negation, restriction, and punishment of childhood sexual rehearsal play probably encourages such anomalies.

Paraphilic imagery creates what may best be called a psychic distance between the paraphiliac and his partner. Inchoately she recognizes that she is a stage dummy for his erotic ventriloquism, so to speak, and she knows that the performance is not her own. She is in the position of a love-blot, unable to play the role of staging the fantasy her partner projects onto her. There is no genuine erotic reciprocity between them. There are rare exceptions, as when a sadist and masochist match together, or when a man with a paraphilia for an amputee partner finds an amputee who authentically fulfills his fantasy, and he, hers, and so on. Such matching in gerontophilia, ephebophilia, and pedophilia is more common than conventionally believed.

GENDER TRANSPOSITIONS. Table 5-3 shows the categories of gender transposition, in which, on the basis of chronicity and degree, masculine and feminine expectancies and stereotypes are interchanged. The arbitrary transpositions have little to do with the functioning of the genitalia, except, perhaps, with respect to decisions about self-commitment to parenthood.

In transexualism, transposition is persistent and total relative to the criterion of the anatomy of the external genitals and the sex of neonatal assignment—so much so that the transexual demands hormonal and surgical reassignment, in order to align the body with the mind. Procedurally, reassignment is a method of rehabilitation not of cure, and as etiological knowledge increases it will probably become outmoded.

In some transexuals, the gender transposition takes place in childhood or adolescence. The nontransexual personality withers away, so to speak, or does not develop, and the transexual one is the only one that family, friends, and acquaintances have ever been thoroughly familiar with. In other transexuals, the transposition does not declare itself until later in life, quite commonly in the forties and under the pressure of an intense life crisis. Two personalities have always been present, each with its own name, wardrobe, and vocation, one of them covert and hypoplastic,

Table 5-3. Transpositions of gender identity/role

	Total	Partial	Arbitrary
Chronic	transexualism	gynecomimesis andromimesis, male androphilia, female gynophilia	androgeny of gender-coded education, work, legal status
Episodic	transvestism	androgynophilia (bisexualism)	androgeny of gender-coded play, body-language, grooming, ornament

except for special transvestitic occasions or ceremonies. Whether under the pressure of a life crisis or simply as the outcome of cumulative change, the covert personality eventually becomes more and more developed and overt. Friends and acquaintances now may know both personalities, the he and the she (this phenomenon is typically male-to-female), the before and the after; and in the transition period they can know them both as they alternate, along with their wardrobes, and as the he progressively dies and the she progressively develops. The contrasts are often extreme, the he an ultra macho male, and the she a femme fatale.

The syndrome of two personalities, each with its own name, its own wardrobe, and its own interests and occupation does not inevitably metamorphose into complete sex-reassignment transexualism. It takes also the form of the syndrome of transvestism (to be distinguished from the symptom of transvestism which is synonymous with cross-dressing). So far, this syndrome has been recorded only in morphologic males. The episode of cross-dressing is unrelentingly dictated by a subjectively experienced distress of great magnitude that cannot be otherwise relieved unless, maybe, it is attenuated by rehearsing the episode in fantasy. Orgasm brings the final relief, but it is not possible without the paraphernalia of cross-dressing in fact or fantasy.

In homosexuality, gender transposition may be reduced to the bare essentials of definition, namely, that in homosexuality two persons with penises, or two with vulvas together have an erotic encounter. No other manifestation of male/female transposition may be involved. In prison, for example (Chapter 4), an otherwise stereotypic male may discover that his penis does not become impotent with a male partner, and so, with another male fantasied as a female partner, he applies, or even imposes his usual male erotic role as the insertor. The insertor thus demonstrates to himself that, despite his former heterosexual self-definition, he does in fact have some degree of bisexual gender identity, at least with respect to copulation and ejaculation, though falling short of falling in love.

At the other extreme, on the other end of the spectrum, is the homosexual, male or female, whose behavior in its entirety is gender-transposed. In gay argot, this pervasively effeminate male is a drag queen (a gynecomimetic). He may take estrogen to grow breasts, but always retains his penis. The female counterpart is a butch dyke (an andromimetic). Some few such individuals eventually define themselves as transexuals, alienated from their own genitalia, but the majority do not.

Most people today who are referred or self-referred to a physician or counselor as homosexual are not drag queens or butch dykes, nor are they, like certain prisoners, situationally homosexual. They follow the medical tradition of classifying people according to their actual or ostensible symptoms and pathology, not their health. More accurately (Chapter 2), they should define themselves as bisexual and then specify the bisexual ratio as 50:50 or 80:20 or whatever.

There are some people who are 100:0 homosexuals, and some who are 0:100 heterosexuals, but they are probably very few, proportionately, in the population at large. Most people have at least a micropotential that would permit situational bisexualism under extreme circumstances. To test yourself against this statement, construct a hypothetical extreme, catch-22 dilemma. For example, a crazed terrorist holds you at bay, at gunpoint, in some place where your chance of escape is nil, say the far ledge at the top of the Empire State Building. His, or her, demand is sexual, its precise content varying according to your sex and that of the terrorist: fellatio, cunnilingus, or anal coitus. Thus, suppose both of you were male, and his demand was "suck my cock or else you go over."

What would be your response? What would it be if he demanded to suck yours? Or, supposing both of you were women, and the demands were likewise for oral sex either way, how would you respond?

You can, of course, make fun of the test, as did one teenager whose reply was: "Now I know why no one could ever get me on top of a high building!" But self-examination goes deeper than joking, for death is annihilation in perpetuity. Most people would be grateful to discover an untapped 0.5 percent bisexual potential in themselves that, without the special situational demand, would have remained forever hidden.

There are other catch-22 test hypotheses on which to test the criterion of when death would tip the scales in its favor—for example, a catch-22 in which the alternatives would be either the gas oven, Hitler style, or being a human experimental subject for transexual surgery and attempted change of G-I/R by enforced brainwashing technique.

Bisexuality has long been stigmatized and morally disapproved, but it has not been classified as a disease. The homosexual component of it, by contrast, like monosexual homosexuality, has been classified as a disease. Before that, it was a sin and heresy (which is consistent with the fact that the Bible nowhere refers to genuine homosexuals, only to homosexual acts between primarily heterosexual men; women are not mentioned). As of the 1975 decision of the American Psychiatric Association, the classification of homosexuality has progressed from sin and sickness to sanctioned social alternative. Today the fact of an erotic encounter or partnership between two people of the same genital anatomy is not considered pathological, nor a sickness. The partners, as in a heterosexual partnership, may or may not be psychopathologically diagnosed. Their partnership, per se, does not warrant a diagnosis. The 1975 change makes good practical sense, for no society could ever afford to maintain enough trained professionals to treat all its homosexuals. Moreover, except in contagious epidemics in which preventive treatment is imposed on each member of an entire community or population without informed consent, the tradition of medicine since Hippocrates has been that the doctor-patient contract is for the relief of the patient's suffering. To define noncomplaining nonsufferers as sick, simply because they constitute a statistical minority, is to confuse the statistical minority with the ideological minority, and the statistical norm with the ideological norm. The sickness classification was really only the old sin classification in disguise. To classify homosexuality as a sickness is analogous to classifying left-handedness as a sickness, as used to be done in school rooms half a century and less ago. Even if there were totally guaranteed ways of changing either homosexuality or left-handedness, it is arguable as to whether change should be imposed nonconsensually. But there is no guaranteed way of effecting change, and so tolerance is the treatment of choice. Tolerance does not abolish or deny a doctor-patient contract on the basis of informed consent. Those homosexuals who make such a contract for treatment often prove to be bisexuals suffering from incompatibility between the two components of their sexuality.

Some writers on homosexuality loosely distinguish masculine or masculinate from effeminate homosexuality in males. They define the masculinate type of homosexual as having a masculine gender identity but a homosexual preference or object choice. The correct conceptualization does not pertain to preference or choice at all. It is that the person has a predominantly masculine G-I/R, the exception being that in an erotic partnership he does what one normally expects of a woman, namely, performs with a person with a penis, even though he may perform only the stereotypic masculine role of being insertor. G-I/R does not pertain to everything masculine or feminine about a person except erotic sexuality. It includes erotic sexuality, as well. Gender identity is not simply a matter of declaring oneself male or female.

HYPOPHILIA. When paraphilic imagery interferes with the functioning of the sex organs during the acceptive phase, the sex organs may manifest some variety of hypophilia. The hypophilic disorders do not invariably mask a paraphilia, but they do so with sufficient frequency that in sex therapy it is essential always to investigate coital imagery and fantasy.

It once was common to categorize the hypophilias simply as impotence and frigidity, a practice now abandoned by the well informed. Table 5-4 shows what is still not universally appreciated, namely, that there are homologous impairments in the man and the woman. The prevalence of the impairment in each pair of homologues is not necessarily the same. For example, it is generally accepted among clinicians, in the absence of epidemiological statistics, that anorgasmia is more prevalent in the female than the male. The surprise for many people is that it is indeed possible for the male to mount and thrust without being able "to come" while his penis remains within the vagina. For men as well as women, as already mentioned, there can be a problem of making the transition from sex above the belt (which is romantic love) to sex below the belt (which is carnal love). In another idiom, this is the transition from the saint to the sinner, or from the madonna to the whore. In some cases, the problem is specific to being married. Thus, a man may be impotent with his wife, on the basis of the hidden premise that copulating with a madonna is equivalent to fucking a whore. It denigrates her to the status of whore. The converse may also occur, namely, in troilism, the paraphilia in which a man can obtain an erection for coitus with his wife only if he first fantasies that she is a whore as he watches her while she has sex with another man, preferably a stranger.

Erotosexual hypofunction may represent a continuation of apathy or

Table 5-4. Hypophilias, male and female
(partial or complete)

Male	Female
coital aninsertia	coital aninsertia
penile anesthesia	vulval anesthesia
anorgasmia	anorgasmia
erectile impotence	vaginal dryness
premature ejaculation	vaginismus
coital pain	dyspareunia

aversion carried over from the proceptive to the acceptive phase. When apathy or aversion is profound, there is no acceptive phase, and hypophilia is total. Hypophilia may, however, be less than total, and it may be limited to specific phenomena of erotosexual participation. For example, participation in oral sex as either performer or recipient, may be an impossibility for some men or women. If one partner is intensely dependent on the odors (pheromones), flavors, and sensations of oral sex for erotosexual arousal, and if the other has an intense aversion to it, compromise may prove unattainable and the partnership may prove unviable.

A similar incompatibility with respect to the use of either the penis or the vagina in penovaginal insertion renders a relationship even more unviable, legally as well as personally. This is the condition of coital aninsertia. It may manifest itself as neglect or denial of one's own penis or vagina, as though it did not exist—a characteristic of, for example, some unoperated transexuals. More commonly, coital aninsertia may manifest itself as a phobic anxiety or panic at having one's vagina penetrated, or one's penis inserted into a vagina.

Insertion phobia is not a problem in those cases in which the chief hyposexual symptom is genital anesthesia or numbness. The penis or vagina performs its insertorial function, but is deficient in inducing erotosexual feeling. If an orgasm is achieved, it too lacks the feeling of climax as judged by prior experience. It is possible that the achievement of orgasm will also be excessively delayed or will fail completely (anorgasmia).

Anorgasmia may manifest itself without genital anesthesia, in which case it represents simply a failure to have a sexual climax. In men it includes failure to ejaculate. Failure to climax may be interpreted subjectively as positive or negative. It is positive if the build-up of erotosexual sensation fades and ceases without a climax, thus creating a pause in readiness for resumption later. It is negative if the build-up of erotosexual sensation neither fades nor is released abruptly in orgasm, thus creating an awareness of frustration. Anorgasmia may be specific to the stimulus input. Thus a man or a woman may be able to climax from masturbation, but not from stimulation with a partner; or when with a certain partner but not another; or with a partner of one sex but not the other. Women more often than men may be less able to climax from penovaginal thrusting than from some other form of stimulation. For some women, oral stimulation of the vulva is orgasmically superior. For others pressure stimulation of the clitoris, the clitoral hood and the labia minora is superior. For some men, oral stimulation of the scrotum may be orgasmically superior. In either sex, augmentation of stimulus input from the nipples or other part of the body may increase the possibility of orgasm.

There is a high degree of idiosyncracy as to the location of the most intense extragenital orgasmic sensitivity, ranging from the lips to the anus, and from pressure spots on the joints and the torso to the fingers and toes. Some of these locations are not simultaneously accessible when there are only two people together. For some people, the stimulation of these extragenital locations may need to be so strong that to another person it would be noxiously painful.

Anorgasmia may be not a primary hypophilic phenomenon, but one that is secondary to failure, in the male, of the penis to become erect or stay erect and, in the female, of the vagina to lubricate or stay lubricated. Vaginal dryness is not given as much attention in sexological texts as is penile impotence, which has long been known as the bane of men.

The antithesis of impotence and anorgasmia in men is premature ejaculation, corresponding to vaginismus in women. In both sexes, the muscles of the genitals contract too soon. In men, the ejaculate typically is lost at the moment the penis comes in contact with the warmth of the vulva or very rapidly after its insertion into the warm vagina, thus curtailing the sensations of thrusting for both partners. Premature ejaculation rarely occurs when the same penis is being masturbated or being fellated. Hence the stop-start method of therapy and the so-called squeeze technique, in which the partner is instructed to stimulate the penis manually and to stop just short of its ejaculation, possibly with a squeeze or pinch to discourage ejaculation. In women, vaginismus represents premature onset of the female postorgasmic refractory period. It is produced by constriction of the perivaginal (pubococcygeal) musculature together with drying of the vagina, thus effectively excluding the penis.

In women, the antithesis of genital anesthesia is dyspareunia which means, etymologically, badly mated, and in current medical usage, difficult or painful coitus, regardless of cause. The same term is seldom applied to men, but they too may experience coital pain. Both sexes may also experience postcoital pain, either in the external genitals or the pelvic cavity. In rare instances, there occurs also a postcoital migraine headache.

In the era before Masters and Johnson, therapy for the hypophilias was for the individual man or woman, not the couple, except that a marriage counselor dealing with a sexual problem might, on occasion, see both partners. Pharmacologic treatment was sometimes resorted to, the prescription being more a matter of trial and error than of rational principle. Testosterone prescribed for impotence, except in unusually rare cases of endocrine deficit, was, and still is, noncontributory to improvement except insofar as it may have a placebo effect. The same may be said of any other present-day medication for any of the hypophilias in the majority of cases.

Another form of treatment was to impart knowledge. Thus, on the assumption that a woman's inadequate sexual functioning (the prime example being anorgasmia or so-called frigidity) was secondary to the man's insufficiency of erotic technique in foreplay, the couple were taught technique. The assumption of ignorance is almost always itself too simple. In most people, ignorance is generally either tolerated, through lack of a standard of comparison, or, if recognized, self-corrected. Self-correction comes about perhaps with the help of talk with companions, or by reading, without recourse to professional help. Those who seek professional help are suffering from something more complex than a void or a gap of ignorance that requires simple filling with education.

For those with a problem too complex for self-correction, the recommended professional help traditionally was some form of psychotherapy based on Freudian doctrine, or perhaps psychoanalysis itself. Psychotherapy was conducted, typically individually, on the principle that the sexual symptoms were secondary to individual personality disorder, and that they would remit if the personality disorder were successfully resolved. The outcome was sometimes successful, sometimes not.

Masters and Johnson not only replaced individual with couple therapy, and the individual therapist with the dual, man-and-woman, therapeutic team but also worked on the principle that if the problem of the sexual dysfunction were resolved first, then the larger problem of the couple relationship would either remit or be subsequently treated in psychotherapy. The Masters and Johnson method may be described as somesthetic as contrasted with ideogogic, in recognition of its grooming, body pleasuring, and sensate focus, among other things. The method spread like wildfire, in large part because it could be practiced by nonpsychiatrist and nonpsychologist therapists. This method can easily degenerate into oversimplified sexual exercises and gymnastics, and an oversimplified zeal in the application of the learning-reinforcement theory fashionably known as behavior modification. It is all but a universal rule of medicine that any form of treatment is likely to work some of the time, at least to bring about a temporary remission of symptoms, because of a placebo effect. In the sexual hypofunctions or insufficiency dysfunctions, the placebo effect is not unexpected, because a prevalent component of the etiology is inhibition or dissociation, which is characteristically unstable and thus lends itself to episodes of remission of symptoms.

An episode of remission may be long-lasting or may end in a relapse. A relapse is likely to occur if, as is all too often the case, the failure of the genitalia to function adequately in coitus signifies, in effect, that the couple are fighting each other with their sex organs. The genitals are more insidious weapons than the arms, the legs, or the voice, but stubbornly effective weapons in a power struggle, nonetheless. A power struggle cannot be resolved by somesthetic means alone. It is necessary, in addition, to engage in what may be called the ideogogic form of therapy, one in which the psychodynamics of the couple relationship is brought into focus, so that the insidious power struggle can be recognized for what it is and, if possible, resolved. Then ensues the possibility of long-term symptomatic improvement. The combination of somesthetic and ideogogic approach to treatment, with the genital and erotic component of the couple's relationship in the foreground rather than the background of focus, is what characterizes the new sex therapy, as it is now coming to be known.

Etiologically, the genital/erotic hypophilias for which the new sex therapy is successful are often referred to as psychogenic. The implication is that they are not organic. The psychogenic versus organic dichotomy is a version of the mind/body dichotomy and is dangerous and unprofitable. It trivializes the significance and severity, and the possible intractability, of the so-called psychogenic syndromes. It leads to misplaced confidence in ability to make an etiological diagnosis, which in turn leads to misdiagnosis. It leads also to muddle-headed hypotheses in research, devoid of attention to the sexual brain which, even though science may not yet be capable of documenting how, is always implicated in the hypophilias and other sexual dysfunctions also. Neuropsychogenic is a safer term than psychogenic.

In all of the hypophilias, and in the hyperphilias and paraphilias as well, the differential diagnosis and prognosis, as well as the method of treatment, requires consideration of the factors listed in Table 5-5. A hypophilia is not a syndrome with a unique etiological origin. Rather it is a syndrome, or possibly a symptom, that, like fever, has different causal origins. Irrespective of its ultimate causal origin or agent, every

Table 5-5. Factors in the etiology of erotic/genital dysfunction

Birth defect	Neoplastic
Hormonal, brain	Traumatic, surgical
Hormonal, target organ	Traumatic, nonsurgical
Toxic, prescribed substance	Vascular
Toxic, nonprescribed substance	Neurologic, peripheral
Infectious	Neuropsychogenic

hypophilia ultimately requires for its expression a pathological change in the way in which pathways of the nervous system, which are still poorly understood, service the genital organs. There are three subsidiary pathways by which this change expresses itself: by directly altering the regulation of the blood supply to the genitalia; by altering the release of hormones that affect genital function; and by altering the release of other tissue chemicals, like prostaglandins, that affect genital function.

Alterations that affect the neurogenital system or any of its three subsidiary pathways may themselves be engendered by birth defects; toxic substances, including drugs, medications or other chemicals; infections; neoplastic growths; mechanical and traumatic anatomic damage either surgical or nonsurgical; and changes in brain chemistries that today defy explanation and that may themselves be engendered by external stimuli, like olfactory and other stimuli from the developmental past or present. Changes in brain chemistries notorious for inducing hypophilic apathy or inertia are those responsible for the syndrome of severe depression. This syndrome, as already mentioned in this chapter, involves an upset of multiple body chemistries and vital functions, including sleep and eating as well as erotosexual function.

Those hypophilias that have developmental origins and that are classified as psychogenic may, in keeping with their classification as hypofunctions, be defined and analyzed in terms of a blockage or inhibition of some aspect of genital and erotosexual responsiveness. The variables responsible for this inhibition cannot yet be spelled out in terms of all the chemical messengers and brain pathways involved. Hence, the classification, psychogenic, signifies that a hypofunction cannot be attributed to any so-called organic cause, like local infection, inflammation, or injury, that brings about a blockage or inhibition of function.

HYPERPHILIA. Logically, the hyperphilias may be considered the obverse of the hypophilias, with the approach to therapy being parallel in both. Not very much is known in a systematic way concerning the hyperphilias, and there is not even a satisfactory catalogue of them, perhaps because they are seldom experienced as a form of suffering. Thus, they are not defined as diseases needing treatment. Too often, they are joked about, ridiculed or bantered as either enviable or morally reprehensible. The terminology is inadequate: nymphomania in the female, and satyriasis, or Don Juanism, in the male. Prostitution, male and female, also is sometimes included.

Prostitution is subsumed under hyperphilia not because of its plurality of customers who pay, but because for some prostitutes it gives easy access to multiple, anonymous, and nonlimerent encounters. If all prostitutes, whether call girls or brothel whores, are viewed only as being entrapped victims of their trade, then those who respond positively to the hyperphilic accumulation of either partners or practices are over-looked. Because males are less often regarded as entrapped victims, call boys and hustlers, whether they serve men or women customers, demon-strate the positive reinforcement of nonlimerent promiscuity. The evi-dence is even more clear among those who neither pay nor are paid, but participate in promiscuous groups, parties, or orgies. Such activities have a long history dating back to antiquity among heterosexuals, but only in the present century of birth control have women been able to participate in them without fear of pregnancy.

Lacking this fear, and traditionally more sexually autonomous than women in our culture, men's homosexual promiscuity groups also have had a lively history, still very much alive in such meeting places as sauna baths, toilet rooms, truck stops, and outdoor "meat racks." Some mem-bers of these groups manifest a form of hyperphilia that is less well documented in the activities of women than in their fantasies of multiple or gang service that some women admit to. This is the polyiterative subtype of hyperphilia, or polyiterophilia. It is fairly well documented in the activities of some homosexual males. Its definitive characteristic is that a man or woman builds up his or her own responsiveness towards orgasm alone or with a partner by reiterating the same activity many times with many different partners in a limited period of time. The activity varies, but it is usually some form of manual, oral, anal, vaginal, or penile manipulation. To illustrate, a homosexual male with the syn-drome of polyiterophilic fellatio will be able to reach an orgasm with his own partner only after accumulating a dozen "blow jobs," that is acts of fellatio, on different men at, say, a steam bath or sauna club.

It hardly needs to be said that there is no fixed standard as to how often is too often in sex, whether in terms of total orgasmic frequency, masturbation frequency, copulatory frequency with or without orgasm, homosexual or heterosexual frequency, or number of partners. The range of variations is wide, from extreme apathy and erotic inertia to a plurality of orgasms on a daily basis. In some partnerships, each partner may be so disparate in orgasmic frequency that no effective compromise is possible.

Extreme sexual frequency is not known to be correlated with hor-monal levels, at least on the basis of today's tests. New tests in the future, especially those that may measure releaser hormones (releasing factors) from brain cells in the hypothalamus and limbic system, may help fill in the gaps in present day knowledge.

Hyperphilia that takes the form of an extreme multiplicity of partners in some instances represents a defect of pair-bonding. Such a defect is commonly a feature of the kind of personality that in the older psychiatric nosology is classified as psychopathic or sociopathic.

Hyperphilia in some cases takes the form of multiphilia, a compulsion always to have a new love affair—a new partner with whom to fall in love and establish a pair-bond. Once the process of establishing the bond is completed, over a period of months or years, the hyperphilic bonder's bonding wanes. Compulsively, he/she abandons the lover, even at the expense of reputation and career, and begins the pathological cycle all over again. Multiphilia carries over into the acceptive phase from the proceptive phase of erotosexualism. Like other forms of hyperphilia, and also hypophilia and paraphilia, multiphilia may be expressed heterosexually, homosexually or, more rarely, bisexually.

Another carry-over from proception to acception pertains to orgasm when one is alone as a sequel to erotosexual imagery exclusively, without pressure or tactual stimulation from oneself or a partner. The prototype of this phenomenon is in males the so-called wet dream that culminates in ejaculatory orgasm while asleep, and in females its counterpart, which also culminates in orgasm. Especially in early adolescence, some boys report nonmasturbatory ejaculation in response to erotic fantasy, with or without input from pictures, narratives, or other perceptual stimulation. The prevalence of the corresponding phenomenon in adolescent girls is uncertain. There are rare cases of recurrent fantasy-induced orgasms that are uncontrollable to an extent that is pathological and extremely unpleasant.

It is a source of distress to some affected individuals that they always fail to establish a pair-bond that has some lasting continuity. The contrary phenomenon is found in some individuals, nosologically classified as schizoid or schizophrenic, who are unable to break a pair-bond, even when the partner has deserted. They pine in the grief of a broken heart. Some such individuals establish a pair-bond, as Dante did with Beatrice, at a distance, or in absentia, without declaring their love directly to the partner. The partner may even be a popular cult hero or heroine represented only in a photograph, idolized as teenagers idolize pop singers. In rare instances, the idolator may commit suicide when an idol dies.

EROTIC SEXUALISM AND THE BRAIN. There is a sexological quip that what goes on between the legs is equalled in importance by what goes on between the ears. All knowledge of brain and behavior, and not only of brain and sexual behavior, is still woefully inadequate, despite steady advances in laboratory animal studies and in the investigation of human clinical syndromes.

From studies of spinal cord injuries in which the cord is completely severed, it is known that the genitalia can function in a partial and disjunctive way on a reflex basis, without connections back and forth to the brain. The condition is known as paraplegia. It involves total paralysis of and loss of sensory feeling from the waist down, loss of continence, and other health problems. Whatever reflex responses the genitals may make to local stimulation, the paraplegic man or woman is unaware of what is happening except by viewing it or palpating it with the hands. Loss of temperature regulation typically renders males sterile, whereas females are capable of pregnancy and delivery. Intercourse is gymnastically very difficult to accomplish. The patient may experience orgasm—a phantom orgasm—in dreams. Otherwise the experience of orgasm as formerly known is lost. The upper part of the body which is sensorily intact may partly compensate for genital orgasmic loss with increased erotic sensation, provided a sexual partnership exists—an aspect of rehabilitation which, until recently, was totally neglected, along with neglect of sexuality in all types of disability and handicap.

At the other end of the spinal cord, studies of brain injury, especially in neurosurgical cases, have shown that the temporal lobe of the brain has a part to play in sexuality in certain instances of hypophilia, hyperphilia, and paraphilia. There is, for example, a case quoted in Money and Ehrhardt (1972) of a safety-pin fetish associated with temporal lobe epilepsy. Both the fetish and the epileptic seizures disappeared when the epileptic focus was successfully removed surgically. In two other published cases, transvestism disappeared following successful temporal lobe surgery for epilepsy.

The temporal lobe of the brain is in part comprised of two limbic system structures, the amygdala and the hippocampus. More central is the septum, another limbic system structure which, according to Paul MacLean, is connected with the tail end of the body, whereas the amygdala is related more to the snout end. MacLean, a leading authority on the limbic system, described this system as the old mammalian brain. It encapsulates the still more archaic reptilian brain and is, in turn, encapsulated by the neocortex, which is most highly evolved in primates. MacLean and his colleagues, working with male squirrel monkeys, traced sexual pathways from the limbic system down through the brain stem to the spinal cord fibers. By stimulating these pathways by way of electrodes implanted at various junctures, they were able to produce erection and ejaculation in the monkeys. Provided with a self-stimulation lever, the monkeys would stimulate themselves, even to the excess of total exhaustion.

The limbic system includes the area of the hypothalamus, the cells and nuclei of which are notably sensitive to steroidal sex hormones. Hormones implanted in this area of the brain at specified locations stimulate the nearby pituitary gland to release its own gonadotropic hormones; and at the other locations they stimulate the release of component parts of mating behavior, for example the lordosis or crouching typical of the female.

The limbic system projects connecting pathways to the neocortex. How these pathways function in sexual eroticism and how the neocortex and the limbic system interact in sexual eroticism still awaits elucidation.

Today's state of knowledge of brain and sexual behavior is still too fragmentary to permit informed therapeutic applications. In West Germany, some attempts have been made to prevent homosexual behavior by means of psychosurgery to the anterior hypothalamus. The results are poorly documented and inconclusive, and the ethics of the procedure have stirred strong debate, and continue to do so.

Regardless of their origins, all variations of sexual behavior, normal and pathological, eventually are coded in the brain as well as in the mind. In today's state of knowledge, however, there is a woeful lack of data as to how brain coding takes place. When facts are lacking, doctrine and dogma fill the gap. So it is that people today tend to become dogmatic about outmoded doctrine of either nature or nurture as being responsible for sexual variations. They waste much time and space in futile argument, as well as futile research, as they try anachronistically to pin down a biological etiology for sexual variation, to the exclusion of a socially learned origin, or vice versa—as, for example, in homosexuality or transexualism.

Many of the paraphilias pose a special challenge to the nature/nurture protagonists. Consider, for example, a fetish for women's silk hose, or for rubber training pants. It seems absurd to conjecture a hereditary or innate determinant that dictates an imperative connection between a stocking fetish or a rubber fetish and sexual arousal. The same may be said of klismaphilia, in which sexual performance is dependent on the partner's prior administration of an enema to the klismaphiliac—a routine that almost transparently has childhood origins in excessive enemas given so that they became erotically arousing. Even so, one cannot dismiss the suspicion that the early enema excess was imposed on a child who in some way or other was overly predisposed or vulnerable to erotic conditioning and stimuli associated therewith. Another child exposed to the same experiences might be erotically indifferent to them, or defiantly rebellious.

There is no exact definition as to what constitutes a developmental predisposition or vulnerability to paraphilia. All the paraphilias, however, are built onto a phyletic substrate that is not, per se, erotic/sexual, but may be enchained in the service of erotic sexuality. Coprophilia is a good example, as is illustrated in the following personal anecdote.

Some years ago, when I visited the Yerkes primate laboratory in Atlanta, Georgia, I saw a newborn chimpanzee in an incubator of the type used for premature human babies. It was there because its captive, imprisoned mother did not know how to keep it alive. Like a human baby in an incubator, it was dressed only in diapers. How, I asked, did a wild chimpanzee mother keep its baby clean from soiling? The answer was that, as in many other species, she licks it clean, just as she licks it clean at birth, bites the umbilical cord, and eats the placenta.

Some months later, I had the chance to ask Margaret Mead if she knew of any societies in which human mothers do the same as do chimpanzee mothers in keeping their babies clean. Her answer was no. Among the people of Bali, in Indonesia, however, small dogs lick the babies clean. When a Balinese mother carries her baby on her thigh in a cloth hammock slung from her shoulders, she is accompanied by her pet dog. The dog's assigned duty is to provide diaper service by licking clean the baby, and the mother, whenever the baby soils. Subsequently I have learned that Eskimo mothers once had a custom of licking their babies clean.

Even though human primates have graduated from using the mother's snout end to keep the baby's tail end clean, it is safe to assume that, as a species, we still possess in the brain the same phyletic circuitry for infant hygiene as do the subhuman primates. Just as males and females have nipples, so also do both sexes have these brain pathways that relate to drinking urine and eating feces. These are the pathways that, when they become associated with neighboring erotic/sexual pathways, produce urophilia and coprophilia as paraphilias. The exact developmental formula whereby this association is facilitated is not known. Simple exposure to urophilia or coprophilia is not enough. Even 500 movies of such practices will not convert the viewer who has no predisposition. Only with a predisposition or unbarriered threshold will a person be capable of becoming a urophiliac or coprophiliac—though with no automatic guarantee of either.

The concept of a predisposing or vulnerability factor pertaining to developmental eroticism and psychosexuality is, by itself alone, too diffuse and speculative. It needs eventually to be reduced to empirical and operationally definable terms, for which today's best guarantee is a theory formulated in terms not of single determinants, but of multideterminants acting sequentially (Chapter 2). Figure 3-1 demonstrates such a formulation, beginning with the dimorphism of the sex chromosomes and ending with the dimorphism of adult G-I/R.

APHRODISIACS. The age-old search for the Fountain of Youth or for the wealth of El Dorado has its erotic/sexual equivalent in the search for an aphrodisiac or love potion, and its procreative equivalent in the search for fertility charms and magic. The latter pertain, obviously, to the third or conceptive phase of eroticism and sexuality. Love potions, love charms, and love magic pertain to the proceptive phase, not of oneself, but one's heedless or apathetic partner. An aphrodisiac proper may pertain also to one's partner, possibly to break down his or her acceptive-phase resistance or reluctance. The woman may sometimes have this aphrodisiac fantasy on behalf of a reluctant mate, but the popular stereotype is of the male in a maniacal state of perpetual priapism desperate to awaken a reluctant partner to wanton lust and erotic abandon. The male who fantasies an aphrodisiac for himself is most likely to do so in connection with the acceptive phase—so as to be able to have more orgasms in a given period, so as to be able to recapture the orgasmic frequency of receding youth, or so as to overcome impotence. The fantasy of stronger orgasms is less a part of the aphrodisiac folklore, except for those who once had stronger ones as a comparison criterion. In men's aphrodisiac folklore, women do not have a repertory of aphrodisiac fantasies for themselves, and women have not yet revealed too much about themselves in this respect. Historically, women have been more concerned with potions for barrenness rather than erotic arousal.

It would be surprising if any one substance could serve multiple aphrodisiac functions, and there is none that can. It is doubtful, indeed, if there is any substance that serves any aphrodisiac function other than, perhaps, to heighten orgasm as subjectively perceived, as is claimed for some street drugs; and, maybe, to reduce reluctance at the proceptive phase, as a low dose of alcohol does for some people.

Apart from powdered rhinocerous horn and various other forms of love magic, the oldest candidate for an aphrodisiac is Spanish fly, a powdered green beetle. Its effect is similar to that of putting the juice of hot peppers on or in the genitalia for its painful and reflex-stimulating effect on urgency of erection, or lubrication, and orgasm. Spanish fly is no aphrodisiac at all, but a painful and dangerous irritant of the mucous membrane of the urethra.

In recent years, there was a flurry of aphrodisiac excitement over L-dopa, a neurotransmitter precursor substance used for the relief of the severe motor incoordination of Parkinson's disease. With additional research, especially on animals, the possible sex-releasing or so-called aphrodisiac effect of L-dopa was not confirmed. L-dopa is related to the biogenic amines that include the brain's neurotransmitter substances, dopamine and serotonin. Though their precise role in erotic/sexual functioning of the brain remains to be discovered, present indications are that dopamine is an erotic/sexual activator and serotonin an inhibitor. It is possible to diminish serotonin by means of a tryptophan-free diet and thus increase sexual activity, according to experiments done on rats by Gessa and associates in Sardinia. Amphetamine and related street drugs are chemically related to the brain's own neurotransmitters. Amphetamine probably potentiates dopamine's erotic/sexual activating effect.

The newly discovered endogenous opiates in the brain, endorphin and enkephalin, are currently under study for their role in either activating or inhibiting erotic/sexual behavior. They are found in high concentrations in the vicinity of erotic/sexual pathways. They interact with dopamine and serotonin, along with other catecholamine and indolamine neurotransmitters.

Among street drugs, tetrahydrocannabinol (the active component of marijuana and hashish), and LSD (and its chemical relatives) have the reputation of heightening eroticism and possibly of prolonging and intensifying the perception of orgasm. Since the effect is not universal and not predictable, the reputed erotic value of these substances would appear to lie in their property of being sensory enhancers. Thus, if a person is erotically indifferent, or spent, then the drug will not be able to activate erotic responsivity. Quaaludes (methaqualone) and cocaine in small doses are claimed by some to delay the onset of orgasm at the plateau phase of feeling, following the excitement phase, and before the orgasmic phase.

The transient vasodilator, amyl nitrite, popularly known as poppers, acts swiftly when it is inhaled to produce not only a vasodilation, but also an accompanying "rush" variously categorized by different people as deplorable (dizziness, nausea, headache) or, conversely, as ecstatic, especially if the inhalation immediately preceded the moment of orgasm (Nickerson et al. 1979).

PORNOGRAPHY OR EROTOGRAPHY. Erotography means erotic writings or pictures, including movies. It is a scientific and impartial term, without the stigmatizing connotation that adheres in customary and legal definition to the term, pornography. Otherwise the two terms are synonymous.

Albeit somewhat facetiously, pornography is sometimes referred to as an aphrodisiac, on the basis, obviously, of the power of the visual or narrative image to induce erotic arousal—a power that is more limited than is commonly assumed.

The principle of the matching-effect dictates that a person can turn-on to the sexually explicit (erotographic) imagery of a book, a picture, or a movie, only if it corresponds to the imagery of his/her own personal turn-on. This is why a person who is not a coprophiliac can view a hundred movies of feces smearing and eating without becoming stirred to an erotic/sexual response.

The principle of satiation dictates that exposure to sexually explicit imagery that matches one's own loses its erotic turn-on efficacy as the novelty effect wears off. Aphroistically stated, the half-life of erotography or pornography is between two to four hours in one's total lifetime. That is to say, for the first two to four hours of exposure, sexually explicit material will evoke an erotic/sexual response, willy nilly. Subsequently, the response is not automatically released by the stimulus, but only if the viewer (or reader) is receptively ready—in the vernacular, horny, or in the right mood—with the personal biological clock properly timed, and perhaps with the partner similarly timed and available. When the conditions are right, then sexually explicit erotica can be used to augment one's sex life, on and off, throughout adulthood.

Exposure to pornography does not turn a person into a sexual maniac. After exposure and response to any type of sexually explicit material, the most that typically happens is a change of sexual timetable: the next sexual experience happens sooner rather than later, but it is the same type of experience (autoerotic, hetero- or homosexual) as one typically has been having. Another possibility, more likely a long-term one, is that the explicit erotic image will unlock an unrealized resource in one's own erotic life. For some people, oral sex may be such an example.

Pornography does not lead step by inexorable step down the pathway of sexual and moral degeneracy. On the contrary, there is some survey evidence to show that boys who grew up to be erotically normal men shared with their age-mates more exposure to explicit erotica, as part of their sub rosa sex education, than did boys who were imprisoned in adulthood as sex offenders.

Empirical findings on the effects of pornography on the individual simply do not square up with social and political dogma concerning its social evil. The social evil of explicit erotica is actually a by-product of its illegality, which enables it to be commercially exploited by the underworld, the personal risks being offset by immense untaxed and undeclared profits (Chapter 12). The same happened with liquor, in Prohibition, the permanent legacy of which is the continuing political power of the Mob. Today is still the era of Prohibition with respect to marijuana and drugs. They, along with explicit erotica, are the prohibited merchandise.

In its 1957 Roth decision, the U.S. Supreme Court first struggled with the impossible assignment of defining pornography in terms of appeal to prurient interest (prurient means itching!); redeeming social value (even cancer has social value for researchers!); and community standards (entire villages were wiped out during the Inquisition, every man, woman and child condemned by the ecclesiastical community to death by burning!). A Supreme Court Justice proclaimed that he recognized pornography when he saw it, even if he couldn't define it. He was closer to the truth than he knew. Pornography is erotically explicit material the reading or viewing of which makes you, as an adult, feel sneaky, because as a child you were threatened with punishment for doing so and thereby breaking society's ultimate taboo. Pornography is in the eye of the beholder. The personal and social price you pay for the taboo is still greater than you ever fully know. In tax money, it costs more to keep a pornography dealer, or anyone, in jail for a year than to send a boy or girl to college.

ANTIAPHRODISIACS. The most well-known antiaphrodisiac myth is that saltpeter, potassium nitrate, is put into the food in all-male institutions, such as a military installation, in order to quell the men's sex drives. Perhaps this myth originated with sailors on long sailing-ship voyages subsisting on a diet of bread and meat pickled in saltpeter brine with no fresh fruit or vegetables. If they lost erotic/sexual vigor, then it was doubtless secondary to vitamin-C deficiency and illness and emaciation (scurvy) than to saltpeter.

In the modern pharmacopoeia, there are two groups of drugs that have erotic/sexual side effects. One group is prescribed for the control of hypertension, for example, guanethidine sulphate. The others are psychiatric tranquilizers, for example, thioridazine (Mellaril). The erotic/sexual side effects are mediated by way of the autonomic nervous system. Their occurrence is unpredictable and individually variable. In males, these side effects include impotence, anorgasmia or, more rarely, orgasm minus the ejaculate. In women, they include impaired lubrication and anorgasmia. In both sexes, there may be a great reduction in erotic/sexual interest and arousal.

In males, surgical castration has long been considered to have a desexing or antiaphrodisiac effect. In subprimates, among those species in which sexual behavior is enchained to hormonal function, such an effect does eventually occur, and in females as well. In some species, however, of which the dog is one, copulatory behavior, or elements of it, may be observed years after castration. In primates, especially human beings, the same applies. Castration does abolish the genital secretions that are governed by gonadal hormones, but it does not automatically abolish all elements of erotic/sexual behavior. Rather, it reduces them and regresses them toward their prepubertal status. A prepubertal boy's penis can erect, and his mind can produce erotic/sexual imagery. The same applies to a castrate. It is for this reason that castration does not automatically abolish the sex-offending behavior of rapists, pedophiliacs, exhibitionists, or other paraphiliacs.

An ethically preferable alternative to surgical castration for sex offenders, in order to save them from prolonged imprisonment, is one that is completely reversible and without dangerous side effects, namely, the use of an antiandrogenic hormone (see Appendix). In males, estrogen is an antiandrogen, the converse of androgen in females. In females, androgen is an erotic/sexual enhancer as well as a somatic virilizer. These effects are well documented in male-to-female and female-to-male transexuals, respectively. For male-to-female transexuals, estrogen-induced breast growth is a positive side effect, but for other males it is negative. Thus, estrogen cannot be used for its antiandrogenic properties as an adjunct to the treatment of sex offenders.

As an alternative, there are two nonfeminizing antiandrogens currently in use—in Europe, cyproterone acetate, and in the Unites States, medroxyprogesterone acetate, a synthetic progestinic hormone. The latter does not produce breast enlargement, whereas the former occasionally may. Both of these hormones are androgen competitors and testicular inhibitors. In large enough doses, they usurp the place of their rival, testosterone, at the cellular level. The molecule of antiandrogen is an intruder, a cuckoo in the nest, so to speak.

Medroxyprogesterone acetate (Depo-Provera) seems to be more effective than its temporary and reversible resemblance to surgical castration as a testicular suppressor might suggest. The difference may well be that the antiandrogen is itself absorbed by brain cells that mediate erotic/sexual behavior, thereby producing an erotic tranquilizing effect. This tranquilizing effect includes a lessened prevalence and a lessened insistence of the imagery which, when translated into behavior, constitutes the paraphilic offense. Progestinic hormones, like medroxyprogesterone acetate, are known to be anesthetic in effect, as is progesterone itself, given in large enough doses.

Antiandrogenic therapy is most effective when combined with counseling therapy. It allows some paraphilic sex offenders for whom psychotherapy, group therapy, behavior modification, legal punishment, or any other treatment given alone is ineffective to gain a measure of self-regulatory control of their offending behavior. When the period of treatment is completed, the improvement may be maintained indefinitely, though long-term follow-up is advisable in order to abort a possible relapse. The chance of continuous, long-term improvement is increased if, as a sequel to hormonal and counseling therapy, the individual has the luck to establish a pair-bond of authentic reciprocity, either by way of gradual change, or in a sudden experience of falling in love. One patient described the before-and-after difference when he equated intercourse prior to treatment as the equivalent of masturbating in his wife's vagina, whereas afterward her erotic responsivity was as important to him as was his own. As a by-product of this change, the once compulsive excess of orgasmic release is no longer obligatory. The orgasm in the mutual relationship of reciprocity is more satisfying. In fact, the paraphiliac's excessive use of the genitals for orgasm prior to treatment bears as little relationship to eroticism, as most people know it, as handwashing does to hygiene in a handwashing-compulsive who washes his hands 200 times a day, until they become raw.

STD (SEXUALLY TRANSMITTED DISEASE). STD is nowadays replacing VD (venereal disease) as the preferred term, in recognition of the fact that erotic/sexual activity involves all of the body, not only the genitalia. Like the threat of pregnancy, the threat of VD has long been used for its would-be antiaphrodisiac effect in sex education curricula. There is no doubt that contagions transmitted chiefly by way of the sex organs are a threat to health and well-being, just as are contagious diseases transmitted chiefly by way of the mouth or any other organs. There is no doubt, also, that the risk of contagion by any route increases as the plurality of contacts increases in any given sample of men and women. People differ with respect to risk-taking in all aspects of living. Some are Las Vegas gamblers, chancing that the worst will never happen. Others are Hartford insurers, chancing that the worst might happen, and insuring against it.

The risk of exposure to STD can be balanced by the precaution of being acquainted with the various syndromes, their symptoms, their prevention, and their treatment (review in Money and Musaph's *Handbook of Sexology* 1977). For the risk-takers, there are some elementary hygienic practices that assist prevention, for example, washing in cold water after exposure, to kill the organisms of syphilis and gonorrhea that may be exposed on external surfaces, and urinating immediately after exposure as a further prophylaxis against urinary tract infection. Above all, regardless of whether the exposure was heterosexual or homosexual, never be too embarrassed or guilty to get a VD check-up which, in most big cities, is free at VD clinics. Neglect is the major personal and public health problem of STD.

6

Ignorance
Besieged and
Assaulted

THE SEXUAL TABOO IN WESTERN CULTURE. No one knows the antiquity of the taboo on sex that permeates our culture. A Biblical origin is tacitly assumed by many who make disparaging remarks about the Judeo-Christian ethic and its accompanying social heritage of antisexualism. As in the case of the Mediterranean legacy of pair-bonding (Chapter 4), however, the ethnographic range of the taboo on sex extends eastward, far beyond the region of Biblical origins, thus suggesting a pre-Biblical origin for the taboo. Irrespective of its origin, the taboo persists in our society today, along with the paradox of the double standard of prudery and publicity that is its inevitable outcome.

Taboo, though it varies from region to region and culture to culture around the world, is a very prevalent phenomenon. A taboo always applies restrictions to an organismic function—to something characteristic of the bodily function or behavior of members of the human species. Ethnographically, one taboo in a society usually outranks others. The great taboos apply to the visible appearance and activities of the sex organs; to the where and how of eliminating body substances; to the kinds of food that may be prepared and eaten; to the strangers and kin with whom one's vocal cords may be used in direct conversations; and to one's conduct with respect to the dying and the dead and their burial places.

The formula for the perpetuation of a taboo in society is like the formula for blackmail; a child in the course of development is threatened or punished for doing the thing that he/she has not yet learned is subject to taboo. To avert further threat or punishment, the child must pay the equivalent of protection money, in this case in the form of shame and/or guilt.

The ultimate function of a taboo is the wielding of power by generating shame and guilt. Once the lever of shame and guilt has been set in place, it can be manipulated not only by parents, but teachers, politicians, and others to control the behavior of those who have been shamed and made guilty. This principle is evident in politics today when, for example, a politician may win support for a covert plan of dictatorial authority by appealing to his constituency to strengthen the nation's moral fiber by means of a campaign to clean up the smut and filth of pornographic magazines and movies. In Asian and Islamic cultures (Chapter 5), the clean-up would include the pornography of kissing scenes in imported American movies, whereas our own moral fiber is threatened only by nude genitalia and copulation, leaving kissing, like violence, uncensored.

It may have been priestly rulers in some remote Cro-Magnon era who invented taboo as a method of controlling the people. The painters of the great cave art at Altamira and Lasceaux represented a people with IQs the equal of ours, and there is no reason to believe that they wasted their intelligence. Indeed, they may have invented complex systems of theological governance early enough for their diffusion far across the globe in great migrations at the conclusion of the last ice age.

The effectiveness of the taboo on sex today greatly handicaps the funding of sex research, the teaching of authentic human sexuality at all ages, and the delivery of effective sexual health care in cases ranging from birth defects of the sex organs to problems of teenage pregnancies, and of erotic partnership in old age. We still lack many simple sexological statistics of who does what, to whom, when and where, and at what ages, because potential informants obey the sexual taboo and censor what they might disclose. Otherwise, they run the risk of self-incrimination.

There are few national sexological statistics, partly because national policy is to keep health statistics chiefly on contagious diseases. Thus, there are national VD statistics, even though they are incomplete owing to underreporting. There are also census figures on legitimacy of offspring and marriage age. But there are no national statistics on congenital sexual defects, on precocious or delayed onset of puberty, or on the frequency of the various sexual malfunctions, and so on.

In a total population of almost 220 million, an estimated 1.2 million American children per year are involved in divorce. Approximately 50 percent of each year's American marriages today end in divorce. Among teenagers, the percentage rises to as high as 80 percent. Also, many teenage parents do not marry. There are approximately one million teenage pregnancies per annum. Three-fifths of the babies are kept by the mother. Half of these mothers are single parents. An estimated one-sixth of all American children live in one-parent households.

Anecdotally, everyone knows that separation and divorce may be the sequel to failure of the erotic/sexual relationship. To some degree the same may apply to failure to establish a joint household initially. Children never divorce their parents, for the parent-child bond is too strong to dissolve. When parents break up, children suffer, often direly. Nonetheless, there are no available data on the possible correlation of erotic/sexual dysfunction or incompatibility with broken pair-bonds, separation, and divorce.

RELIGION, HISTORY, AND EROTICISM. It is common in the history of mankind for religious doctrine to have encompassed erotic imagery and behavior, prescribing it in some cases, proscribing it in others. Some religions have celebrated eroticism, others have negated it. In our own tradition, the early fifth-century Christian fathers preached a doctrine of asceticism and mortification of the flesh. The pendulum began to swing in the twelfth century, the era of the Crusades and the troubadours. This was an age of new religious doctrine, denounced by the church as heresy, that gave prominence to the Mother of God and new tolerance of love and eroticism in pair-bonding as a substitute for arranged marriages in which the matching genealogical power and fortune outweighed falling in love. The troubadours lifted the ban on eroticism in their songs and poems, but only to celebrate an idealized romantic love not fulfilled in sexual intercourse. Along with the new openness in erotic sex, academic formalism and antiscience gave way to a reawakened interest in science. This was the age of Roger Bacon.

The pendulum swung again as the forces of the Inquisition gathered momentum in the fifteenth century, following the papal bull of Innocent VIII in 1484. The spirit of free inquiry was extinguished, and the church became so obsessed with sex as a sin that literally hundreds of thousands of Europeans were tortured to confess erotic encounters with the devil, after which they were then publicly burned alive. Entire villages in southern Germany and Switzerland were exterminated.

Italy escaped the worst excesses of the Inquisition, a situation that no doubt helps account for the fact that the High Renaissance came into full flower in sixteenth-century Italy. From there the new learning spread to the north and was in part responsible for the Reformation, a revolt that the masses, sick from so many burnings, espoused without too much resistance. The Renaissance and the Reformation rehabilitated eroticism after the excesses of the Inquisition, but confined it, in northern Europe and America, within the rigid boundaries of Puritanism and, in southern

Europe, within the traditions of the double standard and the virgin bride. Under Puritanism, woman's status gradually changed. In the notorious misogyny of Heinrich Kramer and Jakob Sprenger, authors of the *Malleus Maleficarum,* handbook of the Inquisition, woman had been the demoniacal temptress, insatiable with carnal lust, who drained man of his seminal strength and bewitched his genitals into impotency and sterility. Puritanism rescued her from the stake by metamorphosing her erotically into a passionless phantom, subjugated by man to be his own extracorporeal womb through which he replenished the earth, unsullied by carnal lust. Not until the twentieth century did couples begin to regain their erotic birthright, minus the threat of eternal damnation.

In the eighteenth century, the Age of Enlightenment, a relatively brief interlude of sexual liberalism was evident in northern Europe, reserved more for the aristocracy than the population at large. The Inquisition still cast its shadow in the form of Fundamentalism, and, in turn, Fundamentalism began to cast a shadow in the form of Victorianism.

Victorianism was less a resurgence of Puritanism, as we are so used to hearing, than a masterful blend of secular and religious dualism in both science and sex. Thus it taught the literalness of Biblical creation, while secularizing the book of Genesis with the theory of evolution. It tabooed sexual frankness but produced Freud and other great founders of sexology. It preached the sanctity of the family, while making big business of prostitution. It imposed a church-appeasing censorship on erotica and ran burlesque shows in its big cities. It warned against the moral and psychic degeneracy of masturbation and encouraged it by supplying no other outlet. It abhorred homosexuality, while segregating boys from girls in adolescent years. Sex was identified as sacred, spiritual, and beautiful, but vetoed until marriage. Simultaneously, it was carnal, lustful, and dirty, but to be shared specifically with the beloved. Victorians believed in universal education, but excluded sexual knowledge from the curriculum. They wanted their children to grow up sexually healthy, but they punished them for showing any signs of healthy primate sexuality in childhood and instilled an abiding sense of guilt.

The move toward liberalism in sexual matters in the present day and age is associated with a greater secularization of sexuality—a greater separation of sex and church. As a reaction to this secularism and a discontent with Christian doctrine, people are dabbling in oriental religions and the occult. But the ultimate import of these trends is that they constitute a new mysticism and antiscientism which, if history is a guide, will consolidate with antisexism.

SEXOLOGY: BACKGROUND HISTORY. In the era of the Inquisition, from the fifteenth to the seventeenth centuries, the principle of guilt by accusation held sway. To be accused of sexual imagery and dreams was to be condemned to death by burning at the stake. The accused person was tortured until a false confession was extorted.

By the eighteenth century, sexual practices took the place of sexual imagery as tell-tale signs of heresy and demonic possession. Oral and anal sex were proscribed as virulent evils, and even variant coital positions other than the male superior (the so-called missionary position) were punishable. Among the virulent evils, the most prevalent, because it afflicted the majority of pubertal boys, was self-pollution, otherwise known as masturbation. Led by the eighteenth-century French physician, Tissot, by the nineteenth-century proponents of the degeneracy doctrine gave masturbation a place of undeserved prominence as the cause of otherwise unexplained illness, especially mental illness. Even so revolutionary a thinker as Freud fell back on the old shibboleths when he proposed not simply a correlational but a causal relationship between latent homosexuality and paranoia.

The doctrine of degeneracy took the place of the doctrine of demon possession as an explanation of all the ills of humankind from epilepsy and tuberculosis to insanity, crime, and poverty. Degeneracy could be acquired by inheritance. It could also be acquired voluntarily, especially by masturbation, and subsequently transmitted down the pedigree.

In today's medicine, the degeneracy doctrine survives only in sexological medicine. It surfaces occasionally in professional writings, and very frequently in the media, notably in the labeling of a sex offender as a sexual degenerate, in much the same way as actors and singers with the early vocal and motor signs of tertiary syphilis were stigmatized in the press earlier in the century. The popular conception is that a sex offender degenerates from bad to worse—for example, from homosexuality to child molesting to lust murder. Such is not the case. The three conditions are separate from one another, and it is extremely rare indeed to find a case in which even two of them coexist.

Only in the present generation has masturbation been rehabilitated as a healthy activity. There are still voices of dissent, notably from the Roman Catholic clergy. In the nineteenth century, antimasturbation fanaticism was exploited legally to exonerate the defendant in a case of child abuse and murder recorded in Mary S. Hartman's *Victorian Murderesses,* and summarized in *Time Magazine,* February 28, 1977, thus:

Women shed no tears over Célestine Doudet when she was tried in Paris in 1855 for beating five young girls, sisters—one to death. The children's father, a fashionable English physician named James Marsden, had put them in the French woman's charge so that she might cure them of masturbation—a practice that Victorians believed caused epilepsy, asthma, paralysis, and madness. Doudet's qualifications for this task were obscure; she had previously been employed as a wardrobe mistress to Queen Victoria, who gave her a warm testimonial.

Once installed in a Paris apartment, Doudet began her course of treatment. She tied the children's wrists and ankles to the bedposts—a common method approved by their father. She also kept them on a starvation diet and subjected them to nasty tortures. On a rare visit to Paris, Marsden attributed his daughters' rickety, emaciated appearance to their persistence in the "secret vice" and ordered up some "preventive belts." Another physician who called upon the girls made a similar diagnosis. Women neighbors, seeing and hearing of the children's plight, managed to start a police investigation. Still Doudet persisted in brutalizing her charges, and one died of skull fracture.

Even after this tragedy, Marsden was reluctant to press charges against Doudet, fearing that exposure of the girls' vice would stain the family honor. When the trial finally took place, it seemed as if the four surviving girls were charged rather than their tormentor. If masturbation was proved, Doudet's lawyer argued, then there was no need to invent mistreatment to explain the dreadful physical condition of the girls.

The issue of whether the sisters did or did not masturbate was never resolved. Doudet claimed that the dead girl had been suicidal because of her uncontrollable masturbation and hit her head against the wall. Acquitted of causing the child's death, the Queen's ex-wardrobe mistress got five years for child abuse.

By the nineteenth century, the evil effects of sex on the body corporeal were extended to the body politic, as exemplified in the laws in many states of the United States narrowly defining the normal and acceptable in human sexuality versus what was abnormal and a "crime against nature." Federal antisexualism was embedded in the infamous Comstock legislation. In the nineteenth century, it was actually self-incriminating and dangerous to be honest with one's doctor, priest, friend, spouse— anyone—about one's sexuality. It was dangerous also to be an investigator of sexuality, and a foregone conclusion that the first serious sexual studies would be of sexual pathology, not of sexual health.

Modern sexology had its beginnings in Krafft-Ebing's *Psychopathia Sexualis,* published in 1886, a forensic psychiatrist's case reports of what today in medicine are called the paraphilias, though in law they continue to be designated as sex crimes and perversions. So as not to offend the susceptibilities of his time, Krafft-Ebing's publisher translated all sexual terms and descriptions into Latin, confronting the reader with freakish bilingualism meaningless to the layman. Even so, the author was professionally ostracized for having written his book.

Ostracism was, to some degree, the fate of all the founders of modern sexology—for example, in England, Havelock Ellis. He published his *Studies in the Psychology of Sex* between 1896 and 1910. The loudest furor of all, however, was generated in 1905 by Freud, no doubt because he proposed a theory not of sexual pathology, but of normalcy—a theory, moreover, that attributed sexuality to infancy and childhood: the oral, anal, and genital phases of development; castration anxiety and the Oedipus complex; and, in girls, penis envy.

All the pioneer sexologists of the nineteenth and early twentieth centuries were physicians, and their primary data were case studies, except for Iwan Bloch who drew also on ethnographic data. The time was not opportune for the study of sexuality in the population at large.

The first comprehensive compilation of data on normal sexuality was also based on case studies. It was gathered early in the twentieth century by Robert L. Dickinson, a gynecologist and the first modern American sexologist. Despite the title, Dickinson's *Human Sex Anatomy* (1933; 2nd edition 1949) gives much information about sexual function, anticipating Masters and Johnson. It also anticipated Kinsey, who knew Dickinson and consulted with him in designing his own epoch-making surveys of American sexuality.

During the years when Kinsey took sexology out of the doctor's office and developed its social-science branch, sexology in the United States was developing also as a branch of animal studies, and as a branch of politics in the thrust of the planned parenthood movement.

SEX SURVEYS: THE KINSEY FINDINGS. Kinsey did sexology an inestimable service by finding out what rank and file Americans actually had to say about their own sexual practices. They admitted much more than the establishment ever expected they would. In effect, they soundly trounced the taboo they had been supposed to live by. The published findings sent shock waves througout Christendom, of which the after-effects continue to be felt. The outraged establishment attacked Kinsey at his weakest point: he had conducted an interview-questionnaire survey without adhering to the rigid statistical rules of true probability sampling. There was, in fact, no possibility of obtaining a truly random probability sample for a sexual study, and there still isn't. Too many people are too shy and inhibited, and too many are fearful of self-incrimination to cooperate. There is, therefore, always a volunteer bias, the significance and extent of which needs to be estimated and allowed for.

The most remarkable feature of the Kinsey surveys is that thousands of people from all walks of life did cooperate with him and his interviewers, and that they admitted so much that, if misused, could have incriminated them as law-breakers. The possibility that they were either liars or freaks was put to rest when subsequent smaller surveys in both the United States and Europe gave confirmatory findings. Thus, although there is still no actual first-hand, observational survey of a representative sample of people regarding what they say and do sexually, there is a replicable body of solid data of what they report they say and do and have done. The Kinsey statistics have proved a boon to subsequent social researchers interested in documenting changes in people's reports of their sexual opinions and behavior.

These changes, in the thirty years since the Kinsey surveys, have been in the general direction of a greater tolerance of the sexual behavior of other people, provided one's own inviolacy is not impinged upon. There has, for example, been an increase in tolerance of the so-called sexual minorities and their practices, as in bisexualism and homosexualism, sadomasochism, and transexualism, for example. The prevalence of these forms of sexual expression seems not to have changed.

So far as their own actual behavior is concerned, people have changed chiefly toward an earlier age at first experiencing sexual intercourse. The old taboo has eased up especially on young women—as might be expected in the age of birth control. Young people live together (in a betrothal arrangement) more openly, and more prevalently than formerly. Other changes in sexual life-style, as in open marriages, consenting adultery, and group sex (swinging) have not been very widespread. Overt instead of covert acceptance of visual erotica, legally defined as pornography, has increased, but is by no means universal. In brief, changes in sexual mores that affect personal behavior have been slow, not dramatic and radical.

Sometimes change takes place in a most unexpected way. In a blue-collar neighborhood of Baltimore, for instance, it has become a status symbol among high school girls to boast of having had an abortion. In actual fact, they have not ever been pregnant and, in a majority of instances, have not begun their sex lives. Most of them have no easy access to contraception. By bragging about abortion, they are creating a climate of acceptability for a teenage sexual relationship. It is a climate that they may not enjoy themselves, but it certainly will prepare them for accepting the teenage sexuality of their successors and, in particular, of their own children.

Since the Kinsey data continue to provide a base line for social surveys, including changes affecting teenagers, they are summarized herewith:

—Kinsey's Report on Male Sexual Behavior: The average male reported from one to four orgasms a week. The incidence gradually declined after the age of 30. Married men had more orgasms per week than did single men, and college graduates fewer than those who did not attend college. Masturbation, nocturnal emissions, and petting to climax were more frequent outlets for college graduates than for those who did not attend college. Premarital, extramarital, and homosexual outlets were more frequent for those with less education than for college graduates. The frequency of intercourse with wives was about the same for all educational levels. Relations with one's wife made up between 80 and

90 percent of all sexual outlets at all ages and educational levels. College graduates showed an increasing proportion of extramarital intercourse with age, whereas those with less education showed a decreasing proportion as they grew older. Patterns of sexual behavior varied with social class. Professional men engaged in more kissing, embracing, and foreplay activities than did mechanics and factory workers. The more-educated also were more apt to be nude when copulating, and to experiment with different sexual positions. About two out of every three male college students experienced premarital intercourse by the time they graduated. The incidence of premarital intercourse was much higher for males of comparable age who finished grade school only. One of Kinsey's figures astonished many people and was used by his critics to cast doubt on the accuracy of all his findings. Slightly more than one-third of his male respondents reported that they had had at least one sexual interaction with another male; 63 percent of males said they had never engaged in a homosexual act; 4 percent that they engaged exclusively in homosexual relations; and 33 percent that they had had varying proportions of heterosexual and homosexual outlets.

—Kinsey's Report on Female Sexual Behavior: Comparing Kinsey's statistics for female sexual behavior with those for males is difficult, because of the differing criteria for orgasm in each sex. Of the sample of married women, 10 percent said they had never reached orgasm at any time in sexual intercourse with their husbands, and one-quarter of the wives had not had an orgasm during the first year of marriage. When college women were compared with less-educated women, masturbation was more frequent for college women and premarital intercourse more frequent for those with less education. About one college woman in five had premarital intercourse compared with almost two in five for those with grade-school education. This difference disappeared after the age of 30. College graduates had more marital intercourse leading to orgasm than did high school graduates. After the age of 25, more of the college graduates had extramarital intercourse than did those with less education. About 2 out of 100 women reported themselves exclusively homosexual (as compared with 4 out of 100 men); about 5 out of 100 were bisexual but predominantly homosexual. College graduates had fewer homosexual relations before the age of 20, and more such contacts after that age, than did women who did not attend college. Homosexual contacts led to orgasm in women proportionately more often than did heterosexual contacts.

In spite of the difficulty of comparing male and female sexual behavior, one can glean from Kinsey's figures that men in the 1940s had more sexual outlets (Table 6–1) and had more partners than did women. More men than women masturbated, engaged in premarital and extramarital intercourse, and had homosexual or animal contacts. In teenage, males had nocturnal emissions (wet dreams) more often than females had orgasm dreams. Women outnumbered men in only one category: petting to climax in teenage, to the exclusion of penovaginal orgasm.

Kinsey concluded that men more than women were aroused by a wide

Table 6-1. Orgasms per week [a]

Age	Single		Married	
	Males	Females	Males	Females
16–20	2.9	0.4	4.7	2.9
31–35	2.4	1.0	2.7	2.3
46–50	1.9	0.9	1.8	1.4

[a] Based on Kinsey, Pomeroy, Martin, & Gebhard 1953.

range of sexual stimuli; had more sexual fantasies; had more sex dreams; reacted more to erotic stories and pictures; talked more about sex; and more often were aroused by watching others in erotic activities. Kinsey's data did not, however, indicate whether these differences were a product of cultural conditioning, or otherwise.

SEX SURVEYS: THE ZELNIK AND KANTNER FINDINGS. Zelnik and Kantner from Johns Hopkins assembled a national probability sample of teenage women in 1971 and in 1976, in order to learn about sexual customs related to family planning and population dynamics. The summary from their 1977 report gives a concisely informative account of several aspects of teenaged sexuality today. It reads as follows:

Data gathered in two nationwide surveys made in 1971 and 1976 provide an opportunity to examine recent changes in prevalence of sexual experience and in contraceptive use among unmarried women aged 15–19. Confining the analysis to unmarried (i.e., never-married) women is a data processing expedient which introduces minor distortions into the findings without, it is believed, altering major conclusions. To have included ever-married women in this analysis would have increased the level of estimated premarital sexual activity, since the vast majority of the married had had intercourse before marriage. The effect on contraceptive practice is harder to judge. Many marriages are precipitated by pregnancy which results either from the failure to use contraception at all, or from ineffective use. On the other hand, the stable courtship arrangements which often preceded marriage are associated, or were in 1971, with better than average contraception.

With respect to sex and contraception, the following findings are most salient:

—Between 1971 and 1976, there was, for both races and at all ages, an increase among unmarried teenage women in the prevalence of premarital intercourse. The validity of the prevalence estimate for 1976 is confirmed by the use of an indirect estimating procedure which is believed to elicit true responses to sensitive questions.

—Knowledge of the time of greatest risk of conception during the menstrual cycle (which is relevant to the use of coitally related methods of contraception) was relatively poor in both 1971 and 1976. Sex education courses helped somewhat; however, among whites (but not blacks) experience and maturity were the better teachers. It is possible that sex education had other, and for this study, unmeasured effects on the use of contraception, the management of pregnancy and other aspects of sex and reproduction.

—Most sexual encounters take place in the home of the girl or her male partner. The older the girl, the more likely it is to be the partner's home.

—Along with increased prevalence of sexual experience, there has been a fairly substantial increase in the number of partners with whom teenage women have ever been involved. This is not a necessary consequence of more sex, and may be related to some stretching of the premarital period by a reduction in the age at first intercourse, as well as by greater postponement of marriage.

—At first intercourse, male partners tend to be teenagers themselves. The most recent partner, on the other hand, tends to be out of his teens and thus, presumably, somewhat harder to reach through programs that are based on some form of institutional catchment.

—The median age at first intercourse, which declined by a few months for both blacks and whites, bears some relationship to the age of menarche among blacks, but not among whites.

—First intercourse among unmarried teenage women is seasonal—summer being the time, apparently, when temptation and opportunity peak together.

—Contraceptive practice among unmarried teenage women improved significantly between 1971 and 1976. The proportions of sexually active unmarried women who always used contraception and who used it at the time of last intercourse increased. This improvement was moderated to some extent by a concurrent though smaller growth in the proportion who never used contraception. These changes appear to have been fostered by changes in the types of contraceptives being used.

—Many more young women used the pill and IUD in 1976 than in 1971. Along with this increase in use of the most effective medical methods of contraception, there has been a substantial decline in the use of the three methods—condom, douche and withdrawal—which were most prominent in 1971. Only among very young teenagers are these the methods of choice.

—Oral contraception is more popular among blacks at every age than among whites. It is, however, for both races, the most popular method.

—The gap between first intercourse and first use of contraception that was observed in 1971 has not narrowed significantly. Those who delay the use of contraception are much more likely than those who do not to have a pregnancy.

—Seemingly, the more committed to sex a young woman is, the more sophisticated is her initial use of contraception. There are striking differences in the first-use profiles of those who have sex only once, those who continue to have sex but use contraception from the start, and those who delay the use of contraception. For these three groups, pill use as the first method goes from less than 10 percent, to over 20 percent, to over 50 percent, respectively; while condom use by the male partner declines from 62, to 41, to 18 percent. Experience with

pregnancy and age at first use of contraception cannot explain these differences.
—About half of the unmarried teenage women who have used oral contraception got their original prescription from a clinic rather than from a private
physician. This contrasts with the practice of older, married women, who rely
much more on the private MD for contraception.
—Whether the first prescription for pills is obtained from a private physician or
from a clinic makes little difference in continuation or effectiveness of subsequent use. The importance of the clinic for contraception among unmarried
teenage women therefore seems to lie in increasing access to oral contraception
by unmarried teens.

Data from these two national surveys indicate that the prevalence of
sexual intercourse is on the rise among young unmarried women in the
United States. Although the majority of female teenagers have not had
intercourse, the magnitude of that majority appears to be diminishing.
More than one-half of those aged 19 or under in 1976 had had intercourse. The surveys also reveal that more of the sexually active are using
contraception, they are using the more effective methods, and they are
using all methods with greater regularity. Although the increasing use of
the pill and the IUD among teenagers should help prevent undesired
pregnancy, questions may also be raised about the desirability of early
and continued use of these contraceptives because of known and suspected increased risk of serious side effects, such as thromboembolic
disease with use of orals, as well as delay and possible impairment of
fertility following discontinuation of pill use.

Some will see in these data cause to lament the passing of the old ways;
others will see the beginning stages of a happier, better adjusted society.
Some will argue that changes are inevitable and will propose various
ways of dealing with them; others will advocate one scheme or another
for turning the tide. Exhortations or simplistic tinkerings, however, can
be expected to have little if any effect. In Japan and the People's Repub-
lic of China, there appears to be little premarital intercourse, at least
among those under age twenty. But both societies are very different
from the United States, and in ways presumably related to behavior of
young people. The methods of contraception that are growing in popularity among American teenagers generally accompany an established
pattern of sexual activity. What is more, it is of no little sociological
significance that most sexually active young unmarried women in the
United States are engaging in that behavior either in their own homes or
in the homes of their partners. This, perhaps, is more telling evidence of
the establishment of sexual activity than any number of statistics.

SEXUAL OBSERVATION: THE FOUR-PHASE RESPONSE CYCLE.
Although Kinsey did in fact make some observational and filmed studies

of human sexuality, and measured some of the physiological parameters of sexual arousal and orgasm, he did not publish them. It remained for Masters and Johnson, who began their sexual research in St. Louis in 1954, publicly to assert the right of physicians and scientists in sexology to make their primary observations and collect their primary data at first hand, instead of by hearsay. Thus, they put themselves in the position of Vesalius, four centuries ago, when he defied the Church and dissected the human cadaver. Masters and Johnson took physiological measurements of people while they were masturbating or copulating and developed a technique, including a transparent probe, for recording and photographing what happens within the vagina during orgasm. They extended their observations to couples whose attempts at copulation were marred by malfunction of the sexual organs of one or both partners, as in impotence and orgasmic failure. For these couples they developed a dual-team method of short-term couple therapy that rapidly was popularized by hundreds of followers and imitators as "the new sex therapy."

Masters and Johnson rediscovered a basic pattern of sexual response for both women and men. It had originally been described by Albert Moll (1912) as "the curve of voluptuousness in four phases: an ascending limb, the equable voluptuous sensation, the acme, and the rapid decline." Masters and Johnson delineated the four phases as:

—The excitement phase. The first physiological change in the male is erection, which occurs almost immediately. In some males, the nipples also become erect. The first change in the female is the moistening of the vaginal lining with lubricating fluid. The nipples also become erect and the breasts swell.
—The plateau phase. The testes of the male increase in size about 50 percent and they are pulled up higher in the scrotum. In the female, the tissues surrounding the outer third of the vagina swell, reducing the diameter of the vaginal opening by as much as 50 percent. In this way the vagina accommodates to different penis dimensions. The deeper portion of the vaginal cavity becomes distended. The clitoris retracts under the hood that covers it. These changes result from the filling of vessels and tissues with extra blood or from increases in muscle tension.
—The orgasmic phase. The penis throbs in rhythmic contractions. The seminal vesicles and prostate gland secrete the seminal fluids into the urethral bulb. Spasmodic muscular contractions at intervals of $8/10$th of a second, eject the semen out of the urethra under pressure, in half a dozen spurts, more or less. Semen may be expelled as far as 2 feet, if the penis is not inserted. In the female orgasm, there are rhythmic muscular contractions of the outer third of the vagina and of the uterus, also at intervals of $8/10$th of a second. Muscles of the anal sphincter contract rhythmically in both sexes. Other muscles throughout the body may also respond, in various patterns. The heart beats faster, blood pressure is elevated, and respiration is increased.

—The resolution phase. The organs and tissues return to their unstimulated condition, some slowly, some more rapidly.

ORGASM. The method of first-hand laboratory observation used by Masters and Johnson confirmed what Dickinson had already said, in contradiction of Freudian doctrine and post-Freudian dogma, namely, that the clitoral and the vaginal orgasm—or the orgasm from any other anatomical focus of stimulation, including the breasts—is simply and without complication an orgasm. To paraphrase Gertrude Stein, a rose is a rose is a rose is an orgasm, regardless of personal differences in the significance and sentiment of how it was attained. This physiological debunking of the myth of the superiority of the vaginal over the clitoral orgasm as the criterion of female erotic maturity undermined orthodox Freudian doctrine and, along with new theory of gender identity/role, required its updating—which is still in progress. It also led to current updating of Freudian theory in response to the valid criticism that, as originally formulated, it incorporated the Victorian sexism of its era, and perpetuated the anachronistic social and political dogma of female inferiority.

In males, the typical experience is of a build-up to one big orgasmic release followed by the refractory period of the resolution phase of rest and relaxation before the next build-up can begin. The length of the refractory interval between orgasms varies from minutes to hours and is partly a function of age, partly of the novelty of the partner, and partly of individual differences that presently are unexplained. Some men have reported a series of lesser, anejaculatory orgasmic peaks, with associated anogenital muscular contractions, prior to the final big one (Robbins and Jensen 1978).

The multiorgasmic phenomenon is prevalent also among women, far more so than among men, though not universally so. A woman is not multiorgasmic on every coital occasion, nor with each partner she may be orgasmic with. Also, a woman may on some occasions experience a series of multiple lesser orgasmic peaks without reaching the big orgasmic climax that heralds the onset of a refractory period during which the vagina dries and contracts and the body rests, relaxed, ready to drift off to sleep. Men and women both, especially as they get older, may feel erotically quite content on some occasions without arriving at the orgasmic grand finale. There are no fixed passing grades for erotic performance! Performing itself is the enjoyment, and there are many ways of performing. The variations, though partly idiosyncratic to each partner and each occasion, are especially a function of what, for want of a better term, may be called the "vibes"—the looks, movements, sounds, smells, tastes, touches, pressures, and warmths—that feedback between two partners. That is why an autoerotic orgasm is quite different from an alloerotic orgasm. It is also why oral and penovaginal orgasms differ, and likewise homoerotic and heteroerotic orgasms. Whether the different orgasmic experiences are ranked as inferior, superior, or equal, is a matter of personal idiosyncracy. The social tolerance of personal idiosyncracy used to be nil. Now it is slowly expanding. Oral sex—fellatio and cunnilingus—is no longer considered abnormal, and the same applies to various other personal and playful erotic idiosyncracies.

Some orgasms are not only different from, but better than others. Water at the end of a dry desert climb is better than water at a riverside swimming picnic. So also with orgasm: the place, the person, the frequency and the recency of orgasmic occurrence all influence the quality of the next one. So also does health, fatigue, age, sex, experience, imagery, novelty, and so forth—but above all, the mutual reciprocity of the partnership, the match for erotic versatility, movement, noise and abandon, the build-up of the proceptive phase, and possibly a drug-induced sensory enhancement.

Whatever the antecedents to an orgasm that is better than others, the final common pathway is the same. The two lovers are able to experience a feeling of unrestrained and untamed abandonment to one another. It is not necessary for them to pay attention either to what the self is doing or what the partner is doing. All the movements take care of themselves, as if reflexively. The sensations greedily absorbed by the vulva, externally and through deep interior pressure, tell the vaginal cavity how to selfishly pulsate, ripple, quiver, and contract on the penis, in order to release itself in orgasm. Reciprocally, the penis selfishly probes and presses, twists a little, withdraws and tantalizes at the portals, and sinks deeply again, it too greedily building up its own orgasmic pleasure. The two bodies writhe, unheedingly. The two minds drift into the oblivion of attending only to their own feeling, so perfectly synchronized that the ecstasy of the one is preordained to be the reciprocal ecstasy of the other. Two minds, mindlessly lost in one another. This is the perfect orgasmic experience. This is how an orgasm sighs, moans, exclaims, expires, exhausts itself into exultant repose. No orgasm is the best. They keep getting better and better.

CYCLICITY AND EROTIC/SEXUAL FUNCTION. Many factors may inhibit or interrupt orgasmic reciprocity, not least of which is insufficient privacy, auditory or visual, especially when there are young children in crowded living quarters and the parents are erotically prudish and secretive. Regardless of hormonal levels, the frequency of coitus during the course of one menstrual cycle in young adult couples screened for psychologic normalcy varies widely. In a 1976 study of eleven couples by

Persky and coworkers, the range of coital frequency per cycle over a total of three cycles was from three to eighteen occasions of coitus, with a mean of eleven.

In subprimate animals, the proceptive, acceptive, and conceptive phases of sexuality correlate closely with the hormonal cycle of estrus, regardless of whether estrus is perpetually cyclic or governed seasonally by climate. In primates, the cycle is menstrual, not estrual, and the proceptive and acceptive phases of the behavioral cycle are less strictly enchained to the hormonal cycle than they are in the estrual cycle. In subhuman primates living in the wild, according to the available evidence, the female's sexual interaction with the male is more enchained to the hormonal cycle of the menses than is the case among human females in their interaction with human males.

The present state of knowledge concerning menstrual fluctuations of estrogen, progesterone, and androgen and their effect on proceptivity and receptivity (acceptivity) in monkeys was updated in 1977 in an exceptionally well-informed review by Baum, Everitt, Herbert, and Keverne. The review concludes with a statement about human beings:

The methods currently being used for studying human sexual behavior make it very difficult to distinguish between proceptivity and receptivity (acceptivity) and hence to ascribe individual roles to various hormones in the way now possible for monkeys. Rhythmic changes in sexual interaction in humans during the menstrual cycle have been reported, although contradictory reports continue to appear and maximum levels are as commonly found early in the follicular phase as at midcycle. It has been suggested that the human female's attractivity may decline during the luteal phase (as in monkeys) and that this can be counteracted in women by taking contraceptive steroids.

The consequence of withdrawing endocrine secretion, or treatment with steroids, have usually been assessed in terms of loss or gain of "libido," although some studies have used other criteria such as incidence of orgasm or "coital satisfaction." It is not clear whether loss of libido indicates changes in receptivity, proceptivity, or both. Furthermore, changes in libido may occur secondarily to those in attractivity, as in monkeys.

Ovariectomy is generally agreed not to diminish the human female's libido consistently, and the same conclusions have been reached in studies of menopausal women. Insofar as comparisons are justified, this correlates with findings on ovariectomized monkeys described above. Adrenalectomy, however (which diminishes androgen) has been found to diminish promptly the human female's libido, whereas giving intact women testosterone stimulates their sexual interest in many cases. This suggests that there may be a role for androgens in the human female's sexuality comparable with that experimentally determined for the rhesus monkey, although exact correspondence awaits further clinical investigation.

ORAL CONTRACEPTION AND EROTIC/SEXUAL FUNCTION.

The foregoing statement continues with a summing up of today's all too sparse knowledge concerning the effect on woman's erotic/sexual function of the hormonal changes induced by the contraceptive pill:

The most common steroid therapy given to women is the contraceptive pill, usually a variable mixture of an estrogen and a progestogen. A number of investigations on the effect of this treatment on libido have been made, with conflicting results. In some cases, libido has been depressed, and this has been a major factor in women's discontinuing their use of the pill. In others, little change has apparently occurred, or libido has even seemed to increase. The way in which such data are collected may have a crucial effect on the apparent change in behavior. Furthermore, effects on behavior, if they occur, may be attributed as much to social factors as to endocrine factors. There are other complications. Clinical depression, of which diminished libido is one symptom, sometimes occurs in women taking contraceptive steroids; the converse, euphoria, may also occur ... women taking the pill excrete less androgen metabolites and have no midcycle peak in either testosterone or estrogen, which may provide an endocrine explanation for some cases of decreased libido.

There has been much inconsistency in findings on the effect of the contraceptive pill on mood and sexuality. A large part, if not all of the inconsistency can probably be attributed to the fact that mood and sexuality are multidetermined, and few studies have been designed for multivariate analysis. In the case of a 1972 study by Cullberg, an attempt is made to deal with multiple variables. The summary of his monograph is as follows:

Three different hormone preparations and one placebo preparation were given to a sample of 322 women volunteers. The hormone preparations contained a constant dose of estrogen (.05 mg ethinyl oestradiol) in combination with varying gestagen (progestin) doses (1.0 mg, .5 mg, and .06 mg norgestral respectively). The compounds could be characterized as strongly gestagenic, medium gestagenic (identical with a commercial oral contraceptive) and estrogenic, according to the dominant physiological effects. The placebo was identical in shape and taste. The medication was given in a double blind, randomized order and taken during a two-month time period.

Overall mental reactions: The mental effects of the hormones showed themselves to be low. In the interview ratings, 14 per cent more individuals of the gestagen dominated medication groups reported adverse mental change in comparison with the placebo group. The estrogen dominated group showed 18 per cent more negative reactions than did the placebo group. The differences from placebo are significant at the .05 level. The mental symptoms were generally mild and mostly of a depressive-dysphoric type.

The self-rating questionnaire for mental change did not show any conclusive evidence of mental change except for the estrogen dominated group which showed a negative change (irritability) in comparison with the placebo group.

Specific somatic and mental symptoms: There are signs of a direct link between gestagen induced weight increase and adverse mental changes, as well as between estrogen induced nausea and mental changes. The subjective reactions towards these physiologic effects of the hormones have some importance for the reporting of mental symptoms, but there is also evidence that hormonally induced mental symptoms appear independently of the somatic reactions. Headache has often been reported as a side effect of oral contraceptive treatment. In the present study no difference was seen in any of the hormone groups as compared with the placebo group.

Nor were any differences found regarding increase or decrease of sexual drive in comparison with the placebo group. There is, however, an association between adverse mental change and lowered sexual interest. These findings could be interpreted as indicative of the absence of any direct negative effects on sexual functions of the hormones used.

Change of menstrual symptoms: Dysmenorrhea was clearly relieved by the gestagen dominated preparations in a dose related response. Estrogen dominated treatment showed no difference from placebo treatment in this respect. Premenstrual tension, as defined by the presence of premenstrual irritability prior to medication differed in response according to type of medication. Here one could observe only nonsignificant trends towards symptom relief with the gestagen dominated medication and impairment with the estrogen dominated medication.

COUPLE SYNCHRONY. There are no clear-cut cyclic rhythms, circadian, seasonal, or of other duration, that influence men's sexual eroticism. The few attempts that have been made to correlate men's orgasmic activity and frequency with circulating testosterone level, irrespective of cyclic regularity, have been inconclusive and inconsistent. The same applies to the possibility that defeat or the stress of competition with or obedience to more authoritarian or dominant males may lower both the testosterone level and the mating activity of the subordinate male.

It is only very recently that research attention has been directed to the possibility that proceptivity and acceptivity in men may fluctuate in synchrony with the hormonal cycle of the woman partner. In 1977, Persky and coworkers found a strong trend for a husband's blood level of testosterone to peak at its maximum value at around seven days after his wife's ovulation, at which time the wife's testosterone level reached its second or postovulatory peak in the menstrual cycle. The behavioral concomitants, if any, of this conjunction of testosterone peaks remain to be investigated.

Another phenomenon of sexual synchrony, still preliminary and unconfirmed, was reported from Australia in 1976 by Henderson. In a study of married couples, she found that, at the time of the female's midcycle temperature low point and subsequent postovulatory rise, the male's basal body temperature underwent a synchronous change, though the elevation was maintained for fewer days in the male than the female. Henderson obtained data also on one homosexual male couple and found that if their basal body temperatures fluctuated, they did so in synchrony. This finding resembles that of McClintock who, in 1971, found that college women living in the same dormitory established menstrual synchrony. It was not necessary for two roommates to know each other's menstrual timetable for synchronization to occur. The same effect occurs if women are experimentally exposed to the underarm odor of a stranger (Hopson 1979).

The most likely hypothesis to explain synchronization in couples or groups is that it is mediated, possibly subliminally, through the sense of smell by way of pheromones or odors. In subhuman primates and other mammals, it is well established that the female at the time of ovulation emits a vaginal odor or pheromone that is for the male an erotic attractant (Chapter 5). It is also established that the human female emits an ovulatory pheromone which chemically is the same as that emitted by the rhesus monkey female and is an attractant for the rhesus male. There is a dearth of information and no definitive investigation on the role of the vaginal pheromone in human male sexuality. Morris and Udry in 1978 reported a properly designed study on 62 young adult couples, all university students, and were not able to demonstrate a pheromonal effect on the frequency of intercourse. They suggested that males may be differentially responsive to pheromone. If so, then some way of identifying those who are responsive will need to be found and further studied.

POSTMENOPAUSAL EROTIC/SEXUAL FUNCTION. The hormonal transmutation of the menopause varies from rapid to gradual. It takes place typically in the fifth or sixth decade of life, at the very latest by age 60. The mechanism of the biological clock that regulates the menopause is not known. In all probability, the process begins in the brain, as the neurotransmitter cells of the hypothalamus change from a cyclic to an acyclic schedule of secreting their neurotransmitter substances—biogenic amines among others. When the hypothalamus goes on an acyclic schedule, it programs the pituitary to do likewise, with an ensuing steady state of gonadotropin secretion that results in an elevation particularly of the gonadotropin FSH (follicle stimulating hormone) in the bloodstream. When pituitary gonadotropins are secreted on an acyclic schedule, then the ovary becomes acyclic also, with a resultant disappearance of cyclic ovulation and menstrual bleeding. With the further passage of time, ovarian function diminshes and the blood level of ovarian estrogen lowers until only a small amount can be detected. Urinary estrogen in the elderly postmenopausal woman is believed to reflect peripheral conversion of steroid precursors and the continued production of estrone from adrenal androstenedione.

Sudden onset of ovarian insufficiency as, for example, in the wake of surgical castration, or of sudden withdrawal of estrogen replacement therapy, induces symptoms of vasomotor insufficiency, experienced as hot flashes, sweating, vertigo, headache, fatigue, and insomnia. These same symptoms accompany the onset of menopause in an estimated 25 percent of women. Eventually, they go into spontaneous remission, though they can, if too severe, be ameliorated by treatment with estrogen. This effect of estrogen on symptoms of vasomotor instability has led to an extensive lay and medical folklore regarding a putative menopausal syndrome of anhedonia, somatic complaints, and hypoeroticism. In 1975, Eisdorfer and Raskind reviewed the published evidence regarding this so-called syndrome and reached the conservative (and arguable) conclusion that if it occurs, only the vasomotor symptoms can be directly attributed to estrogen insufficiency. The prevalence of the syndrome has not been ascertained epidemiologically and almost certainly has been highly exaggerated through lack of adequate statistics. Those whom the syndrome hits, however, it may hit very hard, creating an intense subjective lack of well-being that is in no way helped by the change from spontaneity to perfunctoriness in erotic response to the partner. The return to well-being following replacement therapy with cyclic, low-dose estrogen is dramatic.

There is no universal correlation between estrogen insufficiency and hypoeroticism before, during, or after the menopause. There may be an indirect association after a prolonged period of estrogen insufficiency, secondary to changes in the reproductive anatomy of the type tallied by Masters and Johnson: shrinkage of fatty tissue in the labia majora, involution and loss of elasticity of the vaginal wall, reduced vaginal lubrication, and possible painful uterine contractions. In most things pertaining to human sexuality, normative data are nonexistent. Thus, there are no normative data as to how many postmenopausal women encounter copulatory difficulty secondary to the foregoing somatic changes. Nor is it known whether, and to what degree these changes accelerate or decelerate in relation to erotic inactivity or activity, respectively.

Estrogen/progestin cyclic therapy in low small doses prevents postmenopausal somatic changes in the genitalia, the restoration of vaginal lubrication being of particular significance to the maintenance of erotic activity when vaginal dryness has become a problem. Clinical opinion is divided as to whether the erotic benefits of estrogen replacement are outweighed by suspected adverse side effects, notably hormone-dependent cancer, and, as of 1977, a suspected positive relationship between estrogen and increased risk of heart attack in both sexes. Many women consider the big erotic benefits well worth the small risks.

When vaginal dryness hinders coital activity, and estrogen is not taken, then an exogenous vaginal lubricant is adequate to permit intercourse without discomfort. There are no statistics with respect to masturbation, and also the relationship of masturbation frequency to the availability or unavailability of a partner, and the relationship of the psychosexual status of her husband to a wife's sexual frequency.

Prevalence statistics are lacking also with respect to the frequency of orgasm in postmenopausal women. It is well established, however, that in women who continue an active sex life, the menopause does not interfere with the experience of orgasm. Whether or not they continue an active sex life depends more on the availability of a partner than anything else. In keeping with the mores of their upbringing, unpartnered elderly women are less likely to find a new partner than are their male counterparts. Moreover, men have a shorter life expectancy than do women, thus leaving a surplus of lonely older women (Chapter 4). For women with a partner, the frequency of sexual intercourse diminishes gradually with each advancing decade. Whether it fades altogether, or not, sexual frequency depends more on factors that are individually variable than on those that are specific to aging alone.

EROTIC/SEXUAL GERONTOLOGY IN MALES. There are two doctrines regarding psychosexual and psychoendocrine aging in the male. One is the doctrine of gradual and progressive diminution or winding down, and the other is the doctrine of the male climacteric, first put forward by Marañon in 1929. It is not possible at the present time to arbitrate between these two doctrines, because there are no longitudinal studies in which hormonal and sex-behavioral age changes have been recorded in parallel.

There are also no longitudinal studies in which sex-hormonal age changes have been recorded independently of behavior. The only information presently available is cross sectional, as, for example, in the 1972 study by Vermeulen, Rubens, and Verdonck that showed: "that male senescence is characterized by a decrease in plasma testosterone levels, an increase in testosterone binding and binding capacity, a decrease in metabolic clearance rate, a decreased testosterone production, and a metabolic pattern of testosterone suggestive of hypogonadism, with decrease of the androstenediol formation and preponderance of the 5β over the 5α reductase pathway." The youngest age group in which the foregoing changes first appeared was between 50 and 60 years. More men between 60 and 70 had undergone the same changes, but a good proportion of men between 70 and 80 still had not manifested them, and even by age 90 there was still an occasional man whose hormonal levels were at the same level as the lower limit of the norm for men of 40 or 50.

In the absence of progressive measurements in a longitudinal study, there is no way of knowing whether, in individual men, the hormonal transition of aging is relatively abrupt or gradual. There is also no way of knowing whether the transition is subjectively perceived or not, and if it is perceived, what the perceptions are. According to the doctrine of the male climacteric, the transition represents something of a crisis, though there is no way of differentiating a neuroendocrine crisis from a crisis in career achievement or in the relationship with spouse and offspring.

Because of the routine imperfections and falsifications of memory, retrospective investigations of developmental sexuality in older men are less satisfactory than prospective investigations. The Duke University gerontology studies of sexuality showed that in men the availability of a partner is a prime determinant of an older man's sex life. Because of the greater longevity of women, older men have more available partners than do older women. Also, the older male, conforming to the stereotype of our culture, is more likely than the older female to find a new partner. Having found one, he nonetheless shows a gradual lessening of the frequency of sexual encounters with advancing age, though there is great individual variability.

The longitudinal gerontology studies of sexuality by Clyde E. Martin at the National Institute on Aging have used both retrospective recall and longitudinal developmental data. On the basis of these two sources of information from subjects in the upper educational and socioeconomic bracket, it appears that the earlier and more vigorous the sexuality of youth, the later and more vigorous the sexuality of aging. In addition, it appears that lessening frequency of erection and/or ejaculation, with or without a partner, is not experienced as a traumatic deprivation in probably the majority of men who are healthy in body and mind.

From anecdotal clinical reports, it appears likely that the psychosexual concomitants of aging comprise lessened frequency of erection and ejaculation, longer time to achieve full erection, greater likelihood of incomplete erection, earlier loss of complete erection, longer refractory period between erections and/or orgasms, greater likelihood of ejaculatory delay, greater likelihood of nonejaculatory copulation (or masturbation) with or without the subjective feeling of orgasm, and continued appreciation of erotic sensuousness despite the foregoing changes.

Despite the lack of systematic confirmatory statistics it seems likely, as a general principle, that with advancing age a man's erotic performance becomes more dependent on the visual imagery of arousal in the procep-

tive phase and less responsive to tactual stimulation of the genitals themselves. There is something of a paradox here. It lies in the fact that the
neural mechanism of erection can function reflexly through the lower
spinal cord independently of the brain. One proof of this autonomy is
found in cases of paraplegia (Chapter 5) that are characterized by spinal
cord injury, with complete severance of the cord and hence total decon-
nection of the genital organs from the brain. In the paraplegic, it is
possible to apply genital tactual stimulation to induce an erection of the
penis, totally unbeknownst to the patient, unless he either sees it or
palpates it with his hand.

This reflex activation of the genitals extends probably also to secretion
of the seminal fluids and to their spasmodic ejaculation in orgasm. Erection, emission, ejaculation and detumescence each are neurally independent of one another, though normally coordinated, presumably not
peripherally, but centrally, in the brain.

On first thought, one might assume that in the absence of peripheral
disease or impairment, tactual stimulation would be sufficient to ensure
genital response in either sex, regardless of age. Such is very much the
case early in adolescence, when the slightest touch may trigger a genital
response. It is not the case, however, in many instances of sexual inadequacy, sluggishness, or hypofunction. Regardless of age, in such instances, the spinal cord genital circuits appear unable to function on
their own. Apparently they need to be reinforced with added stimuli
generated from erotic imagery and fantasy in the brain. This fantasy-
imagery need not be exclusively visual, though probably it is primarily
so. The partner as represented in the fantasy may possibly be represented fictively, in absentia. However, the response of the genitals to the
stimulus image is more effective if the partner is actually present, per-
ceptually, and involved as a participant in the staging of the fantasy.

This hypothesis of greater dependency on erotic imagery and fantasy
for genital arousal with advancing age, if correct, would fit in with the
popular conception that "life begins at forty." Implicit in this saying is
the idea that the older person has fewer restraints than when younger on
living out erotic fantasies, especially with a new partner who perfectly
performs his/her fantasy role. Thus can one account for a change in
erotic behavior in some older people that seems greatly out of character
relative to their earlier, more moralistic erotic orthodoxy. In popular
parlance, this change turns a man into a dirty old man.

The wide range of individual variability in geriatric eroticism exists
independently of partner availability and regardless of the prior history
and quality of a long-term erotic relationship.

There is no conclusive evidence presently available as to the effectiveness of androgen supplementation therapy on male sexual function in

old age, nor of potentially adverse side effects. However, there are individual reports of positive sex-organ response to such therapy in terms of improved sexual performance. Without statistical evidence from a group of cases, however, it is not possible to distinguish the effects of hormonal supplementation from the effects of stimulus novelty, and the effects of visual or imagistic arousal from those of tactual arousal. The age-effects of hormonal supplementation on the occurrence and frequency of erotic imagery are unknown.

HORMONES AND MONOMORPHIC PARTNERSHIPS. When techniques for measuring sex steroids in the bloodstream and/or urine first became available to clinical case management in the 1930s, the very names of the hormones made it inevitable that some investigators would hypothesize a lack of male or female hormone as the cause of male or female homosexuality, respectively. Attempts to prove the hypothesis gave inconsistent, inconclusive, or contradictory evidence. Likewise, correlative attempts, on the basis of trial and error, to treat homosexuality hormonally failed. Androgen given to male homosexuals either had no effect or, possibly, increased the frequency of homosexual activity. Lesbians, always ignored by both law and medicine as compared with male homosexuals, were seldom treated with estrogen but, if they were, there was no effect on their having a partnership with a female.

The precision radioimmunoassay techniques of blood-hormonal measurements in the mid-1960s ushered in a new flurry of attempts to correlate hormones and homosexual behavior. None of the studies has been so designed as to take account of multivariate determinism, but simply to prove a rather naive assumption that matching with a same-sex partner is hormonally ordained. The sample size and criteria of selection have varied, as have the procedures for determining hormonal levels, the hormones measured, and the precautions to safeguard against diurnal fluctuations in hormone secretion.

To date, there are few studies that have addressed the possibility that the hypothalamic-pituitary-gonadal system may be different with respect to homosexuality. One is a study by Dörner and coworkers in East Berlin of the feedback effect of an injection of conjugated estrogens (Premarin) on the hypothalamic-pituitary regulation of the release of pituitary luteinizing hormone (LH). The subjects were heterosexual, bisexual, and homosexual males admitted to a hospital for venereal or skin disease. Homosexual males were reported to manifest a primary decrease in serum LH level, followed by a secondary rebound effect to levels above the initial values. A similar, though stronger rebound occurs in heterosexual females, whereas in heterosexual males and in bisexuals the rebound that followed the primary decrease did not exceed initial values.

Another study is more recent (1978) and was published by Seyler and a group of collaborators in New England. They test-treated female-to-male transexual candidates with the feminizing drug, diethylstilbestrol (DES) orally for a week and then gave an injection of LHRH (luteinizing-hormone releasing hormone). In normal heterosexual women, such treatment is followed by increased release from the pituitary of the gonadotropins LH and FSH (follicle stimulating hormone). In the female-to-male transexuals, this increase was conspicuously impaired and closely resembled the low response found in normal heterosexual men. The best hypothesis to explain this finding is that in the female-to-male transexuals the hypothalamic pathways in the brain were subject prenatally to hormonal influences similar to those typical of males in utero. These prenatal hormonal influences were not sufficient to prevent the pubertal onset of menstruation and fertility, with normal pituitary and ovarian hormone levels. But they probably did set the stage behaviorally so that transexualism could more easily differentiate in the gender identity, postnatally.

In other studies of pituitary function in male homosexuality, there has been no test-dosage of an injected hormone, but simply a blood-plasma measurement of the pituitary's own spontaneously secreted gonado-tropic hormones, LH and FSH. Kolodny and associates in 1972 reported elevated LH levels in some volunteer homosexual subjects who rated as 5 or 6, the predominantly or exclusively homosexual ratings on the Kinsey scale of heterosexuality/bisexuality/homosexuality. The exact number of subjects with elevated LH was not specified, but four received special mention because they had, in addition to high LH, high FSH and azoospermia—which suggests that they represent an as yet unrecognized psychoendocrine syndrome. In two cases only, pituitary prolactin level was also elevated.

Increased prevalence of elevated LH was found also by Doerr and associates in a 1976 study of homosexuals given ratings of 4, 5, or 6 on the Kinsey scale. By contrast, Tourney and associates in 1975 found no significant difference in gonadotropin (LH and FSH) levels in a homosexual as compared with a heterosexual group. The same applies to the most meticulously designed study yet done, the one reported by Parks and coauthors in 1974. They took blood samples every day for a month, thus eliminating as a source of error the potential distorting effect of day-to-day fluctuations in hormonal output, which are of great magnitude. They also tested youths institutionalized as juvenile offenders, which presumably eliminated the potential distorting effect of unreported medications or illicit drugs and alcohol.

The foregoing findings indicate that many homosexuals cannot be differentiated from heterosexuals on the basis of tests of pituitary function, but they do permit the speculation that there may be some dif-

ferential in hypothalamic-pituitary programing before birth that expe-
dites, though does not preordain the differentiation of a homosexual, a
bisexual, or a heterosexual gender-identity or psychosexual status in the
postnatal developmental years. By contrast, the findings from measurements of the gonadal hormones, the sex steroids themselves, invite
no theoretical speculation, for they are inconsistent. Their levels in
homosexuals as compared with heterosexual controls have variously
been found to be the same, lower, or higher. Such inconsistency may be
secondary to sample size, method of sample selection, differences in
laboratory technique, the difference in hormonal products that are measured in urine as compared with blood, diurnal fluctuations in the
amount of steroid hormone released into the bloodstream from the
gonads and from the adrenal cortices as well, the time period and frequency with which blood samples are drawn, recency of sexual experience, and the possible intrusion of effects of recent sleeplessness, toxic
drugs, and so on.

PUSHING HORMONES BEYOND THE LIMIT. Putting sex hormones and homosexuality into the same equation is a great scientific
temptation. It is too easy to assume the premise that male hormone
causes male behavior and female hormone causes female behavior, and
to design an experimental test. Likewise, it is too easy to equate mood
fluctuations, and fluctuations in sexual activity with hormonal fluctuations (estrogen and progesterone) of the menstrual cycle and, again, to
design an experimental test.

The findings of these experiments have been and continue to be inconsistent, but people want positive correlations so much that they all but
follow the old maxim—don't bother me with your facts; my mind is
already made up. The issues are of sufficient importance to a great many
people that here follows a scholars' listing of references.

Regarding steroid hormone levels (androgen or estrogen and their
derivatives) in homosexuality, some studies reported a hormonal deficiency, some no difference, and some an elevation.

A below-average level of testosterone was reported by Loraine and
coauthors (1971) and, for a subgroup of their homosexual volunteers, by
Kolodny and coauthors (1971). Evans (1972) confirmed a finding first
reported by Margolese (1970) of a lower ratio of androsterone to
etiocholanolone, both of which are urinary metabolites, waste products,
of steroid hormones from the adrenal cortices as well as the gonads.
They do not give information about the levels of the biologically active
hormones of which they are the waste products. Another measure of
urinary hormonal waste, the total 17-ketosteroids, was at the same level
in both homosexuals and heterosexuals.

An above average level of plasma testosterone in homosexuals was reported by Brodie and coauthors (1974) and by Tourney and coauthors (1975). Plasma estrogen (estradiol and estrone) was reported higher by Doerr and coauthors (1973 and 1976), who also found dihydrotestosterone and the percentage of free testosterone (both utilizable intracellularly) to be higher in homosexuals than heterosexual controls, though total testosterone levels (free and bound) as determined in the 1973 study did not differentiate the two groups.

Other studies that failed to differentiate homosexuals from heterosexuals on the basis of testosterone levels are those of Birk and coauthors (1973), Barlow and coauthors (1974), Parks and coauthors (1974), and Pillard and coauthors (1974). Tourney and coauthors (1975), in the same study in which they found plasma testosterone higher in homosexuals than heterosexuals, found no difference between the groups with respect to androstenedione (a precursor of testosterone) and dehydroepiandrosterone.

Hormonal studies of female homosexuals have been fewer than those of male homosexuals, perhaps because of the empirical difficulties engendered by the hormonal fluctuations of the menstrual cycle. Loraine and coauthors (1970), on the basis of four cases, suggested that the urinary levels of LH and testosterone may be higher and the level of estrogen lower in lesbians than controls. Griffiths and coauthors (1974) studied the urinary output of estrogenic, androgenic, and adrenocortical steroids in forty-two lesbian subjects, and found that no consistent pattern emerged.

The most likely conclusion to be drawn regarding hormonal and sexual eroticism is that the attempt to correlate the sex of one erotic partner with urinary or blood levels of the other partner's steroids in adulthood is naive and doomed to failure. The hormones of adolescence and adulthood activate programs of erotic-sexual behavior, but they do not originate them. To understand their origins, it is necessary to take account of the hormonal programing of fetal life, and of the subsequent developmental learning experiences of childhood that have as profound an influence on psychosexual status and gender-identity as they do, in another context, on native language or native dietary composition and menu habits.

An analogous statement applies to the attempt to correlate the levels of hormones in the cycle of the menses with cycles of mood level, the extent of sexual desire, or the frequency of sexual participation or activity. For those interested in doing their own intellectual sleuthing, the following references will reveal the inconsistencies of claims regarding the menstrual cycle and fluctuations of mood and behavior: Benedek and Rubenstien (1939*a,b*), Coppen and Kessel (1963), Dalton (1959,

1964), Glass et al. (1971), Gottschalk et al. (1962), Ivey and Bardwick (1968), Janowsky et al. (1969), Kane et al. (1967), Lamb et al. (1953), MacKinnon et al. (1959), Mandell and Mandell (1967), May (1976), McCance et al. (1937), Moos (1968), Moos et al. (1969), Morton et al. (1953), Shainess (1961), Smith and Sauder (1969), Stenn and Klinge (1972), Wetzel et al. (1971).

References demonstrating inconsistencies of claims regarding fluctuations in woman's sexuality and eroticism, including effects of the contraceptive pill, are: Davis (1929), Frölich et al. (1976), Hamburg et al. (1968), Hart (1960), James (1971), Janiger et al. (1972), Kane et al. (1969), Luschen and Pierce (1972), Markowitz and Brender (1977), Masters and Johnson (1966), McCance et al. (1937), McCauley and Ehrhardt (1976), Michael (1972), Morris and Udry (1978), O'Connor et al. (1974), Persky et al. (1977, 1978), Spitz et al. (1975), Udry and Morris (1968, 1970, 1973).

Inconsistencies today do not necessarily persist tomorrow. Animal experiments on primates eventually should help to get the story clear, and improvements in technology should increase the trustworthiness of what is found in human studies.

Minimizing
versus Maximizing Sex
Differences

GENITAL RELATIVISM. As registered on your birth certificate and other documents, your sex denotes, on the basis of the anatomy between your legs, your civil status as either male or female. You are given no other option, for the dichotomy of male and female has long been accepted axiomatically as an eternal verity. Onto it has been grafted the cultural practice, universally taken for granted in our culture, of maximizing the differences, behavioral included, between the sexes, rather than maximizing the similarities.

The male/female dichotomy is not, in fact, an absolute one. Just as the dichotomy of day and night breaks down in the land of the midnight sun, so also the male/female dichotomy fails in certain test cases. Among fish, for example, there are some species that alternate between being fertile as male and as female during different phases of the life cycle (see below).

Among mammals, there is no known corresponding example of hermaphroditic alternation of fertility. In mammals, hermaphroditism, also known as intersexuality, manifests itself as the end product of an incomplete degree of differentiation of the neutral or undifferentiated genital ducts of the embryo into the male or female organs of the full-term fetus. It is possible, as already indicated in Chapter 3, for a chromosomally female (46,XX) embryo that is overexposed to an excess of male sex hormone prenatally, to be born with two fertile ovaries, a uterus, and fallopian tubes internally, and a normal-looking penis and empty scrotum, externally. Conversely, it is possible for a chromosomally male (46, XY) embryo to be underexposed to hormonal masculinization and to be born, in consequence, with the genital appearance of a normal female. Internally, the uterus is vestigial and the testicles, typically undescended, are sterile. In another variation of male hermaphroditism, internal and external differentiation proceeds as expected in embryonic and fetal life, except that the mullerian ducts do not vestigiate, as they should do, but differentiate into a uterus and fallopian tubes, that herniate into the scrotum. Thus the baby is born as a boy with a uterus.

Complete incongruity between the internal and the external genital anatomy, as in the foregoing examples, occurs but is not the rule in human hermaphroditism. More commonly the hermaphroditic baby is born looking "sexually unfinished." In other words, from visual inspection alone, one cannot decide whether the phallic organ is an enlarged clitoris or a hypospadiac penis (that is to say, a penis with an open gutter in the place of a urinary tube); nor whether the opening below the phallic organ represents incomplete fusion of the scrotum, or too much fusion of the labia majora.

Congenital indeterminacy of sex does not always involve the gross reproductive anatomy, but may be covert, involving only the sex chromosomes and the gonads. Thus, in Klinefelter's syndrome, the genital appearance is that of a male, except for a small penis and small, infertile testes, but the chromosomal sex is indeterminate, 47,XXY, instead of the expected 46,XY. That is to say, there is one chromosome too many, and the extra one is an X. Another syndrome of sex-chromosomal indeterminacy is Turner's syndrome, in which the genital appearance is female, except for the internal defect of agenesis of the ovaries. The sex-chromosomal status is 45,X instead of the expected 46,XX, or 46,XY.

The prevalence of the 47,XXY syndrome is 1 per 500 male births, and of the 45,X syndrome, 1 per 2.500 female births. The prevalence of syndromes involving hermaphroditic ambiguity of the sexual anatomy has not yet been ascertained, but it may be conjectured as ranging between 1 per 1000 and 1 per 5000 births.

The significance of these figures lies not so much in the actual numbers of persons involved as in demonstrating that nature herself is less absolute in creating sexual dimorphism than we human beings are in thinking about it. When the figures on chromosomal and morphologic hermaphroditism are expanded to include so-called psychic hermaphroditism, then nature's relativism regarding sex differences is even more apparent. The long social tradition to which we are heirs, by contrast, maximizes sex differences rather than sex similarities.

SEX REVERSAL. In human beings, as in mammals generally, there is no backtracking once the morphologic sex differentiation of the fetus has taken place. A penis cannot be induced to shrink and change into a clitoris, and a clitoris, although it will enlarge somewhat under treatment with androgen will not turn into a penis—it will not even enlarge enough to permit further surgical masculinization into a penis. Among mammals, nature's plan is to resolve the original state of hermaphroditism or indeterminism once and for all, early in development, and from then on the sexual anatomy remains fixed. But this familiar pattern is not a universal verity. Among birds, in some species of fish, and in other lower forms of life the dimorphism of sex is more flexible.

Earthworms, for example, are said to be monoecious. That is, they are simultaneous hermaphrodites able to produce ova and sperm simultaneously. They maintain their monoecious status throughout life. They are able to use their sex organs either in self-fertilization or in mutual exchange fertilization with another earthworm. Oysters are another hermaphroditic species. They do not self-fertilize, but reproduce sometimes as a male, sometimes as a female. They are able to alternate their sex and fertility in response to changes in water temperature, food availability, or season.

Among fish with backbones, there are several species that are able to change from male to female and vice versa. That is, they are consecutive or sequential hermaphrodites. They are said to be dioecious in that the male and the female forms are distinctly dimorphic. Thus a change of sex involves not only a change of fertility but also a metamorphosis of other bodily features. In some species, there is only one such metamorphosis per lifetime; in others, more than one. The metamorphosis may be a function of age or of some other variable. The variable inducing a change of sex may be behavioral, as it is in one species of cleaner fish, *Labroides dimidiatus.* Groups of these small fish travel with a large fish, feeding on the algae and parasites they clean from its gills and mouth. The cleaner group is comprised of perhaps a dozen females and one male leader, the largest of the group. If the leader disappears or is taken from the group, then the void in leadership is filled by the largest female of the group. In her new role, this female begins to metamorphose into a male. Over a period of a week or two, the new leader undergoes hormonal changes that increase the body size and change the reproductive fertility to that of a male. The formerly vestigial male reproductive structures mature and the formerly female structures vestigiate. Instead of eggs, the erstwhile female produces sperms to fertilize the eggs of others. The entire process may be reversed, should the former male leader return to the group.

In addition to those species that manifest spontaneous change or reversal of sex, there are others in whom developmental reversal has been achieved on a once only basis. For example, if contrasex hormone is added to their swimming water, fingerlings of the small killifish, *Oryzias latipes*, also known as medaka, can be induced to differentiate and mature as fertile adults in the sex opposite that of their chromosomal sex. The same phenomenon can be demonstrated in genetic male frogs which, as tadpoles, have been exposed to estrogen in their swimming water. With genetic females of the same species, *Xenopus laevis,* a more complex experiment is necessary in order to have testes instead of ovaries, namely, grafting two testes into the developing chromosomal female instead of simply dissolving androgen in the swimming water.

Among human beings, and, in fact, among all mammals, there are no examples of hermaphroditism in which a single individual is self-fertilizing or able to be fertile as both male and female. The primordial hermaphroditic bipotentiality of the gonads and the internal ducts is the same for mammals as it is for lower species, so that in science fiction it is plausible to imagine the interchangeable metamorphosis of ovary and testis in adult mammals, as in the sex-reversing lower species. It is even more science-fictional to imagine the metamorphosis in adulthood of the internal reproductive anatomy, whereby the mullerian organs or the wolffian organs would metamorphose, the one fully mature set vestigiating to be replaced by the proliferation of the vestigial remnants of the other.

No matter how mind-boggling science-fiction sex fantasies may be, there is a point to raising them. Science-fiction has an uncanny history of becoming science-fact within half a century or so. Thus, humankind may unravel the secret of how nature goes about programing spontaneous sex reversal in some species and apply that secret to human beings. The concept of reversal embryology is not too far fetched in this present age of molecular genetics and recombinant DNA. Nature has already prepared the way by producing in transexuals people who would unhesitatingly give informed consent to treatment that would induce their reproductive anatomy, internal and external, to regress to a state of being embryonically undifferentiated, and then reprogramed to differentiate as the anatomy of the other sex.

What can be envisaged for transexuals—male-to-female, or female-to-male—can be envisaged for nontransexuals as well. Sex reversal for nontransexuals, however, would raise horrendous problems of the ethics of informed consent. Only transexuals have their minds spontaneously sex-reversed and at odds with their stubbornly nonreversed reproductive genitopelvic anatomy. The reversal that exists in their minds by definition exists also in their brains. Whether the reversal in the brain was programed there prenatally or postnatally, or both, is still a scientifically unresolved issue. All that is known is that the reversal, having once taken place, is extraordinarily tenacious and long-lasting. So also is, respectively, the masculinity or femininity of the ordinary person's behavior and mental life.

SEX-IRREDUCIBLE ROLES. In the final analysis, the irreducible difference between the sexes is that men impregnate, and women menstruate, gestate, and lactate. For you personally, these differences constitute the basis of your sex-irreducible role, in which is conjoined your sex-erotic role and your sex-procreative role. Of course, it is not imperative that a man should actually impregnate in order to qualify as a man, nor that a woman should either menstruate, gestate, or lactate in order to qualify as a woman. It is rather that these differences are the definitive ones that cannot be interchanged without changing the very concept of male and female—at least for the remainder of the twentieth century.

From embryonic life onward, the differentiation and functioning of the sex organs is under the governance of hormones: steroidal (sex) hormones from the gonads themselves, which are regulated by peptide hormones (gonadotropins) from the pituitary gland, which are regulated by smaller peptide hormones (releasing hormones or releasing factors) from cells in the hypothalamus of the brain.

The sex steroids are secreted chiefly by the gonads—the ovaries or the testes. To some extent they come also from the adrenocortical glands, of which the primary steroidal hormone is cortisol, a close biochemical relative. It is possible that the cells of some target organs that utilize one of the sex hormones may themselves change the hormone's molecular structure. The liver is known to play an active role in the breakdown of circulating hormone. This fact of hormonal change within the body means that hormones circulating and measured in the bloodstream do not precisely reflect what is happening hormonally within cells. Cellular uptake studies are also required.

There are three categories of sex steroid: androgen, estrogen, and progestin. Variant forms of each occur within the body and can be synthesized in the laboratory. Biochemically, all three are closely related. Their biochemical origin is in cholesterol, and their synthetic sequence is from cholesterol to pregnenolone (a precursor of progesterone) to androgen to estrogen. Etymologically, progesterone was named for its role in gestation, androgen for its role in males (andros=man), and estrogen for its role in female estrus, or heat, at the time of ovulation in lower animals. The etymology is misleading, for all three hormones circulate in the bloodstream of both sexes. The sexes differ in the amount of each hormone present, not in its absolute presence or absence.

The proportionate level of estrogen in males as compared with females varies according to the female's menstrual phase, and ranges from an average 30 percent postmenstrually, to 2 percent at the peak period of ovulation when the female's estrogen secretion is at its maximum. The corresponding proportions for progesterone are 100 percent premenstrually, and 6 percent at the female's progestinic peak period, which is after ovulation and before the premenstrual decline in preparation for menstruation.

The average level of androgen in females as compared with males is 6 percent, though it has been calculated as high as 20 percent.

In the case of all three hormones, the ratios given do not discriminate between bound and free or circulating blood levels of the hormone, but they do indicate the relativity of the amounts secreted.

SEX-DERIVATIVE ROLES. The sex steroids govern not only the differentiation of the procreative organs and their postpubertal function but also, for example, the sex difference in the anatomy of urination. In four-legged mammals, there are likely to be differences in urinary posture. The dog is a familiar example. The male lifts his leg and urinates in small dribbles as he marks a sequence of vertical projections with urinary pheromones, as attractants to the bitch in heat and warnings to other male intruders. The bitch squats to urinate in a more steady stream. In the sheep, if a ewe is experimentally masculinized with androgen prenatally, even if her urinary anatomy is not changed, the physiology of urination may be. Thus, she stands as does a normal ewe, but the urine comes out in a pulsatile trickle, as in a ram, instead of a continuous flow.

Human males and females do not differ in urinary flow, but they do differ in the expeditiousness of being able to stand to urinate. This difference fascinates very young children in late infancy, at around the time of learning to use a toilet facility. Boys can, of course, urinate while sitting and girls can do so while standing. Thus urinary posture is not a sex difference that is utterly irreducible. That is, it has many of the qualities of a sex-adjunctive role.

With the advent of the hormonal surge of puberty, the sex steroids govern the growth and development of those sex-derivative bodily characteristics that are usually denoted as secondary sexual characteristics. Some of them, like the growth of breasts under the stimulus of estrogen in preparation for lactation later, are clearly related to eroticism and procreation, whereas others are not. Balding of the man's head, for example, bears no known relationship to the male erotic and procreative roles, yet it is under the governance of androgen and can be prevented by removal of the testes or suppression of their function with antiandrogen. Elsewhere on the body, androgen governs not the loss but the growth of hair. If there is a direct erotic/procreative connection between hair on the face and body, then it has not yet been scientifically demonstrated. The same applies to the androgen-deepened voice.

The situation is somewhat different with respect to the effect of the anabolic or growth-promoting property of androgen on bone and muscle. Men on the whole are taller and longer-boned than women, more muscularly powerful and less supplied with subcutaneous fat padding. These masculinizing features do not appear in the chromosomal male whose body at puberty is androgen-insensitive (the androgen-insensitivity syndrome). Nor do they appear in those chromosomal male hermaphrodites, assigned and reared as girls, who are given not androgen but estrogen replacement hormone to induce pubertal development.

In many, but not all subhuman species (the hamster is one exception), greater brute strength is characteristic of the male. Husbandmen for centuries have been impressed by the reduction in brute strength induced by castration of domestic animals. This reduction is commonly accompanied by a reduction in competitive courtship fighting, in fighting for hierarchical dominance, and in attacking intruders. From the folklore of animal husbandry, science has borrowed the concept that androgen is the aggression hormone (Chapter 8) and that aggression is a sex-related or sex-supplemental trait. The example of the lioness that kills for her mate as well as her young is sufficient to require qualification of this concept: it is necessary always to specify the context and the stimulus if one is to do justice to the facts in linking aggression to sexual dimorphism.

SEX-ADJUNCTIVE ROLES. In human affairs, one can readily concede that in prehistory the brute strength of the male, plus the constraints of pregnancy and lactation in the female, became the basis of sex-adjunctive division of labor. Thus the man ranged more widely, hunting and defending, and the woman was more constrained. She not only gestated and nursed the baby but also prepared food for children and older members of her troop. In today's world, the rigid stereotyping of sex-adjunctive vocational roles has become anachronistic. The invention and development of labor-saving devices and machines and of infant feeding formulas (Chapters 8 and 9) allow for a sharing of roles, so that they become shared human roles and not sex-stereotypic roles.

Across species, nature is extraordinarily variable with respect to whether individuals live in herds, troops, or alone; whether group members arrange themselves in a hierarchy of dominance; and whether one sex assumes dominance over the other. In the human species, there is no definitive and incontrovertible evidence of a hormonally regulated phyletic program that destines males to be dominant over females either erotically or in domestic politics. In the absence of conclusive evidence, scientists tend toward doctrinal positions. Social theorists are inclined to underrate the derivative influence of hormones on sex-divergent roles in human beings. By contrast, animal experimentalists and sociobiologists, impressed with the close linkage, especially in the lower species, between hormones and behavior in sex-erotic and sex-derivative roles, are inclined to underrate the extent to which sex-divergent roles in human beings are not hormone–dependent, but hormone-adjunctive, culturally coded, and learned.

Cultural coding begins very early. In fact, it begins in the delivery room, where the first thing said after the emergence of the baby from the vagina is not about its anatomy as a whole, but about its genitals. People must know immediately whether to say he or she. The very language dictates that the neonate be referred to not on the basis of what we all share anatomically, but on the basis of the anatomical difference between the legs.

The pronouns are only the tip of the iceberg, so to speak. They are a symbol of the he-schema and the she-schema that, as a sequel to our own personal histories of identification and reciprocation, shape all of our interactions with other people, even newborn babies. It is all too easy to assume, as most researchers have done, that behavioral differences between newborn boys and girls are not only newborn but inborn differences. Even in the first few hours or days of a baby's life, however, its own behavior, no matter what it is like, is responded to by other people on the basis of the sexual status they attribute to it. Hence, the importance of nursery color-coding, blue for boys and pink for girls, and any other insignia of sexual status with which parents decorate their babies as guides to the uninformed. If pictures or movies of a small baby are taken so as to give no clue as to the baby's sex, people who look at them interpret the features and actions differentially on the basis of what sex they believe the baby to be. Their interpretations are sex-stereotyped! The same thing happens in a parallel experiment with movies of transexuals. The adjectives and adverbs that viewers use to describe what they see depend on whether they know the subject's status as a transexual, for example, male-to-female, or simply accept her as a woman (unpublished data).

It is not necessary to dispute the inborn existence or nonexistence of a difference in the behavior of newborn boys and girls in order to establish that there is a difference in the way they are responded to by others. It is sufficient simply to acknowledge that people do respond differently and that, in consequence, even on day one of life it is impossible to record or measure inborn differences uncontaminated by the social interaction with the environment. To illustrate, Thoman and Gaulin-Kremer in their 1977 review recorded that primiparous mothers of newborn daughters, as compared with sons, talked to them more, smiled at them more, and stimulated them more during feedings on the second day of life. Mothers talk to daughters more than to sons throughout infancy.

Another illustration is that, among older infants, girls were more likely to be disciplined by withdrawal of affection, whereas boys received physical punishment.

A rather dramatic illustration of a differential in the social response to newborn boys and girls is that, over a large portion of the globe, genital mutilation is considered more suited to boys than girls. There are vast regions of Africa above the equator where girls are genitally mutilated, namely, by clitoral circumcision, clitoral extirpation, or complete vulvectomy and infibulation. In the latter, the denuded surfaces of the labia are sewn together, leaving only one small orifice for the escape of urine, and eventually of menstrual blood. Coitus is impossible without surgical reopening of the vagina, nuptially. Scarring may render childbirth impossible.

In cultures where girls are genitally mutilated, boys also are similarly treated, namely, by being circumcised. But male circumcision is geographically far more widespread. It is obligatory in Moslem cultures. In twentieth-century Christian America, it has become very widely practiced, apparently as a Gentile cultural borrowing from Jewish ritual. The prevalent age for male circumcision is in the early newborn period. The operation is usually done rather brutally, without anesthetic, as is the case for African girls also. Afterward the raw tip of the penis is exposed to urine and hurts.

In behavioral studies of sex differences in the newborn, no one thought to control for the possible effect of circumcision until Richards, Bernal, and Brackbill published their study in 1976. They compared newborn boys in England, where circumcision is not fashionable, with those in the United States, where it is. With suitable scientific caution, they were modest in presenting their conclusion, and acknowledged that replication of their findings is desirable. The thrust of the data clearly favors the hypothesis that neonatal sex differences in behavior that characterize American research, and have not been confirmed in British research, are a product of the neonatal effects of circumcision rather than of sex, per se.

Through lack of research, there is very little that can be said about the effect of circumcision or of female genital mutilation on adult eroticism. Some males circumcised in adulthood have reported no discernible difference in erotic feeling and orgasm; some have reported more staying power prior to climaxing. The only available female data come from a small group of women with congenital hypertrophy of the clitoris who elected in favor of surgical clitoridectomy in adulthood. They do not become deprived of erotic sensation and orgasm, but they have not been adept at verbalizing a possible qualitative difference. Male-to-female transexuals, after surgical reassignment, claim not to have lost a feeling of climax, though the majority allow that it is more diffuse and less spasmodic.

There is no evidence one way or the other that circumcision of either the male or the female, or more radical mutilation of the latter, has a direct part to play in regulating the ratio of dominance and submission in an erotic partnership between a man and a woman. It is rather that cultural regulations governing dominance and submission also govern what is done to the genitals in ritual surgery.

There is no conclusive evidence that either chromosomes or hormones have a direct part to play in regulating the ratio of dominance and submission in an erotic partnership between a man and a woman. As among nonhuman primates, females and males both may initiate erotic invitations of one another, and both may cooperate dominantly as well as submissively. It has long been the cultural tradition in our society that women are erotically submissive, permissive, passive, and receptive. Correspondingly, it has long been a fact of history that, except for courtesans and harlots, women reared in our society have been acculturated into obedience to the tradition. Science, victim of its own obedience to the teleological dogma of instinct or drive, has falsely imputed woman's cultural obedience—and the reciprocal stereotyping of male eroticism—to a hormonally fueled biological drive. The correct imputation is that sex-stereotyping or sex-coding of roles is a product of a frequently arbitrary cultural history.

SEX-ARBITRARY ROLES. The sex-coding of roles is to a large extent arbitrary and capricious, even though one may trace or conjecture a tangential association between an arbitrarily sex-coded trait and a sex-irreducible or a sex-derivative one. For example, it is arbitrary that women, but not men, should paint their nails and eyelids in a variety of colors. Nonetheless, the idea that women and not men should paint their bodies is consistent with the traditional sex-adjunctive role whereby men dominate women and other men. The high-ranking man outclasses his rivals by displaying his woman as a subordinate whom he can afford to keep in well-groomed, well-dressed idleness. Under different traditions, the man may be more decorated than the female—as in precolonial Polynesia, where the male warrior's face was heavily tatooed.

The length of the haircut provides another example of arbitrary sex-coding. As the flapper age took shape in the 1920s, among the old-guard it was tantamount to breaking a religious sacrament for a woman to follow the new fashion of having her hair cut short. For men, a haircut was an emblem of modern masculinity until the age of the Beatles, in the 1960s, when the long-hair style of the seventeenth century was revived. Traditional males were outraged. Fathers reviled their long-haired sons, convinced that their long hair meant moral degeneracy and homosexual effeminacy. They overlooked the noneffeminate evidence of beardedness, or sideburns and moustache, also part of the new fashion.

The rage over haircuts, along with objection to unisex clothing styles, indicates that we are in our society dependent on visible insignia of sex for rapid recognition of and orientation toward the sex of a stranger, the sexual anatomy itself being covered. There are literally hundreds of arbitrary sex-codings of behavior in addition to those related to grooming and clothing. A whole science of sexual dimorphism of body language is still only in its infancy. Sex-coding applies to demeanor, manners, and etiquette in the everyday social interaction of males and females. It applies also to the games, recreations, and pastimes they engage in, to the work deemed suitable for them to do, to the educational and occupational activities deemed seemly for them to become proficient in (girls are expected to underachieve in mathematics, so by teenage the majority oblige!), and to their legal status.

Arbitrary sex-coding applies also to the way men and women talk. Men's and women's vocabularies are different in the frequency with which some words are used. Their idiomatic expressions and exclamations are to a certain degree different, but it is in breathing and intonation that the difference is greatest. The sexy voice of a woman advertising on television, for example, is not the same as that of a man using sex appeal for advertising purposes.

Surprisingly, vocal sex-coding is related to speech differences that are a mark of social class. Thus, for many men, it is sissy and effeminate to talk with the accent of the educated and wealthy. In a trade-off between sex and wealth, they maintain their masculine image by solemnly acquiescing to inferior socioeconomic status. They are, of course, oblivious to the fact that they are conspiring with their oppressors to maintain social inequity. The same principle affects women also, but for them its primary manifestation has been, for generations, their exclusion and self-exclusion from men's careers at any socioeconomic level. Men's talk was too uncouth for their refined ears it was claimed. To some extent this arbitrary stereotype is still maintained.

In traditional psychology, attention to sex-coded roles has been greatest among social and developmental psychologists. They refer to them simply as sex roles, and to their transmission as sex-role learning. Insofar as they do not differentiate between sex-irreducible, sex-derivative, sex-adjunctive, and sex-arbitrary roles, they often write as though human beings were dolls without genitals (Chapter 2). That leads to problems of what is innate versus what is acquired that they cannot resolve—another resurfacing of the fruitless nature/nurture controversy. It leads also to a prudish neglect of the manifestations of sex-erotic roles in the play and the development of infancy and prepuberty. Erotic sexuality in child development is still taboo to explicit scientific investigation (Chapter 4).

Rage over a change in the sexual dimorphism of haircuts indicates also that a change of an arbitrarily sex-coded role becomes interpreted as a veritable threat to one's genitalia and a challenge to one's basic sex-irreducible role, and to sex-derivative roles as well. The four role components of one's overall sexual self—of one's total G/I-R—constitute a pervasive unity. A threat to one becomes experienced as a threat to the whole. A person experiences his/her own G/I-R as a unity, virtually sacrosanct and God-given, or at least as an attributed product of genetics or other innate determinants. Small wonder, then, that the impartiality of science has often been replaced by social doctrine and the dogma of politics, as in the controversy generated by the liberation movement. The wonder of this controversy is that it all applies only to historically arbitrary decisions regarding the decorative, recreational, educational, vocational, and legal roles of men and women. One might think, at times, judging by the heat of the argument, that liberation of the sexes pertains to whether men will forfeit their manhood and women their womanhood in their erotic and procreative roles.

SEX REVOLUTION AND THE TIDE OF HISTORY. In 1876, at the Philadelphia Exhibition, one of the nation's first centennial birthday presents to itself was the first public display of the rubber condom, the male contraceptive that was a product of a new technique—the vulcanization of rubber. The birth control age did not get under way in earnest, however, until the late 1920s, when, with the latex rubber technique, skin-thin condoms could be mass-produced and mass-distributed very cheaply. Since then, development of spermicides, the diaphragm, the Pill, and the IUD have expanded the techniques of contraception; and since then vasectomy, tubal ligation and early abortion have become less socially stigmatized. Further technical improvements in both male and female contraception are still being researched.

Conception control, like the control of fire-making in an earlier epoch, profoundly affects your life-style, whoever you are and wherever you are. It sets you apart in history, among the first two generations of human beings who are able, after puberty and prior to the menopause, to separate recreational from procreational sex and to begin your recreational sex life in a betrothal relationship (Chapter 4) while preparing yourself for parenthood.

The human race is noteworthy for being unable either to discard its new cultural artifacts, once they have been discovered or invented, or to fully assimilate them without divisive factionalism and onerous struggle over change versus preservation of the status quo. The struggle to for-mulate a new morality of nonpromiscuous sexual partnerships that are recreational rather than procreational touches all of our lives. It is par-ticularly acute during adolescence, when it can be the source of cruelly abrasive power struggles between parents and teenagers. They are struggles that cannot be legislated away, and, quite apart from the inven-tion of contraception, the idea of recreational sex is not a whimsical irresponsibility of some morally degenerate imagination. Rather it is a technically feasible possibility that has become an urgent moral impera-tive in a world that is increasingly overpopulated and already has begun to experience the effects of overexploiting its ecological resources.

Overpopulation is to some extent a by-product of twentieth-century medical technology, which has increased the life expectancy from the fifth to the eighth decade since 1900. Childbearing parents no longer die during their childbearing years to the extent that they used to.

At the beginning of the life span, reproductive fertility begins sooner than it used to. The reasons are unclear, but the statistics are not: the age of puberty has been lowering by four months every ten years for the past century and more. In the eighteenth century, when J. S. Bach was or-ganist and choirmaster at St. Thomas Church in Leipzig, the choirboys sang soprano until age seventeen or older. Today their voices break at age twelve or thirteen. In times past, the interval between puberty in late teenage and legal adulthood at age twenty-one did not put too great a demand on youth with respect to establishing a sexual partnership and parenthood. The onset of normal puberty today can be as young as age nine in girls and eleven in boys. It is unreasonable to expect these young people to wait until their early twenties, when they are academically and economically prepared for parenthood, before they establish themselves in a romantic and erotic pair-bond.

Earlier puberty, increased longevity, world population excess—these are currents in the tide of history that sweep over us in the age of birth control and leave us with no choice except to work out a new ethic of recreational and procreational sex.

The parental generation has not, by and large, done very well in helping its teenagers work out this new ethic of boy and girl together. One feature of the omnipresent taboo on sex is that it prescribes an avoidance of frankness between people of disparate ages, especially be-tween adults and adolescents and children, especially their own, regard-ing the intimacies of personal sexuality (Chapter 4). This age-avoidancy masquerades in a self-righteous way as a protection of the innocence of youth. It prevents parents from relating to their own children and ado-lescents on the basis of what they remember of their own childhood and adolescence. Instead, it requires that parents adopt a role-stereotype of parenthood. They step into the shoes of their own parents and, identify-ing with them, play the mommy and daddy role as faithfully as if they were following a script on stage. Quite explicitly, as they sit talking about the sex education of their own children, they may disapprove of the way their parents handled sex education with them, and may profess that they themselves will do differently with their own offspring—beginning tomorrow! But tomorrow becomes indefinitely postponed, the victim of perpetual procrastination that allows the status quo to persist.

SEX DESTEREOTYPING IN CHILDHOOD SEX EDUCATION.
Among children, one product of this procrastination in the earlier years, before they are old enough to have independent access to books or other reliable sources of information, is that they establish their juvenile con-cepts of role differences between the sexes rather arbitrarily. Denied knowledge of the basis of the sex-irreducible roles in the genitals them-selves, children rely instead on knowledge of the derivative, adjunctive, or arbitrarily coded sex roles. By the rules of infantile reasoning, they are entitled to the logic that the sexes are definitively discriminated on the basis of names, clothing, haircut, and sex-stereotyped behavior of a general type. They are entitled even to a logic of sexual meta-morphosis—that a girl can grow a penis as readily as breasts, or that a boy can become a girl by having his penis drop off. Some children have, in fact, given voice to precisely such logic of gender inconstancy, which is in childhood an indicator of G-I/R confusion that in adulthood becomes a homosexual G-I/R or an impairment of a heterosexual G-I/R.

Without the security of knowing that the genitalia and their procrea-tive function give ultimate authority to all other sex-divergent roles, children may readily attribute too much authority to sex-coding of roles that is, in actuality, quite arbitrary. They have nothing else to go by. "Only boys can be Batman! Only girls can be in the playhouse!" These and many other sex stereotypes were common among the boys and girls of her preschool grade before Stephanie Waxman wrote for them her graphic essay, *What Is a Girl? What Is a Boy?* Her initial efforts to encourage sex-decoding of some of their play and their sexist treat-ment of one another were in vain. "I blamed their parents, other teachers, television—things over which I had no control," she wrote. Then one day she was startled into a fresh point of view when a boy dared to confide to her his question, "Will I always be a boy?" In her notebook there were similar queries:

—If I was a boy baby, will I always be a boy?
—Will my sister grow a penis when she grows up?
—What do fathers look like without their clothes on?
—What else falls out beside teeth?

Gradually I realized [Waxman wrote] that the children's need to divide along sex lines was part of their struggle to discover their sexual identity. For the first time I differentiated between sex role (a set of behaviors) and sexual identity (a self-concept). In carefully playing down the differences between the sexes and encouraging the similarities, I had disregarded the children's need for elementary information about sexual differences. They really didn't know the [basic] difference between a girl and a boy, but they knew they were supposed to be one or the other. Naturally, they used the sexist models our society offers.

Waxman's book deliberately broke the age-avoidancy, and intimacy-avoidancy taboo. Here, in this book, an adult admitted to very young people that the genitals may be photographed and displayed as proof of the ultimate and irreducible criterion and bulwark of sex difference. Supported by so impregnable a bulwark, Waxman was safely able to present photographic examples of boys and girls whose behavior contravened the conventional rigidities of sex-coding. A boy cries, but he is no less a boy because he does so. A girl lifts a heavy building block, without becoming less a girl for doing so—and so on, with many different examples. "It worked," the author reported. "When the children got the information they needed, they didn't have to exclude and stereotype each other to form a secure sexual identity. They felt good about their bodies and about being girls and boys."

Waxman did not advance her program for older children. Had she done so, pictures of genital nudity would not have been sufficient. Older children require also evasion-free pictures and explanations of copulation, pregnancy, and birth. By around age seven or eight, boys and girls can assimilate this information step by step and relate it to the fertilization of egg and sperm. When the logistics of copulation are presented explicitly and graphically before the hormones of puberty render children more sensitive to the erotic-arousal effect of the material, then after puberty the same material, because of the familiarity or satiation effect, can be encountered more matter-of-factly, with less erotic arousal, in accordance with the proprieties of learning and teaching.

In the present sociosexual era, it is difficult for most parents to give explicit information about copulation to their own children. They may plan not to replay the role of their own parents, keeping silent, but the magnetism of that role in the end wins out. Parents do, indeed, obey the twin dictates of the sexual taboo regarding age-avoidancy and intimacy-avoidancy. Thus there is no alternative but to have at least one generation of sex educators who are specifically trained to break the ice of silence that covers both the physiology and sociology of sex. Their training will prepare them to transmit the specifics not only of procreation but also of love and pair-bonding. Sex education and love education belong together.

Sex and love education do not turn children into libertines. By analogy, religious education that includes detailed knowledge of crucifixion, complete with graphics and sculptures of Christ bleeding on the cross, does not send children home from Sunday school to play the role of Pontius Pilate or of Roman centurions, crucifying their dolls or their playmates. The explanation is that crucifixion education includes concepts and precepts regarding the morality of the Crucifixion. So it is that sex education and love education, when correctly given, include concepts and precepts regarding the morality of both copulation and love-bonding. The ethnographic and historical relativity of concepts and precepts of sex and love constitute part of the curriculum.

PUPPY-LOVE: JUVENILE PAIR-BONDING. When it occurs, juvenile pair-bonding with a friend of the other sex provides a child with a first-hand experience of another basic phenomenon of sex roles, namely, the reciprocal attachment or bonding of one sex to the other, otherwise known as being in love. The dogma of the latency period has effectively sealed off scientific investigation into this aspect of child development. Thus the prevalence, age, and durability of juvenile love affairs have never been ascertained. They do, however, occur and, as part of healthy childhood development, witness the following transcript.

This transcript was taken from an interview with a young father who was rooming-in with his small son. The boy was admitted to the hospital for surgery to correct a birth defect of the penis. The mother had stayed at home with three other infants. The father was articulate and interested in matters pertaining to his son's juvenile G-I/R development, for there had been a period of neonatal uncertainty as to whether the child should be assigned as a boy or girl. Hence the father's ease in drawing on his own biography. Referring to a woman who had beat her son when she found him playing sex with a girl, and who thought she had done right, he said:

I guess she thought she was right, but I don't. A boy's got to find out sooner or later. Why beat him because he's trying it young? I tried it. I didn't know what the hell I was doing, but I tried it. I was five or six I guess; I really can't remember. As a matter of fact, I fell in love with my cousin, first cousin, at eight years old. I remember that. I'll never forget that.

It was the first time I'd seen her. She was a red-head, and she was bright. She was good-looking. She had freckles on her face. She came to visit us for a week or ten days. We had a small house then, and all the cousins had to sleep with us. So Cathy, that's her name, she would sleep with me, but at the other end of the bed, head to toe. We were both the same age. And the way she would sleep, she would always push down in the bed, and my foot would be up between her legs. And it was very warm there! I would be wiggling my toes between her legs. She wouldn't be doin' nothin', but she would take her feet and start wiggling them between my legs.

Then we would just continue on, I don't know if we thought of ourselves having an affair or sexual intercourse or anything. I don't recall whether I felt for her vagina or not, but I know we did something. I mean we got on top of each other. And she had her panties off, and I had my underwear off.

The whole time she was there, we would wait until everybody would go to sleep, and then we'd get together and get out of the bed, quietly, not waking my little brother and the other girls, onto the floor. Or go in the kitchen, or outside and sit on the back porch.

You know, right now, she and I are just like this (demonstrating)—tight. We're real close. . . . She used to write to me till after she found out I was married. She didn't like the idea of me getting married, because she always said I thought you were going to wait for me, and all this. And I would say something like, well, you know, they wouldn't let us get married, no way. And she would say something like, we'll just wait till we get old enough to where we wouldn't need anybody's consent but our own.

[In comparing his feelings for Cathy and for his wife, he said:] "Well, I really couldn't say, because I've never really compared them. I love my wife, quite naturally, and I don't know what you'd call it between Cathy and me. When I found out that we were related, I thought it would be incest, between first cousins. I think I tried to change my feelings for her. I'm not saying that I did it. I can't explain the feelings that I feel toward her. I doubt if she could explain her feelings toward me either. I guess the reason why we don't write each other is because we've told each other that we wouldn't contact any more, unless we accidentally run up on each other. But it seems as if she's been trying sort of to keep up with me. When I joined the service, she found out, and six months later she joined the service. Same branch. But where she's stationed I don't know. She doesn't know where I'm stationed, because I didn't tell even my family, in case she'd find out. . . .

After I was married and back from California, she came to visit home. She called on the phone, and she was talking to my wife first, and my wife told me to pick up the phone. She and I were talking, and my wife was eavesdropping on the other end. And she was talking to me as if I was her long lost love. . . . We drove out to my mother's house, where she was staying. Before I stopped the car, she was embracing me not like relatives, but as if we were really lovers. And my wife didn't like this!

The inquiry turned to whether he and Cathy had been in love at age eight. "I don't know. I guess you could say love. It might be; it might not. If it was love, well, I guess you could say yes. People say it's puppy-love, but I don't know if it was puppy-love. It wouldn't be going on. Every time we see each other now it wouldn't continue as puppy-love." He compared his feelings for Cathy at age eight and in teenage: "I think it was the same thing. It feels the same thing. I often dream about her, and I did then too. I would always talk about her, and occasionally I do now.

Not to my wife, of course, but around my mother or dad, or my sisters and brothers. So I don't see any difference in it." In adulthood, they had once come very close to having sex together, but didn't. "We were trying to figure out whether we should continue and do it or not. We didn't know, so we just messed around, and then got up."

To label a juvenile love attachment as puppy-love is to trivialize it and underestimate its developmental significance. At a later age, the same kind of down-playing is achieved when an affair is written off as an infatuation. In neither case is the family willing to take the match seriously and give its approval in marriage. One harks back here to the tradition of the arranged marriage, in which the union of family power, prestige, and wealth rivaled in importance fertility and the attachment of the couple in love. In this way, sex difference was maximized in the interest of the metaphorical checkbook rather than the well-being of the couple and their prospective family. Marriage, and with it divorce, always involve, epigrammatically, love or the checkbook, or both.

CRUSHES AND HERO-WORSHIP. Puppy-love is not defined in terms of the exact age of the partners, but rather in terms of their being heterosexual and young enough to be the suitable targets of the bantering of their older siblings and family. This same bantering or joking relationship does not apply to those young people whose first experience of pair-bonding in prepuberty is known in the vernacular as a crush.

A crush mixes the bondedness of a love affair with the bondedness of hero-worship. Though it is not age-limited, hero-worship is predominantly a phenomenon of childhood and youth. The hero is, in some way or other a mentor, a somewhat older person to be emulated, a person after whom to model oneself. The maximal environment for learning takes place when a learner so admires, emulates, and hero-worships a teacher that learning becomes a form of identification with that teacher in which what the teacher knows becomes something to incorporate into one's own knowledge.

The admiration of hero-worship easily veers over in fantasy to having the admiration returned, and that degree of complementarity or reciprocity readily may become romantically tinged. It may grow into a fantasy of a full-blown love affair, especially as childhood yields to puberty and adolescence. Whereas in fantasy the love affair is two-way, in actuality it is more likely one-sided. In other words, the younger person has a crush on the older one.

Insofar as it is romantically and erotically tinged, a younger person's crush on an older person is more likely to be heterosexual than homosexual, though the latter also occurs. Without the tinge of romance and eroticism, identification with the hero becomes part of the way in which a young person's nonerotic G-I/R becomes consolidated and expanded.

This same consolidation process goes on among children of similar age and the same sex, many of whom pass through a prepubertal sex-segregated phase of despising age-mates of the opposite sex and their sex-stereotyped play and other activities.

Some children at this age develop a very special relationship with a same-sex friend who in either chronologic or social age is a year or two older. The relationship may have all the hallmarks of hero-worship of the older by the younger partner. Then the relationship becomes very intense, and the pair-bonded dependency of each on the other is extreme. They replicate one another in their interests. They may share a common creative bent, as in writing poetry, painting, acting, or dancing. For some such pairs, the shared interest may, instead, be in delinquency or, in very rare cases, psychopathology.

If a hero-worship relationship between two younger people becomes romanticized, it qualifies as a crush. To a variable degree it may then become sensuous, with hugging and kissing, especially between girls, for whom such closeness is not socially stigmatized. For either boys or girls, a crush may also become eroticized and sexualized, as, for example, if the two spend time together in overnight visits or on trips or at camp. This sexual-rehearsal phase of the relationship fades when they reach the age of boyfriend-girlfriend relationships and graduates into the heterosexuality of adolescence and adulthood. Such sexual rehearsal is a preparation for erotic sexuality in general and not specifically for either homosexuality or heterosexuality or bisexuality in adulthood. In later adolescence, the two friends see less of each other and become less intense in their relationship. They are quite likely to maintain contact, off and on, throughout life.

LOVE AS ADDICTION. Regardless of age, a crush, hero-worship or falling in love, along with other pair-bonded relationships, may be regarded as the prototype of addiction. The person who has fallen in love becomes addicted to the love partner—obsessed and preoccupied with the next "fix" of being together or talking together. In the paraphilias, (Chapter 5), the love partner becomes replaced, in part or in toto, by some intrusion. A fetish, for example, a shoe fetish, insists on being included in the imagery of erotic arousal. A fetishist is addicted to his fetish. A transvestite's addiction to his women's clothes is another example. No matter how many times he disposes of them, in an attempt to escape their erotic demands on him, sooner or later he compulsively replaces them. In a women's wear store, he is like an alcoholic in a distillery. For the zoophiliac, the addiction is to his/her pet. And so on; and always the addiction has its genesis in childhood.

The displacement paraphilias, of which exhibitionism and voyeurism are prime examples, also have their genesis in childhood. Here the intrusion that becomes an addiction is some part of the ordinary proceptive process of erotic arousal, like being on display as a potential sexual partner, or looking over a potential sexual partner. The male exhibitionist (the female exhibitionist is either very rare or goes unreported by the males to whom she exhibits) is a person who has become addicted to the surprise, shock, or terror of an unwarned female to whom he flashes or displays his penis in a public place. The voyeur's addiction, essential to erotic arousal, is to spying, usually through a window, on unsuspecting people getting undressed or having sexual intercourse.

One part of the explanation of why the love addictions of the paraphilias have their origin in childhood is that the sexual taboo is strongly imposed on children in our society. It is part of our cultural strategy to obtain children's overall obedience and conformity via the all-out veto on eroticism and sex. There is no corresponding all-out veto on aggression and violence. Sex and violence are traded off against one another as negative and positive, respectively. That is why a goodly proportion of the sex offenses have a degree of violence in them—as, in fact, in lesser degree, do many nonoffending sexual encounters.

Some children grow up unable to become love-addicted, that is, they are deficient in becoming pair-bonded as lovers. Such a deficit tends to be associated, inter alia, with Klinefelter's (47,XXY) syndrome in males, and with hypopituitarism in either sex (Chapter 5). The extent to which this deficit may belong to other syndromes, some perhaps still unnamed, is unknown, but is undoubtedly greater than is usually believed. There are also some children who are much delayed in reaching the pair-bonding stage.

Some children grow up to become not pair-bonded, but addicted instead to a nonerotic, nonsexual substitute. Thus some people are addicted to carbohydrate and eat food in place of having a partner sexually and erotically. Others become addicted to pharmacologic products and become bonded to them at the expense of love-bonding and performing sexually with a partner. Alcohol is the most universal of the addictive replacements for sex with a partner, most commonly the spouse. Some street drugs, notably morphine derivatives, are analogous. Both sexes are affected, but males are more incapacitated than females, by reason of becoming impotent.

One of the least understood characteristics of an addiction is that, like the negative and positive poles of an electric current, or the negative and positive of a photograph, an addiction exists between two people, just as the pair-bonding of love exists between two people. There are some dramatic examples of this two-way process, as when one partner in a marriage is a chronic alcoholic and the other a chronic martyr to the other's alcoholism. If the alcoholic should reform or die, then the other may transform from being a martyr and total abstainer to being a chronic alcoholic.

So complete a role-reversal is relatively uncommon. By contrast, the phenomenon of role-reciprocity or role-collusion is common, and remarkably so in the erotic/sexual addictions of the paraphilias. Thus the martyr-wife of a sadist may for half a century accommodate to her husband's inability to reach orgasm unless he vilifies, humiliates, restrains, disciplines, injures, and tortures her. Conversely, a husband may, if he is a masochist, demand his wife to be the dominatrix. After the orgasm is achieved, the sadism or masochism, respectively, may recede into the background, and the man may be repentant and mortified at what he has put his wife through (almost always the man is the instigator, whether as sadist or masochist). With the logic of a lawyer's mind, one might easily tell the wife to separate and divorce. But legal logic is not the logic of role-collusion, and so the couple stays intact. In those relatively rare instances in which they together get into sexological therapy, it eventually emerges that if the offender's behavior changes for the better, then the offended one can't cope and deteriorates into either somatic or psychopathologic illness, or both.

In the present state of knowledge, the extent to which the accommodation of the partner to a paraphiliac's addiction begins as a mutual attraction (Chapter 4) is not known. It is known, however, that the degree of accommodation of the one partner to the other may develop so as to have extraordinary tenacity, as is always the case in the psychology of abuse and abuser, martyr and tyrant, and slave and master. Herein lies the explanation of why the therapy of sex addictions must, virtually without exception, be couple therapy in order to be effective. It needs great patience and much time.

Though unconventional, it is not as odd as it might sound to speak of the love-addicted and to classify the rituals of the paraphilias among the addictions. It is more usual to reserve the term, addiction, for substance abuse, it being understood that the substances of abuse are either swallowed, inhaled, or injected into the blood stream. There is no reason why the products to which one is addicted should be restricted to such methods of entry into the self. They might equally well include products that enter through the eyes and, perhaps with some assistance from the other senses, become mental images in the brain, as is the case predominantly in the love addictions. Once past their point of entry, they activate the brain and its chemistries of neurotransmission—all of which is not too far removed from the way in which opium and its derivatives activate the brain by competing with the brain's own recently discovered opiate-like neurotransmitters, the endorphins.

8

Dimorphism and
Fighting, Assertion,
and Dominance

TESTOSTERONE AND AGGRESSION. A great many people of both sexes, scientists included, accept the idea of aggression as an innate characteristic of the male. The idea that males are more aggressive than females is a veritable platitude. Animal experimentalists elevate it practically to a law of nature, for they are impressed, as farmers have been impressed since time immemorial, by the increased docility of male animals that have been castrated. The changes of castration are now known, on the basis of twentieth-century hormonal knowledge, to be the product of the loss of the testicular hormone, testosterone. The same hormone circulates in the bloodstream of females as well as males, but in proportionately lesser amount (Chapter 7). Whether the lesser amount influences behavior less cannot be assumed a priori. In human females, for example, their low testosterone level is sufficient for the growth of pubic and axillary hair, though not for body hair and a beard, which requires more. There is presumptive evidence from animal experiments and human clinical observations that, low-leveled as it is, testosterone in women is both sufficient and necessary for the subjective experience of being "horny," to use the vernacular term for wanting coitus.

Because male hormone is, strictly speaking, a misnomer for testosterone, and because aggression is conventionally defined as more typical of males than females, regardless either of species or stimulus context, testosterone is by many investigators given the status of the aggression hormone, and much time and effort is expended experimentally to prove that it is.

A parallel, but more updated version of this syllogism is that because males have a Y chromosome that females do not, and because males are, by definition, the more aggressive, therefore, the Y chromosome is the aggression chromosome. Enamored of alliteration, media writers quite erroneously have dubbed Y the crime chromosome, especially in those special individuals who have two of them (47,XYY).

The trouble with both folk and scientific dogma of aggression as a hormone-determined, sexually dimorphic trait is that aggression is conceptualized to be a motivational well-spring of power, a cauldron of underground steam, so to speak, forever hissing and blowing off its cap. Such a teleological conceptualization is too amorphous. For scientific accuracy, aggression needs to be conceptually analyzed into at least three categories: fighting, assertion, and dominance. These are three different forms of behavior, and each varies with respect to the stimuli that elicit it, though there may be some overlap.

PHENOMENOLOGICAL DISTINCTIONS. Fighting is a good Anglo-Saxon word that means exactly what it says: fighting or making an attack, either as the initiator or, in self-defense, as the respondent. In the preliminary phase, it is threat. Carried out, it becomes attack. Threat and attack both are self-assertive. To assert oneself means to maneuver in some way to claim one's priority, one's rights, or one's position. Assertion may involve fighting and attack, but it may also be covert and subtle. In human beings, it may be verbal rather than assaultive.

Self-assertion may involve rivalry for dominance. Dominating means exercising control and authority over another, or others. Dominance may be achieved with or without fighting. Fighting, or even power maneuvering, is not necessary when other people acknowledge one's authority, power, privilege, or leadership.

Among species that live together in social groups or troops, as do most of the primates, human beings included, it is common for dominance in one of its forms to pertain to the hierarchy of authority or leadership. Then individuals may jockey for position in the dominance hierarchy. The challenge may include fighting. A priori, it is possible that individuals will arrange and rearrange themselves in a dominance hierarchy, irrespective of sex. Alternatively, it may always be a couple, male and female, that constitutes the unit that jockeys for power in the dominance hierarchy—in which case they may contribute equally, or the male may assist the female, or the female the male. If the individuals act singly, then the sexes may segregate, with females in one hierarchy and males in the other; or only one sex may form a dominance hierarchy, while members of the other sex range singly, rather than in groups, except at mating time. Then, at mating time, it may be that males compete together to mate with one or more females; or that females compete together to mate with one or more males; or that mating occurs without competition.

There is no empirical and complete catalogue of all the variations on competitive and noncompetitive mating found in nature. The range is broad. Because of mankind's extensive acquaintance with domestic herds, we are very familiar with the concept of competitive rivalry and fighting among males for dominance in mating. Beyond the barnyard, elephant seals provide an example. When these mammals leave the sea for their rocky breeding grounds, males assault and lacerate one another in territorial and harem defense and competition. They turn their crowded breeding grounds into a charnel house of newborn pups crushed to death, haphazard victims of their ungainly lunging.

Little known at the opposite extreme is the behavior of lekking in which males do not fight to breed, but congregate at a lekking site and wait to be selected by a female. Lekking has been reported in a few species of ground-living birds, a South American bat, and two species of African antelope, the lechwe of the Kafue river area and the kob of Uganda. At a lek, as described in 1976 by Shuster, male antelopes are in close proximity, but each has his own small territorial space. They engage in ritualistic lekking courtship displays, regardless of whether females are present or not. Females enter a lek to mate, and they choose a mate for the purpose. The social status of males on a lek is unequal, and it is usual to observe most or all females on a lek with a single male on "prime" territory. Only a small percentage of males do most of the breeding.

Antelopes are phyletically close to oxen, sheep, and goats, the males of which do not lek, but fight for access to a breeding female.

In some species, notably birds, matings are noncompetitive, monogamous, and permanent. Penguins and greylag geese are examples.

In primate troops that have been studied in the wild, mating is partly competitive and partly shared. In some species, the amount of dominance assertion and jealousy over a female mate varies according to whether the female is ovulating or not. When she is not ovulating, her dominant mate is relatively indifferent if other males mate with her.

Fighting, when it occurs in relation to social dominance, is not exclusively a matter of in-feuding for position and mating privilege within the troop. Defense against intruders and predators may also be a function of an individual's position within the social dominance hierarchy. Thus, it might be the older and more dominant males that keep intruders from encroaching on their home territory and that attack marauding predators. Or, it might be that the older, dominant ones stay close by the troop and send younger, less dominant ones to the periphery to attack the predator.

It is not always the male that does the fighting. The predator itself, for example, may be a female fighting to kill to feed her young, as commonly is the case among carnivores. When her young themselves are threatened or under attack, a female is likely to be fiercely aggressive—another reminder that aggression is not exclusively a masculine prerogative.

Fighting to kill for food is not equivalent to fighting to protect the young. Nor is there equivalence between fighting to defend the troop, fighting to obtain or maintain dominance within the troop, fighting to possess a mate, or fighting to dominate a mate. It is necessary always to specify the stimulus context in which fighting is elicited, for it is variable according to sex and species.

The degree to which either male or female dominates the other is also species variable. In most rodents, for example, the male fights more than the female and dominates her. The female hamster, by contrast, is more belligerent than her smaller mate and dominates him.

GENETIC AND PRENATAL HORMONAL PROGRAMING. Within a given species, fighting may vary according to genetic strain. Thus it is possible to produce an inbred strain of aggressive mice in which the males are guaranteed to attack one another more readily and viciously than males of an inbred strain of pacific mice. Even the aggressive strain will appear peaceful, however, until the stimulus situation provokes fighting. Two males of the aggressive strain will not fight if they have sufficient territorial distance between them. It is only when they are crowded in too close proximity that they attack one another, contesting the territorial boundaries that each would otherwise mark off, using his own pheromonal marker substance.

Not only is it possible for genetics, but also for prenatal hormonal programing to set the threshold for agonistic as compared with pacific behavior. The prenatal hormonal effect can be demonstrated experimentally. The standard procedure is to remove the source of androgen from the fetal male, or to add a surplus of androgen to the fetal female. In rats, which are extremely immature at birth, there is a period of two to three days after birth when the same effects can be achieved. Treatment of the male is either surgical castration, or temporary suppression of testicular function by injection of an antiandrogenic hormone. Treatment of the female is by injection of testosterone. These early treatments have a permanent effect on sexually dimorphic brain pathways that program the release of fighting behavior later in life. After reaching the age of sexual maturity, the animals are given fighting tests, with and without injections of sex hormone. In general, injections of testosterone are more efficacious than injections of estrogen plus progesterone (the combination that is normal in females), but the latter will also act as a primer, at least in rodents. Far more important than the hormone injected at the time of testing is the history of what happened prenatally or neonatally. Males that were deprived of androgen during the critical early period of brain formation behave more like ordinary females when tested, whereas females overdosed with androgen at the same period behave more like ordinary males.

Rats are among those species in which the programing of both fighting and sexual behavior is rather strictly under hormonal governance, with relatively little leeway for individually learned variations. Primates are less enslaved by hormones and more open to the modifying effects of postnatal social learning. Female rhesus monkeys androgenized in utero are born with ambiguous-looking, masculinized external genitals. In childhood play, they are more rough-and-tumble than ordinary females, and they show more playful threat and fighting. In adolescence, the proportional increase in fighting is less in evidence.

In human beings, the corresponding phenomena can be studied not experimentally, but only in experiments of nature, that is to say, in clinical syndromes. The adrenogenital syndrome (Chapter 3) is the most appropriate, by way of illustration, for girls with this condition are heavily androgenized in utero. Like their monkey counterparts, above, they show a high level of kinetic energy expenditure in childhood, the equivalent of rough-and-tumble play, especially in athletic sports. They do not, however, manifest a proportional increase in agonistic play, nor in actual threats and fights. The same applies to those of their brothers (chromosomally 46,XY) who have the same syndrome, and who were similarly exposed to an excess of androgen prenatally. In adolescence and adulthood, both females and males with the adrenogenital syndrome continue not to manifest a disproportionate amount of fighting or other forms of aggression and assertiveness.

HISTORY AND MALE DOMINANCE. All told, among human beings, there is no substantial experimental evidence that sex hormones, either before birth or at puberty, are directly responsible for sexual dimorphism of aggression, assertion, or dominance, and, in particular, for the domination of one mate by the other. Male domination of the female, with or without fighting, is of immense importance in human history. It has long been a characteristic of the patriarchal cultural traditions to which we are heir. Those traditions were formerly taken for granted as God-given, or as preordained by nature. Now they are being questioned and opened to serious scientific investigation, as well as to political militancy. Passions run high. The patriarchists are adamant in justifying their power against the liberationists, who are militant in claiming their own. Male chauvinists and nativists point to the many species in which male dominance sets the pattern of relations between the sexes and neglect to mention the many exceptions. They discount the long cultural and legal reinforcement of male dominance in patriarchal cultures, ours among them, since before recorded history.

Phyletically and nativistically there is a basic sexual dimorphism that helps to account for the long history of woman's domination by man. It is the irreducible dimorphism, already noted in Chapter 7, namely, that, whereas men impregnate, women menstruate, gestate, and lactate. Being pregnant and having infants to breast feed decreased woman's mobility in the early history of the human race and made her more sedentary than man. Even as recently as the era of the American Revolution, the expected life span, even for those who belonged to the 50 percent who survived the first five years of life, was as low as thirty-five years. Thus a woman spent all the years of her maturity either pregnant, lactating, or caring for juveniles, too fettered to assert her dominance over men, unless she was one of the few who survived to become a powerful grandmaternal matriarch of the clan.

If one interpolates from the evidence of various other primate species, then it is probable that human males, in the era of prehistory, were not only more free-ranging than women but also were phyletically programed to keep intruders and marauders away from the troop's territorial boundaries and to protect the troop against carnivorous predators. It is not unreasonable to conjecture that on these phyletic beginnings the developments of cultural history were grafted. The institution of slavery must have had a profound effect. Men enforcing domination over other men, gave a model for their enforcing domination over their own women. Without slavery, kingdoms, cities and temples could scarcely have been built, for their building necessitates that some have less in order that others may have more.

There is no dateline for the origin of kingdoms and the unequal distribution of power in society. One knows, however, that Cro-Magnon man (Chapter 6) some 30,000 years ago was creating highly sophisticated works of sculpture, and his cave paintings some few thousand years later have likewise survived until today. The creation of such art required intelligence equal to the best of our own. One may justifiably conjecture that such high intelligence did not go to waste and did not expend itself only on art. Social organization and religious doctrine, which includes the primacy and power of Adam over Eve, are likely products of this high intelligence. These products may well have been dispersed over far distances at the conclusion of the last ice age—another justifiable conjecture, for there is remarkable similarity in the elements of social and family organization and of religious principles throughout the Old World and Asia. It is in the New World, tropical Africa, mountainous

New Guinea and nearby islands, and Australia that one finds cultures or remnants of cultures most divergent from our own.

It is not sufficient to look to phylogeny alone to understand today's dominance of woman by today's man. The social heritage to which today's man and woman are heir is equally important. Most of that heritage can be reconstructed only in conjecture and hypothesis, from archeological fragments and radioactive dating, up to a scant six millennia ago when the invention of writing left a legacy of detail formerly completely lost.

THE PLATITUDES OF HISTORY IN CHILD-REARING. The platitudes of history that shape aggression, assertiveness and dominance in the relationships of today's young boy and girl are bestowed on them in nursery myths, in toys and the games to play with them, and in adult customs of how to bring up children, write books for them, educate them, and entertain them. To be a boy is to be macho, to have weapons, to have fights, and to kill, at first in play, then maybe later in war. To be a boy is also to be powerful with a penis and to do things with it unmentionable to adults. Then at adolescence, in boys' talk only, to be a boy is to brag about penis conquests and then to settle for a desultory sex life in adulthood, but to keep bragging about what a stud one is, modeling oneself on the image of a bull, a ram, or a stallion, servicing a herd. At home, to be a man is to wrest sex from an apathetic wife distracted by the proximity of the children. Or else it is forcibly to coerce sex upon an unwilling wife whose duty is to obey instructions and do what she is told, in return for favors rendered by the checkbook.

To be a girl is to be sweet, to be a sugar or a honey, to have dolls, to play house and be the mother. To be a girl is not to fight, but to wheedle and cajole, to manipulate behind the scenes and deviously control by being pretty and coquettish. To be a girl is to not know about having a vulva, but to know about kissing and cuddling, being modest and winsome, and winning a man, and then to discover at puberty that the vagina is the source of "the curse." It is to be confronted with the claim that men want women only for their bodies, and that women have to give in, because men have the power, and that there is no escape—for where can one escape when there are children?

Not all biographies embody these platitudes of history as oppressively and bleakly as above portrayed. Yet the stereotypes are at large in our culture, and they do indeed program into young people an image of the dominant male and the subservient female that becomes second nature to many of them. They may become so deeply engrained that they are mistaken for first nature.

So powerful are the platitudes, that serious-minded scientists dismiss them as a legacy of social history and turn instead to social evolutionary theory, currently undergoing a resurgence as sociobiology. It is folly to do so. It is true that we human beings cannot understand ourselves without recourse to our phyletic heritage. It is equally true that we cannot understand ourselves without recourse to our social heritage. Both perspectives are essential to a refined understanding of the sexual dimorphism of aggression, assertiveness, and dominance in the redefinition of man and woman together in today's changing traditions of love, pair-bonding, and marriage.

EQUALITY OF DOMINANCE. Redefinition of the relationship of men and women together on the basis of equality of dominance is not a matter of idle or trivial concern. Rather, it is a cultural imperative of the present age of the evolution of humankind on earth. This is the age of overpopulation of the earth with homo sapiens. Momentously, it is also the age of birth control. Now is the first time since we human beings became human that we have been able to regulate the number of offspring that we will have without regulating the frequency of our copulations. We do not need multiple pregnancies, for there are already too many of us, and the survival rate of infants is spectacularly increased. Each child grows up to reach the age of reproductive maturity four months earlier than its counterpart ten years ago, for the age of puberty has been going down by four months each ten years for at least a century and a half (Chapter 7). Girls have a longer period of reproductive maturity before the onset of the menopause than did their mothers and grandmothers. Both sexes expect to live into their seventies, the females longer than the males, whereas, as recently as the beginning of the twentieth century, the life expectancy was forty-five years.

All of these changes influence in turn the relationship between the sexes, for they no longer are required to dedicate the major portion of a short-lived existence to reciprocal service in the procreation and care of children. Man and woman both can anticipate many years of nonprocreational independence—years of autonomy and authority over their own destinies, neither subservient to the other, and neither dominant over the other.

In addition, during the years of child-rearing, men and women are no longer dependent on the division of labor for which they are so differently equipped. Though formula feeding and baby foods are not ideal in neonatal life, later they enable the father to be more active in the care of his young infant than was possible prior to the development of these products (Chapter 9). The invention of labor-saving devices and heavy machinery and equipment enables the mother to undertake, without impediment, the same heavy tasks that formerly only her husband had the brute strength to accomplish.

Already embarked on redefining the distribution of labor, it is little wonder that men and women are also embarked on redefining their mutual dominance, assertiveness, and aggression.

THE PERSISTENCE OF ANACHRONISM. There is much that needs to be redefined. One may smile and be a little indulgent, perhaps, of sexist conceptions of female psychology promulgated in the nineteenth century, but it is a shock to see similar ideas still put forth, anachronistically, in the 1970s. A nineteenth-century example can be found in the writings of the criminologist, Cesare Lombroso, as quoted by Marvin E. Wolfgang. A contemporary example comes from the fourth edition (1971) of *Obstretrics and Gynecology,* a textbook written by two men, J. R. Willson and C. T. Beecham, and one woman, E. R. Carrington.

Lombroso believed that, among those whom he labeled born criminals, males predominated, but that women were more ferocious. The normal woman, he argued, is naturally less sensitive to pain than is a man. Wanting sensitiveness, she is less compassionate. Woman also, Lombroso argued, is childlike, in that she has a deficient moral sense, and is revengeful, jealous, and "inclined to vengeances of a refined cruelty." These defects in most women, however, are neutralized "by piety, maternity, want of passion, sexual coldness, weakness, and an undeveloped intelligence." In cases where such neutralization fails, then a woman is transformed into "a born criminal more terrible than any man."

Willson, Beecham, and Carrington are not concerned with explaining the female offender, as was Lombroso, but with defining, on the basis of an anachronistic Freudian and sexist slant, the psychology of women as wives and mothers. They juxtapose feminine narcissism, masochism, and passivity against masculine narcissism, aggression, and activity. The woman is not as active or aggressive as the male, they claim, because of her constitution and lesser muscular development. Her sexual organ is receptive and cannot easily be used actively or aggressively. As a young girl, the female has oedipal feelings toward her father. Her assumption of feminine traits makes her desire for and attraction toward him compatible with loving and pleasing her mother. The parents and the culture both encourage the girl in her feminine ways. She grows up to love differently than men do.

The woman falls in love with the idea of being loved [the authors write], whereas the man loves an object for the pleasure it will give. The woman receives gratification from the idea of being loved and bases an increased sense of her own value on her image of the person who loves her. She says, I am valuable, important, etc. because he loves me. This type of narcissism finds expression in many aspects of a woman's life, the most obvious being her interest in clothes, personal appearance, and beauty. Such interest is normal and entirely feminine if its main object is to have someone admire and love her. It is subverted when it becomes an end in itself. Every phase of a woman's life is influenced by narcissism. To an adolescent and young woman it gives impetus to her efforts to attract a man. As a wife it allows her to be gratified by the success and achievements of her husband. In pregnancy and labor it expands her conception of herself in that she is going to reproduce and give her husband a gift of a child.

The authors regard ordinary feminine masochism as not being neurotic. In a woman's life, they say, the idea of suffering is an essential part,

since every woman has to face the fear of childbirth and the fear of the pain that is attached to this. Pain is not an integral part of the male's concept of his role. He can fantasy a life without physical pain that does not produce a conflict in his sexual identity. The woman cannot do this. Every aspect of a woman's life is colored by her ability to accept the masochism that is a part of her feminine role. As a young girl being courted she must *allow* herself to be won by the man she chooses. In the role of a wife she often must submit her own needs to build up the personality and strivings of her husband and family. Sexually there is always an element of rape in that the male organ penetrates. As a mother she sacrifices her own needs to those of her children. Finally, she must accept her children's marriage and separation from her.

[Feminine passivity allows a young woman] to put great efforts into making herself attractive, so that the male will pursue her while she seemingly waits. As a wife she must show interest in the home and in the well-being of its occupants. She must accept the idea that she is given things by her husband and even by her children, rather than assuming an active and aggressive role in attaining these things for herself. Sexually she must be passive and receptive to the male.

A balance between narcissism, masochism, and passivity is the mark of maturity. "Too much feminine narcissism without masochism and passivity produces a self-centered woman interested only in attaining love and admiration from those around her. There is no element of giving. Too much feminine masochism without the protective narcissism produces a woman who sacrifices herself without idea of rewards. The overly passive woman is continually waiting to receive without any willingness to give of herself in a masochistic or narcissistic manner." No formula is given whereby narcissism, masochism, and passivity can be kept in balance, as it is asserted they must be; and there is no formula for the proper control of opposing masculine elements of the personality. Implicitly, the burden of responsibility rests with the individual as a matter of choice and willingness to conform to the criteria set forth.

What actually happens is that the cultural stereotype embodied in this writing becomes imposed on a girl from infancy onward by those who themselves are the agents of its transmission, whether or not they are obstetricians and gynecologists. Developmentally, the girl either assimilates or disassimilates the stereotype, in much the same way as she either assimilates or disassimilates the foreign accent of her parents, should they happen to be immigrants who speak English with an accent. If the stereotype has been assimilated by her sisters and brothers, by other family members, and above all by her peer group, then its impact is pervasive and intrusively irresistible. She assimilates it until it takes on the appearance not of second nature, but of first nature. That is to say, it is mistakenly labeled as hereditary, constitutional, or biological in origin. Among each new generation of students exposed to the textbook that expounds it, the mistake is perpetuated until enough rebel and the book goes out of fashion or is revised. As of 1975, that revision did occur in the fifth edition of Willson, Beecham, and Carrington. Students of that text will no longer be prone to confuse arbitrarily sex-coded roles and stereotypes with the nonarbitrary sex roles of reproduction and infant care. They will not perpetuate anachronisms of sex among their patients, their children, and, in turn, their own students.

Dimorphism and Parenting

THE ROOTS OF ROLES: MENSTRUATION, PREGNANCY, CHILDBIRTH. English nouns are no longer classified as masculine or feminine, as are those of other European languages, though we still may refer admiringly to a ship, or a car, or an angler's proud catch as she. The sun is a god, and the moon a goddess. The dichotomy of sex is more than a criterion of genitalia, it is a basic principle of categorization. The principle is no more ubiquitously applied than in the categorization of activities and artifacts as men's or women's. One sees the process at work when new artifacts appear. When tobacco and coffee first were introduced to Europe from the New World, they were men's products. As recently as until World War II, ladies did not smoke in public without being considered brazen hussies or harlots. Whiskey was a man's drink long before it became acceptable for women. Cars, usurping the place of horses, were established initially as men's business, and their mechanics and repairs remain so, even though women now may be their owners and drivers, except where prohibited, as in Saudi Arabia. Today rockets and space gear are men's prerogatives, and women are only recently being allowed to train to be astronauts.

Just as the gender and the etymology of words can be traced to Latin or Sanskrit roots, so also the sex attribution of vocational or recreational activities can be traced to its roots in the procreative difference of the mother and father of one's family (Chapter 7). The connection with the dichotomy of procreation may be and often is tortuous and tenuous in the extreme. Alternatively, it may be very direct and obvious, as in the exclusion of males from having anything to do with rituals of menstruation and pregnancy.

Freud familiarized society with the doctrines of penis envy and the castration complex for girls and women. Pregnancy envy and the lactation complex are the corresponding, and not so well known, doctrines for boys and men. Pregnancy envy is institutionalized in some ethnic societies in the custom of the couvade, in which a man experiences symptoms of pregnancy and delivery like those of a woman and may claim a secret confinement. In black Amerafrican urban culture, among homosexuals with a strongly feminine G-I/R, there exists a folklore, according to which a male can become rectally pregnant and deliver a blood-clot fetus, a "blood baby," as an early miscarriage. Male-to-female transexuals are explicit in their envy of breasts and pregnancy.

It is, of course, far-fetched and science-fictional, even in this new age of extrauterine conception or test-tube babies, so-called, to consider that not only a barren woman but also a man could obtain a human egg from a donor bank, have it fertilized and implanted in a "slave" chimpanzee, and delivered at term. Yet, such an idea is thinkable and could eventually occur. The imagination can even concede that, before the end of the next century, as already mentioned in Chapter 7, a reverse process of embryology might be set in motion, thus allowing a male to generate a uterus in which to gestate a fetus. The very preposterousness of this idea serves the purpose of shocking the intellect into trying to answer the queries: "Would I or wouldn't I try it? If yes, why? If not, why not?" For women there are similar queries about being able to procreate as the father of a child.

MAN MIDWIVES. As in many ethnic societies untouched by modern medicine, in Western society, childbirth formerly was women's work and an exclusive prerogative of women. It was immodest for a woman to exhibit her genitalia to a man not her husband, even in childbirth, and shameful for the man not her husband to see them. The first man midwives, as obstetricians were initially called, were required to do their examinations and deliveries under the cover of a sheet.

Male physicians made their entry into obstetrical medicine as the Middle Ages yielded to Renaissance medical scholarship in the sixteenth century. In the seventeenth century, Paris was a leading center for the training of men along with women as midwives. Obstetrical forceps were invented early in the seventeenth century by Peter Chamberlen, a member of a French Hugenot refugee family in southern England, seven of whom in three generations were surgeon midwives (but not chartered and registered physicians). They were renowned for their successful interventions in difficult deliveries and guarded the secret of their method until, in the eighteenth century, the use of forceps became universally adopted. Professionally chartered and licensed, men physicians excluded nonphysician midwives from advanced training and licensure. In the nineteenth century, the profession of midwifery was eclipsed by obstetrics, and this status has persisted until the present.

It took male physicians approximately three centuries to lay siege to the birth chamber and, having won it, to rebuild it as a delivery room. They had broken the power and persistence of the mores that defined delivery as gender-coded, women's work, and they were not about to dilute their victory by sharing it with other men who were not physicians. It was not until the mid-twentieth century that the rigidity of gender-coding of work and play was still further eroded so that, finally, the father could be present to assist his wife in the delivery of his own child. The way for his entry was prepared by the movement toward natural childbirth, or prepared childbirth, associated with the names of Grantly Dick-Read, in England; Lamaze (who studied in Russia); Vellay, and Leboyer, in France. In America, Robert Bradley proselytized the new movement under the name of husband-coach childbirth.

NEONATAL PARENT/CHILD-BONDING. For the woman in delivery, it is supportive and reassuring to have her man with her. There is another bonus, however, this one for the baby, namely, that father-infant pair-bonding becomes established in synchrony with mother-infant pair-bonding. Thenceforth, both will have a corresponding degree of attachment to the child. A stable equilibrium between the three becomes more readily established. The father does not become an outsider. His parentalism is fully mobilized, and he is able to perform it and enjoy it more intensively.

Neonatal pair-bonding between parent and baby involves eye contact and finger contact. In the *Handbook of Sexology*, Trause, Kennell, and Klaus give information adapted as follows: A mother presented with her nude, full-term infant begins with fingertip touching of the infant's extremities. Within a few minutes she proceeds to massage, with encompassing palm contact of the infant's trunk. Mothers of premature infants also follow a small portion of this sequence, but proceed at a much slower rate. When mothers are given their fully clothed infants, it takes several days for them to move to palmar stroking of the trunk. Fathers go through some of the same routine. In home deliveries, where the mother rather than a doctor has been in control, she cradles her infant in her arms immediately after its birth and begins touching its face with her fingertips.

Mothers also show a strong interest in eye-to-eye contact with both full-term and premature infants. "Let me see your eyes," and "Open your eyes and I'll know you love me," are actual statements recorded on tape.

Mothers who had early contact with their infants looked at them significantly more often than did late-contact mothers during a subsequently filmed feeding session at the time of discharge. At age 42 months, the early-contact and the late-contact babies had average IQs of 99 and 85, respectively, and there was a correlation (r=0.71) between IQ and the amount of time the mothers had spent looking at their babies during a filmed feeding at age one month. Mothers of full-term babies, experimentally given one hour of extra contact with the baby in the first three hours after birth and a total of fifteen hours extra contact in the first three days, two years later conversed differently with their children than did control mothers. They used twice as many questions, more words per proposition, fewer content words, more adjectives, and fewer commands.

Prolonged separation of mothers of premature babies, as compared with early contact was associated with an increased chance that the mother might subsequently give up the baby or obtain a divorce.

The one comment on fathers in the foregoing suggests that they are not categorically different from mothers in neonatal parent/infant-bonding. Both parents share the same responses in what appears to follow the formula (Chapter 3) of behavior that is sex-shared/threshold dimorphic. The clear exception to this formula is lactation and breast feeding, which certainly is exception enough.

BREAST FEEDING. It is true that a newborn baby can be fed on other than human milk, in which case either the mother, the father, an older sibling, or a hired helper can substitute for one another. However, nonhuman milk has disadvantages. It does not have the same human bioprotective qualities for a human infant as does a mother's milk. Human milk, for example, provides the baby with immunological protection in the early weeks of life while its own immune system is immature. In nutritional value, it perfectly fulfills the baby's requirement, quantitatively as well as qualitatively, when the mother is healthy. In special cases, like congenital thyroid deficiency in the baby, the mother's milk can supply the missing hormone and so prevent hypothyroid impairment of the brain and intelligence during the early period of life when it is most vulnerable.

Independently of the nutritional principles involved, breast feeding also provides both mother and child with sensuous experience. In the mother this sensuousness may approach the sensuous quality of orgasm. It is a positive factor in the mother-child interaction. The sensuousness of body contact and movement, as in stroking and rocking, is an imperative for the child's total well-being and, especially, for a healthy psychosocial and erotosexual status in subsequent development.

Too much is at risk when mother and baby do not breast feed. The traditional system of the distribution of labor between the sexes, with the mother at home with her children and the father away at work, allowed the mother to breast feed. This system is a rational and logical one, but not the only one. For the mother with a nondomestic career, society can formulate different, workable systems of maternity leave, maternity shift scheduling, nursery care of breast-feeding babies, and so forth.

Men's preordained exclusion from feeding babies with breast milk could have been circumvented, hypothetically, had the history of sex-coded roles been different. Absurd though it may sound, men could have extended their dominance over women so that women's milk was dairy-farmed and collected for distribution to fathers who would feed it to their babies—a practice not too extraordinarily different from that of hiring a wet nurse as a substitute for a nursing mother. Then men may have included the domestic preparation of meals, instead of only the commercial preparation of meals, as male sex-coded work. Fame as chefs would have been relegated to women, in such a sex-revised society.

Unrevised, society's sex-coding of meal preparation was, in a presuffragist society of rigidly sex-coded work and play, for women only. Not only did men demand complete emancipation from the kitchen, but, especially in homes with sufficient help, women demanded that men be completely excluded from the kitchen: that was the domain where woman could reign over man, tyrannizing over him through his belly or ingratiating herself through his palate. Only the use of her sex organs in the bed chamber gave her comparable dimensions of power over him and that power she at times resorted to, also.

SAMENESS, DIFFERENCE, AND PRENATAL HORMONALIZA-TION. Apart from suckling at the breasts, there is no component of human parent-infant care that is either absolutely mother-specific, or absolutely father-specific. Single-parent households, according to the evidence of everyday observation, lend support to this statement, as does also the evidence of parenting in both male-to-female and female-to-male transexuals, though systematic tabulations have not yet been made. Interchangeability of maternal and paternal parentalism does not necessarily mean equivalence. Rather, it means that the behavior is sex-shared and may or may not be threshold dimorphic, dependent on individual differences. Mothers are not all identical, nor are fathers. On the contrary, the stereotype of the sanctity of motherhood notwithstanding, the parentalism of some mothers, as well as of some fathers, may be pathologically impaired to such an extreme degree that it expresses itself in traumatic abuse and neglect of one or more offspring. In the battered-child syndrome, both somatic and intellectual growth may be permanently impaired, and parentally inflicted injuries may be lethal.

Among the multiple origins of individual differences in parenting, prenatal sex-hormonalization of the brain may be included. Not much human evidence can yet be marshaled in support of this statement, but in the annals of intersexuality (hermaphroditism) it is known that in chromosomal and gonadal females masculinized in utero and reared and rehabilitated as males, parenting as adoptive fathers is without complication. The obverse applies to chromosomal and gonadal males, demasculinized in utero and reared and rehabilitated as women, parenting as adoptive mothers.

As of the present, there are no data on parenting in monkeys born hermaphroditic by reason of treatment in utero with sex hormones. Among subprimate mammals, none has been more intensively studied than the rat. In West Berlin, Neumann and colleagues antiandrogenized unborn male rats with cyproterone acetate so that they were born feminized. Subsequently they were gonadectomized and at the age of maturity treated with female hormones. Hormones govern rodent procreative behavior rather authoritarianly. In these animals, the combined effect of prenatal plus postnatal hormonal feminization permitted lactation, though insufficiently to keep a borrowed litter alive. It also induced retrieval of the young and care of them in the nest.

PARENTALISM IN MALE RATS AND MONKEYS. Hormonal manipulation, either before or after birth, is not a prerequisite to elicitation of maternalism in male rats. Rosenblatt some years ago showed that when exposed to newborn pups (nourished elsewhere by females) for from five to seven days, normal male rats would begin licking and retrieving them to the nest. Building the nest was not included. For nest-building to occur, the level of progesterone, the hormone that governs nest-building, needed to be higher. To induce licking and retrieval of the young to the nest, it was sufficient simply to break the threshold of the male's indifference by persistently exposing him to the stimulus of the helpless young. Juvenile females need less persistence, and gravid or newly delivered mothers need no persistence at all, only a brief exposure.

Hormonal governance of procreative and parental behavior in primates is less rigid and authoritarian than in rodents, but more so than in human beings. In the wild, primate species are quite variable in the degree to which adult males interact with the young. The males of some New World species assume almost all infant care, except for the mother's nursing and brief cleaning of the infant.

Rhesus males in the wild are seldom observed parenting their young, but parental behavior can be elicited by manipulating the stimulus environment, such as by depriving an adult male of all contact with members of his troop except a baby. As reported in 1977, Mitchell allowed isolated adult male rhesus monkeys each to rear a lone infant. The males adopted and cared for the infants like mothers do, but with minor differences. With males, the infant had less ventral-ventral contact than with mothers; the male-infant attachment increased, whereas mother-infant attachment lessened over time; males protected infants by approaching the threat, whereas mothers retrieved them and withdrew; and males played more frequently and intensely with their infants than did mothers. Like mothers, males protested separation from their infants. The males "often reacted violently," Mitchell reported, "usually by pacing and attempting to remove the barrier separating them from the infant." Some males would bite themselves repeatedly, inflicting superficial and sometimes severe wounds. The infants made many distress calls and postures. Reunited, the couple would cling to each other and then resume play.

Adopting an infant proved to be possible for males that had been rendered psychotic by having themselves been reared in isolation, motherless since earliest infancy. "Initially," Mitchell wrote, "these bizarre and abnormal males did not protect their infants and appeared to be arbitrarily, though not excessively, aggressive toward them. Eventually, however, they did protect their infants and, more importantly, they came to groom and play with them. The infants did not imitate any of the bizarre behavior of their isolate cagemates and they did not suffer any severe trauma or social deprivation." If the pair were separated, the infant reacted with even violent protest and calls of distress. One little infant repeatedly threw herself against the barrier separating her from her bizarre caretaker. She had strong affection for him and, like the other infants, was able to grow up adequately socialized, despite his odd behavior. More correctly, perhaps, it should be said that the infants were able to normalize their abnormal foster fathers, socializing them.

Rats, monkeys, and human beings—all three show that maternalism is a sexist word, and so is paternalism. Parentalism that both the sexes in our own species show is neither male nor female, but human. It is, of course, compatible with the pair-bond of the parents while, concurrently, it enlarges their pair-bond into a trio-bond.

Dimorphism and Mathematical, Verbal, and Praxic Reasoning

SEMANTICS, ETIOLOGY, AND MEASUREMENT. It has been a cornerstone of traditional attitudes toward dimorphism of gender roles from Greek and Roman times until the present century that males and females should be educated differently. In fact, for centuries it was assumed that it was unbecoming for a female to be educated at all, except in the arts of domesticity and child-rearing. By an easy process of circular reasoning, it became a tradition not only that women were poorly educated, but also that they were ill-suited to education. Untrained in the logic and rationality of men's knowledge, they were said, by a further process of circular reasoning, to be emotional rather than logical, intuitive rather than rational, and impulsive rather than reasonable. Restricted to the home, rather than sharing the activities of men, they were also characterized as passive rather than active. Forbidden to be assertive and straightforward, they were damned as devious and deceptive. Men and women, it was firmly believed, think differently, not because they learned differently, just as Greeks and Romans learned a different native language, but because of a God-given difference in endowment comparable in significance to the difference in their sex organs, even though not necessarily attributed to the same embryonic hormonal mechanisms responsible for the dimorphism of their genitalia, respectively.

The twentieth-century education of women notwithstanding, the belief in an innate difference in the way men and women think is still widespread and powerful. Insidiously, this belief has penetrated scientific thinking. Psychologists and other behavioral scientists have spent an extraordinary amount of effort to prove, and equally to disprove, it. So much effort has been expended in vain, for it has led only to a great compilation of evidence of sex difference in the intellectual and the academic achievements of men and women, respectively, but not to the origins of the difference in nature or nurture.

It is an academic legacy from antiquity that scholars look for teleological powers or forces in their attempt to formulate explanations for what happens in the universe, including what happens in the human mind (Chapter 2). So it is that psychologists, and before them philosophers, have long postulated abilities or aptitudes to explain human achievements. Rather naively, they have also tried to measure these abilities, as if there were some way of assessing ability apart from achievement, when in fact there is not. One may postulate that achievement demonstrates the existence of ability, but it does so only by inference, not quantitatively. Ability cannot reveal itself except in performance or achievement. There is no way of apportioning a test score between ability and achievement, and there is no way of assessing the two independently of one another. Achievement may run parallel with ability, but it does not indicate whether there was more ability than was used, nor does failure to achieve prove that ability is lacking.

Scales that purport to measure ability do not do so, because it is not possible to construct ability scales that have a genuine zero. Deprived of genuine measurement, the researcher must resort to counting units or degrees of specific aspects of performance. The only clue to unmanifested ability is through introspection, and the only person one can introspect is oneself. One may recognize in oneself great ability or lack of it, but such introspective recognition has no consensual validity. For science, the only admissible data concerning ability come from what people do or say. These are data that the observer can see, hear, touch, or perhaps smell or taste (Chapter 2)—either directly or after they have been processed by an instrument that can pick up stimuli that the human senses cannot register. By whatever way data are generated, however, ability is already so inextricably contaminated by the medium whereby it manifests itself that any quantitative estimate of ability per se resolves into a matter of faith.

To avoid the pitfalls of attempting to talk about sex differences in ability, one may resort to using the term "reasoning" rather than "ability" as in intellectual reasoning, mathematical and computational reasoning, spatial and praxic reasoning, verbal reasoning, and so on. Hereafter, in this presentation such terminology is employed, rather than the terminology of perception, cognition, intelligence, and the like.

Behavior geneticists have, naturally enough, heredity being their business, looked to heredity for an explanation of sex differences in reasoning abilities. It is extremely rare, however, apart from a few genetic syndromes, to link any aspect of human behavior directly to heredity. Even in syndrome studies, Huntington's chorea, for example, it is not possible to specify a one-on-one direct link between the genetic defect and a particular anomaly or type of thought or behavior. There are intervening variables between genetics and behavior. They usually are so complex that there is no way yet known to science to spell them out. This complexity applies to the relationship between genetics and nonerotic behavior that, as commonly encountered, is sexually dimorphic. It is reasonably certain on the basis of today's evidence that the direct contribution of the dimorphic sex chromosomes to the programing of sexual dimorphism of human behavior of any type ends once the chromosomes have directed the neutral gonadal tissues to differentiate as testes or as ovaries. Thenceforth, the work of programing sexual dimorphism in development is taken over by the presence or absence of hormones secreted by the gonads.

There are no genes that by themselves directly create instincts or other anlagen of behavioral patterns destined to unfold as dimorphically male or female. Likewise, there is no prenatal hormone—nor any other known substance or combination of substances—that directly creates sexually segregated and dimorphic instincts or forms of reasoning or other behavior. It does appear, however, on the basis of evidence so far available, that prenatal hormones (which themselves may be genetically regulated) are able to establish trends or dispositions toward a few sexually dimorphic forms of behavior. The principle is that a given hormone changes the threshold for the eventual emergence of a certain type of behavior. Threshold is the key word (Chapter 3). It is not that males are endowed with one kind of behavior and females with another. The behavior is shared. It is the threshold for its emergence that is sexually dimorphic.

There are no known sex-different thresholds that directly regulate behavior of the type that one refers to as rational, logical, or of the intellect. Thus there is no known evidence of a sex-dimorphic threshold that directly regulates proficiency or performance in mathematical reasoning, computational reasoning, spatial reasoning, praxic reasoning, musical reasoning, verbal reasoning, or any other form of reasoning. Whatever innate difference, if any, that might be uncovered between males and females in these respects, it is not a difference in the final product, namely, reasoning itself, but in an elemental component or threshold on which that final product is developmentally elaborated. Between the elemental component or threshold and the final product there are intervening variables, and they undoubtedly are complex. Undoubtedly, also, they involve postnatal social stimuli and learning and not only prenatal determinants. The etiological or causal principle involved here is neither nature nor nurture, but the two in interaction, as in the model provided by ethologists in their theory of imprinting (Chapter 4). That is to say, a phyletically programed releasing mechanism must match up with a phyletically prescribed releaser stimulus before a given pattern of behavior can developmentally express itself. The matching must take place at a phyletically prescribed period of the life cycle. Otherwise the given behavior pattern will forever be unable fully to express itself. If the behavior manifests itself at the prescribed time, it becomes a permanent part of the individual's repertory, as fixed and indwelling as if it had been programed into the brain by heredity alone. If the match between releasing mechanism and releaser stimulus is a mismatch, or if the timing is off, then the faulty behavioral product that ensues also becomes fixed and indwelling. There is an analogy here with an immune mechanism that fails: the residual pathology that ensues when an immune mechanism is faulty may induce a lifetime's impairment.

MATHEMATICAL REASONING. Phenomenologically, it is well documented that, within the western cultural tradition of learning, if not elsewhere, men as a group outstrip women as a group in mathematical (and mechanical) achievement. Though there is no supporting evidence, it is possible to hypothesize a correlation of this sex disparity with the sex difference in hormonal puberty, for the sex difference in mathematical or computational achievement is not clearly in evidence among children. Maccoby and Jacklin in their 1974 survey of sex differences, concluded that: "The earliest measures of some aspect of quantitative ability begins at about age 3 with measures of number conservation, soon followed by enumeration. . . . There appear to be no sex differences in performance on these tasks during the preschool years, or in the mastery of numerical operations and concepts during the early school years, except in disadvantaged populations. . . . The majority of studies on more representative samples show no sex differences up to adolescence."

Of course it is highly possible that the sex difference in mathematical reasoning that shows up by adolescence has nothing whatsoever to do with hormonal puberty (Chapter 3). The more parsimonious explanation is that it is one of the arbitrary fruits of sex-coded stereotyping of roles, so basic to our cultural tradition, and the learning of those roles throughout childhood. Reinforcement for conformity and ostracism for noncomformity can be either explicit or covert. Half a century ago in the elementary and junior high schools of New Zealand, boys who disliked mathematics classes would elect to do extra mathematics assignments rather than attend singing classes, for refusal to sing was considered a badge of masculinity there. Had the same boys lived in Wales, or in a New Orleans jazz culture, singing would have been a mark of masculinity.

There is an analogy between the relative underrepresentation of women in the ranks of high mathematical achievement and the relative underrepresentation of Roman Catholic males in the ranks of high scientific achievement. As reported in a 1974 study by Hardy, males reared in the Roman Catholic academic tradition, in which doctrinal thinking is more prevalent than empirical thinking, achieved fewer of the highest awards and honors of science than did Protestant and Jewish men. Doctrinal thinking favors a career in theology or law, rather than science. Underrepresentation does not, of course, exclude a minority of exceptionally brilliant, highly achieved individuals. Thus, a minority of highly achieved scientists are Roman Catholic men and, likewise, another academic minority are women, despite the sexist obstacles that blocked their way to fame (Ernest 1976, Hughes 1977).

Another possible explanation for the fact that a sex difference in mathematical achievement does not show up until adolescence might be that it is a delayed-action, maturational effect, not necessarily related to hormonal puberty. If so, then one might hypothesize it to be a delayed-action effect of what has elsewhere been called the Adam principle (Chapter 3). Such hypothesis-making is highly conjectural and qualifies as entirely science fictional until such time as a methodology might be found for testing the hypothesis.

According to the Adam principle, prenatal androgen influences the developing central nervous system in a sexually dimorphic way. In primates, the actual neural influence is inferred. The empirical observations so far have been limited to showing a correlation between prenatal androgenization and postnatal behavioral manifestations. As indicated earlier in this chapter, what actually happens neurally is not the turning on or off of female or male behavior, but the priming of thresholds governing the release of certain types of behavior. The behavior itself is sex-shared, but the threshold for its manifestation is sex-different, in other words sex-dimorphic. The types of behavior involved are phyletically elementary and basic, so they may be behaviorally characterized as belonging to a category of phyletic elements, components, attributes, or mechanisms that become incorporated into more complex behavioral manifestations. Sneezing in response to light or to sexual arousal (Everett 1964) is a phyletic mechanism, though one that is not sexually dimorphic. Cradling and rocking a small baby is a phyletic mechanism: it is sex-shared and dimorphic only in the sense that it is more readily elicited in women than men.

Three of the proposed sex-shared, threshold-dimorphic mechanisms

(Table 3-1) attributed to prenatal hormonization according to the Adam principle, may be drawn upon in order to formulate a fictive hypothesis concerning the etiology of a sex difference in the male-prevalence of mathematical attainment. First, male-prevalent roaming and territorial mapping may be associated with a special cognitional responsivity to visuognosic stimuli, that is to visually known spatial, shape, and directional stimuli; and to visuopraxic, that is visual-constructional stimuli; and to the logic of combined space-form-directional-praxic reasoning. This kind of reasoning is quantitative and thus is allied to computational and mathematical reasoning. Second, male-prevalent kinetic energy expenditure may become channeled into the kinds of play, such as competitive ball games, which put a premium on hand-eye (visuognosic-visuopraxic) coordination and skills. Third, the hypothesized male-prevalence of the visual image as a stimulus to erotic approach may become allied to nonerotic visuognosic (space-form) reasoning, and so on, ultimately, to mathematical reasoning.

It is not possible to make a definitive statement concerning the possible role of the foregoing phyletic mechanisms in the development of sexual dimorphism in mathematical reasoning. Empirically, not enough variables have proved amenable to being held constant so as to permit genuine fact-finding. Nor has there been much light thrown on the issue through the study of cytogenetic and clinical syndromes of the type mentioned in Chapter 3.

Prenatal androgenization of genetic (46,XX) females with the adrenogenital syndrome is not noteworthy for subsequent specific superiority in mathematical reasoning, even in those affected 46,XX individuals who have been reared as boys. The superiority, when it is present, as is commonly the case, is across-the-board and includes verbal as well as mathematical reasoning. The same across-the-board superiority also characterizes genetic (46,XY) males with the adrenogenital syndrome.

Prenatal deandrogenization of genetic (46,XY) males, notably in the androgen insensitivity syndrome, is not noteworthy for specific inferiority in mathematical or computational reasoning. Such reasoning is normally distributed in the population of affected individuals so far tested, as is verbal reasoning—likewise the nonverbal and verbal IQ.

Prenatal total lack of gonadal steroids occurs in girls with the cytogenetic anomaly (45,X and related mosaics or translocations) of Turner's syndrome, because with one sex chromosome missing, the embryo typically develops gonadal streaks instead of either ovaries or testes. Hypothetically, the absence of gonadal steroids—which signifies a total failure of the Adam principle—may be responsible for the specific cognitional deficit that is prevalent in Turner's syndrome. This deficit involves impaired visuognosis (space-form blindness), visuopraxis (constructional deficit), and directionality (direction-sense deficit). It is associated with a lesser degree of computational and mathematical deficit. In the present state of knowledge, one may not confidently link this cognitional deficit to the absence of fetal gonadal steroids. It may be the product of some other anomaly of embryochemistry that directly affects the brain. Thus it may be one of many somatic anomalies of somatic differentiation, including cardiac and kidney anomalies, that are excessively prevalent in Turner's syndrome. This nonhormonal etiology is favored because prenatal sex-hormonal failure is apparently universal in Turner's syndrome, but the specific cognitional deficit is not.

VERBAL REASONING. Unlike the sex difference in mathematical performance that favors males, the difference in language performance that favors females does not await adolescence to show itself: it has been recorded from infancy through grade school. It affects reading as well as spoken language before, during, and after adolescence. Thus puberty has not been invoked as etiologically responsible.

The earlier the appearance of a sex difference, the greater the likelihood that developmentalists will attempt to attribute it to an innate determinant. But this has not been so with respect to female prevalence of superiority in language development. Here one suspects that the prevalence of male investigators has inchoately influenced the fashionability of hypotheses: men unwittingly are predisposed to hypotheses that do not undermine the tenet of male superiority in anything except childbearing. Thus a genetic explanation for the verbal superiority of females has not been widely proposed.

On the contrary, the most popular hypothesis of the superiority of girls in language development is not nativistic, but nurturistic. Mothers, it is said, have a special bond, linguistic and otherwise, with daughters, insofar as girls may identify in perpetuity with their mothers, whereas boys must break from the mother-infant bond and identify with their fathers. The boy's change-over is postulated to be developmentally traumatic, with the result that the ensuing verbal reasoning and achievement of boys, by and large, is actually underachievement.

The barrier to acceptance of the above concept is that it neglects the developmental role of complementation or reciprocation to the opposite-sexed parent and proportionally overemphasizes identification with the same-sexed parent, whereas, both principles actually are at work, simultaneously, Moreover, they are at work in the development of both boys and girls. Each sex has the developmental task of establishing dimorphic responsiveness vis-à-vis the sex of the stimulus person.

It is a truism to say that culture builds on nature and is constrained by the limits set by nature: there would be no moon-culture of sex differences among human beings abandoned on the moon, for without a system of life support supplied from earth, in obedience to the constraints of being human, humankind would not survive on the moon.

Thus, as in the case of mathematical reasoning, so also in language development and verbal reasoning, one may look not to culture alone but also to the phyletic mechanisms on which culture may build, in order to explain an observed developmental sex difference. Hypothetically, there are two possible phyletic mechanisms that one may fictively invoke in connection with female-prevalence of developmental verbal superiority.

The first hypothesis pertains to sensitivity to vocal signals, especially signals of hunger and distress, made by the neonate and young infant. It is well known in folk knowledge that whereas a mother with a young baby is able to sleep through the ordinary distracting noises of the night, she is trigger-sensitive to stirrings of the baby, even at some distance. It is also well known that the father, too, can awaken to the same whimpers and attend to the baby's needs, especially if he has sole responsibility for the baby during the sleeping hours. Obviously, then, here is yet another example of a sex-shared, threshold-dimorphic response. The issue is whether the sex-different threshold is a product simply of postnatal conditioning and habituation, or whether it is set by a prenatal, species-shared phyletic mechanism. As in many other fundamentals of human behavior, the issue cannot yet be resolved conclusively, for systematic research is exceedingly sparse. However, there is an important lead to be found in what was originally a serendipitous experimental finding of Koranyi and his associates in Pécs, Hungary.

The experiment as planned was designed to monitor under various conditions electrical activity of multiple cell units (multiple unit activity) in different brain regions, including the anterior hypothalamus. The experimental animals, cats, lived with microelectrodes permanently and safely implanted into the brain. They were tested on many different occasions. It so happened that one experimental animal became pregnant and delivered a litter of kittens. Experimentally, she was too valuable to exclude from further study. So, she was brought with her kittens into the testing room. There, on one occasion, it was observed that the recording traced on paper by an EEG (brainwave) pen was highly erratic. This erraticism could have been written off as an experimental error. Instead, the investigator was astute enough to recognize that it occurred only when the hungry kittens in the litter box meowed, calling for their mother to feed them. The sound of their hungry call triggered a response in various parts of the brain, particularly, as subsequent investigation showed, in the amygdala. Subsequent investigation showed also that a mother cat's sensitivity to the call of her kittens rose sharply during the period of lactation. This increase in sensitivity is regulated by lactogenic hormone or possibly some other substance in the bloodstream. This point was proved using mice as the experimental animals.

When plasma from a lactating mouse-mother was injected into virgin females or into males, it produced a dramatic change in their parental behavior: primed with lactogenic plasma, these other animals required only twelve hours, instead of seven to nine days, of exposure to helpless young pups in order to become maternally responsive to their distress signals. In other words, the lactogenic plasma effect worked by lowering the threshold of stimulus sensitivity and response.

It is not yet clear whether the above lactogenic effect is exclusively a postpubertal phenomenon, or whether it may be partly prenatal as well. That is to say, a prenatal hormonal influence, epitomized in the foregoing as the Adam principle, may possibly make the male always somewhat less receptive than the female to the sounds of the young. If so, then one could invoke this phyletic mechanism in an attempt to explain the greater developmental sensitivity of most girls, as compared with most boys, to the sounds and usage of language. The same mechanism might differ among members of the same sex and thus would explain individual same-sex differences.

There is another hypothesis that may be generated from a second postulated phyletic mechanism to explain the female prevalence of language superiority. This second postulated phyletic mechanism, another product of the Adam principle, as mentioned in the foregoing, is that males have a lower threshold of sensitivity to the visual image with respect to the arousal of erotic initiative. If so, then the hypothesis would be that female prevalence of superiority in language is a counterpart of male prevalence of spatial-praxic-mathematical superiority. The trouble with this hypothesis, however, is that it fits badly with the observed phenomenon that female prevalence of language superiority includes visual, written language and reading, as well as spoken language. Reading disability (dyslexic) problems are notoriously more prevalent in boys than girls (Money 1962, 1966). By way of explaining this paradox, one may here offer the hypothesis that it is in the conjunction between auditory and visual language that boys' problems are generated, whereas, for some unknown reason, no similar problem of conjunction affects girls. Alternatively, one may develop a hypothesis based on the commonly recorded evidence that all manner of school problems are male-prevalent, possibly on the basis of a male prevalence of high kinetic energy expenditure, plus a concomitant high threshold barrier to sitting still to learn, as is required in a typical school classroom.

The study of clinical syndromes does not offer much help in elucidating female prevalence of verbal linguistic superiority. Syndromes of partial or complete prenatal deandrogenization of the 46,XY fetus are not noteworthy for subsequent specific language superiority. Nor, in reverse, are syndromes of prenatal androgenization of the 46,XX fetus noteworthy for language inferiority. In them, linguistic competence is adequate or superior. To complicate matters further, individuals with Turner's syndrome, with the symptom of so-called space-form deficit (with concomitant computational and mathematical deficit), are not noteworthy for prevalence of reading disability. In fact, in Turner's syndrome it is rather that linguistic facility becomes the basis of verbalizing formulas to circumvent the problems of spatial and praxic reasoning. Turner's syndrome is seldom diagnosed as early as the age of learning to read, so there is no clear evidence as to whether Turner girls may or may not have early problems with letter and word rotations. If they do, then they overcome them rather rapidly.

All in all, the balance of evidence at the present time is that language excellence, like mathematical excellence, while based on an individual talent, is programed postnatally more than prenatally, and is chiefly a product of socially transmitted sex stereotyping. Here, perhaps, may lie a clue to the paradox that, despite the female prevalence of linguistic excellence, the great names of literature, drama, and rhetoric in civilization have been prevalently male. In all literate civilizations, high academic achievement, regardless of subject matter, has always been prevalently sex stereotyped as male. By contrast, women have been excluded, both covertly and overtly, from academic opportunity. The subtle pressures of exclusion continue today (Ernest 1976, Hughes 1977).

PRAXIC REASONING. The psychology of sex differences in reasoning is incomplete without reference to what may be termed, borrowing a term from neurology, praxic reasoning. Praxis is the constructing of things in three dimensions, or recognizing them three-dimensionally by touch, or visualizing them as a three-dimensional image from a two-dimensional constructional plan or diagram. Praxis involves shapes and spatial reasoning, but from the visual-manual, rather than from the exclusively visual or exclusively manual viewpoint.

Praxic reasoning, it goes without saying, is an integral part of many occupations traditionally sex-coded as masculine: pattern-making, die-casting, mechanics, engineering, and architecture, for example. It is also integral to traditional woman's work, as in weaving, designing and sewing clothing, and in pottery-making. Thus there is no basis in the traditional sex-coding of occupations for assuming a sex-prevalence of praxic reasoning.

Many tests of praxic reasoning include items that might equally well be included in a test of spatial reasoning. In today's psychology the two types of reasoning are not very clearly distinguished. Thus it is more a matter of folklore than of empirical fact that women are said to be defective in mechanical aptitude. Among women themselves, it is an added part of the folklore that they should feign mechanical ineptitude, especially in the presence of men, so that they can appear helpless and in need of a man's help. Thus a woman who is accomplished as a musical instrumentalist may perform with total incompetence at opening a door with, say, a combination lock or a chain lock, the technique of which she could have readily mastered at age eight.

Because praxic and spatial reasoning are still not well distinguished in scientific empiricism, there exists a lack of tests purported to measure praxic reasoning per se. Thus there is little empirical evidence on which to generate hypotheses regarding the prenatal, postnatal, hormonal, or cultural genesis of a sex difference in the chronology of maturation of the two hemispheres of the brain (Chapter 3).

The basis of this tenuous hemispheric hypothesis is the well-documented neurological evidence that, during the years of infancy, one hemisphere of the brain develops dominance over the other as the language hemisphere. At birth, both hemispheres are equipotential, so that if one should become injured or incapacitated neonatally, the other would take over in the establishment of native language. After native language has become established, however, injury to the language pathways (situated in the temporal and parietal lobes) of the language hemisphere irretrievably interferes with speech and language comprehension.

The majority of human beings, males and females, are right-handed. For right-handed people, the language-dominant hemisphere of the brain is typically the left one. This is a well-established fact according to both neurological and neurosurgical evidence. It is not so well established that the subdominant hemisphere is the hemisphere that prevails in the control of spatial and praxic reasoning, but the evidence in support of this hypothesis has some clinical and experimental support. Evidence in support of a preprogramed sex difference in maturation of the two hemispheres in childhood is tenuous at best. Thus it is still purely conjectural to hypothesize that in girls the dominant, language hemisphere is preprogramed to mature more rapidly, whereas, in boys it is the later maturation of this hemisphere that gives them a headstart in the contrahemispheric maturation of spatial and praxic reasoning. Indeed, the cause-effect relationship could be the other way around.

Until further evidence settles the issue, it is still the most secure hypothesis that an observed sex difference in praxic reasoning is more a product of cultural than of nativistic determinants.

IDIOGRAPHIC FLEXIBILITY. Should it eventually transpire that prenatal determinants of dimorphic sex differences in reasoning are more definitive than concluded herein, then one issue still will remain, namely, the matter of individual differences. No one today would dare to assume that all male fetuses have an identical prenatal history, and certainly not an identical genetic history. Likewise with female fetuses. On the prenatal criterion alone, therefore, it is inhumane to expect, or dictate, that all female babies should be molded into a uniform sex stereotype postnatally; and, respectively, all male babies likewise. The lesson of clinical syndromes (such as the adrenogenital syndrome) alone should be enough to support humanistic respect for idiographic uniqueness or deviation from the statistical norm and with it developmental divergence from society's ideological norm.

Idiographic prenatal divergency from the phyletic statistical norm is not, however, the only criterion of respect for the individual. Idiographic differences built in as a product of individual postnatal programing may become as fixed and indelible as if programed genetically or by prenatal hormonization (Chapter 2). These manifestations of individuality are equally deserving of humanistic respect as are those that are prenatally programed. The principle here involved is that it is inhumane to attempt to force all boys and girls, respectively, down uniform sex-stereotypic pathways—just as it is inhumane forcibly to prevent others from following those pathways.

This is not to say that individuals and societies have total control over the sex differentiation of reasoning in their future development, as some nurturists might claim. Conversely, it is not to say that they have no control, as some nativists might claim. It says simply that increased flexibility in sex-coded roles in reasoning is both possible and desirable. That is to say, that individuals can safely be allowed by society to be themselves, even in disobedience to today's sex-coded customs.

Recently Great Britain shifted from its age-old currency tradition of pounds, shillings, and pence to the decimal system of currency. An intensive, public educational system preceded the change. Then, at a given date, at midnight, an entire population became legally obliged to adopt the new system. Many were antagonized at first, but now they acquiesce. The new generation knows only the decimal system. For them the old system is a burdensome and useless anachronism. A similar overnight change is scheduled to take place in both Britain and the United States, as they prepare to change to the decimal system of measurement. So also might it be that at some future date our presently outdated system of sex-sterotyped modalities of reasoning may be legally abolished at the hour of midnight. Then perhaps many other outdated sex-stereotpyes may follow suit.

Such a change would, of course, entail various other changes in the logistics of sex-sharing, especially sharing the career of parenthood and child-care. The irreducible sex differences in procreation would not thereby be abolished. Nor would eroticism in pair-bondedness be threatened. Being equal in mathematical, verbal, or praxic reasoning is not incompatible with being pair-bonded in love, marriage, and parenthood. Quite to the contrary, being compatibly pair-bonded may for some people prove to be the key that unlocks intellectual creativity.

VOCATIONAL AND EROTIC SYNCHRONY. The way in which erotic life and work life may be interlocked or synchronized is still scientifically a largely unexplored territory, but it becomes evident in the clinic. In adolescence, for example, it is quite common for a high-school or college student to be at risk to become vocationally wrecked on the shoals of underachievement at the same time as the priorities of love, sex, and pair-bonding are threatened with wreckage and need attention. A fairly routine problem during these years is one of distinguishing between liking and being in love. The person you simply like may be madly in love with you, or you may be madly in love with someone who simply likes you. Or you may be madly ready to fall in love without someone to become attached to, which is what some people rather imprecisely, for want of a better expression, label being in love with love. Over and beyond the distinction between being friends and being in love is the moral decision of when to begin one's sex life. This issue may become very confounding for the adolescent who is different, a homosexual, for example, or a bisexual, or pedophile, or any other kind of paraphiliac.

The interlocking of sex life and work life is not exclusively an issue of adolescence. It is quite common also in middle life. The wife and mother, for example, whose daily life has become a monotony of domestic servitude, finds that she has lost all enthusiasm for sex with her husband, whereas it blooms afresh in the excitement of a new love affair, with its promise of change and novelty, work included. The same sort of thing may happen to the woman whose career is in the market place, though there one sees more men affected. As his career becomes more monotonous, his boss more overbearing, and his job tenure more threatened, a man's sex life may also become more dispirited and marked by apathy and dysfunction, especially the dysfunction of impotence.

There are some specific cases that particularly dramatize the interlocking of an improvement in sex life with an improvement in work productivity. One such case is that of a man born with a congenital deformity of the sex organs (Money et al. 1955). Despite surgical repair, his penis was no more than 6.5 cm (2.5 in) long when erect. A widow at his place of work bantered him into an affair, the prospects of which scared him, until he jested about holding the olympic record for the world's smallest penis, and she did not back down. The erotic and orgasmic exuberance of their total disinhibition in bed had no parallel in his prior experience. Simultaneously, his work output changed from small traditional songs to vast, synthetic tone poems that had no parallel in his prior compositions. After a few months he terminated the affair rather than have it disrupt his marriage and family life. As it phased out, so also did his electronic music, and for the next twenty years he wrote only songs.

Not only are artists subject to work and erotic blockages and releases in synchrony. A similar phenomenon has been observed in the severely mentally retarded. The case in point is that of a boy with congenital hypothyroidism, whose intelligence for years grew slowly, leaving his IQ around 50. But it kept growing, stimulated with appropriate learning experiences, well into young adulthood. Then, with the onset of his one and only love affair and marriage, there was a burst of further vocational productivity, accelerated intellectual growth, and IQ gain. He embarked on a special study program in calculation, aided by his wife, whose handicap was motoric rather than intellectual. By age 32, his IQ had elevated to 76 (Money, Clarke, and Beck 1978).

Vocational and erotic synchrony may also become synchronized with ethnic conflict. The illustrative case here is that of a man, exceptionally handsome and highly proficient, who sometimes used his nickname, Billy, and sometimes his formal name, William (unpublished data). Billy was a product of the urban, black-ghetto, street-corner culture, and gay. He spent his time cruising, going places with gay friends, and drinking. When a long-standing gay love affair broke up catastrophically, he became an alcoholic for a while and came perilously close to destroying not only his ex-lover but also William and his career. Billy did not go to work when he took over from William, and as an artist he was eclipsed under a work blockage. William was the artist, and he held a high-ranking, well-paid job as an illustrator. William admired his white-descended grandmother who partially reared him, and through her influence he climbed the educational ladder out of the ghetto. He dressed expensively and in a conservative style, quite different from the raffish style of Billy. Even his speech and body language differed from Billy's, and his sex life was different. William often referred to Billy as being like a male whore, whereas William established long-term partnerships. He gradually discovered himself to be bisexual. In bed with his woman partner he was more constrained than when with a man, except on an occasion when he had both partners together in a three-way turn-on. It was when his love life was going well for him as William that his vocational productivity reached its peak and his art was at its most creative—and that was a very distinguished creativity indeed.

11

The Genealogy
of Concepts in
Psychohormonal
Sexology

SYMPATHIES, VITAL FORCES, AND INTERNAL SECRETIONS.
Sexology is the science that until the 1970s dared not, in respectable
company, speak its name. By other scientists it was ridiculed as pornographic or shut off as shameful and illicit. Yet, from Aristotle to John
Hunter, various other life sciences, among them endocrinology and its
psychohormonal subspecialty, psychoendocrinology (hormonal behaviorology), owed their early origins to the sexological enigma of sexual
dimorphism and differentiation.

The sexological genealogy of endocrinology and its psychohormonal
subspecialty begins with sexual transplants at the end of the eighteenth
century when John Hunter (1728-93), the English anatomist and surgeon, demonstrated surgical transplantation effects in chickens. He
showed that the spur from the leg of a young hen would attain the larger
size of a cock's spur if transplanted to a cock, and that the immature spur
from a young cock would grow only to the smaller, female size, if transplanted to a hen. He succeeded also in transplanting the cock testis to the
abdominal cavity of the hen. Three anatomical specimens preserved in
the Hunterian Museum in London today bear witness to the successful
transplant of the testis into the female host.

Hunter did not report his testicular transplants in detail, nor the conclusions he drew from them regarding masculinization of the hen. It is
actually possible that he refrained from publicizing what he had discovered, so as to avoid an accusation of witchcraft. It was one of the tenets of
the Inquisition, from which he was not far removed in time, that witchcraft could be recognized by the witch's demonic power to denature
people sexually, and to do the same with farm animals, rendering them

187

infertile, impotent, or otherwise sexually altered. Perhaps, also, Hunter may have been somewhat disappointed in his findings, for he later wrote that he had "formerly transplanted the testicles of a cock into the abdomen of a hen, and they had sometimes taken root there, but not frequently, and then had never come to perfection."

According to the prevailing doctrine of the time, assorted living principles, vital forces, or sympathies (from which the current term, sympathetic nervous system, derives) allowed an organ or part of the body to grow and function in harmony with other organs and parts, and thus ensured the unity of the organism. There was no firm doctrine of how a sympathy exerted its influence, and no such doctrine emerged from Hunter's demonstrations. They were, in fact, the first demonstrations that internal secretions from a gland travel in the bloodstream and influence other organs and tissues; but it would take another century before that principle would be fully formulated and applied. A partial formulation was recorded in 1849, when Arnold A. Berthold, in Goettingen, repeated Hunter's testicular transplant experiments and concluded that something from the testis had acted upon the blood. Replication of Berthold's demonstration proved difficult and, like Hunter's, its significance for science was at first neglected and subsequently rediscovered.

In nineteenth-century French biomedical doctrine, Claude Bernard's general concept of internal secretions became linked to the very ancient, premedical priestly doctrine (the source of antimasturbation and related Biblical doctrine) of the conservation of vital force by the conservation of semen. The neurobiologist, Brown-Séguard, tested on dogs the hypothesis that sperm extract from a vigorous animal would reinvigorate an elderly one. Finally, in 1889, he performed the experiment that made him famous, namely, injecting under his own skin extracts obtained from sperm, tissue of testis, and from blood obtained from the testicular vein of dog and guinea pig. He was cautious about the possibility of autosuggestion, but eventually became empirically convinced that an internal secretion present in testicular extract (*liquide orchitique*) was responsible, and that it did indeed invigorate the elderly and the infirm. Brown-Séguard's evidence was inconclusive, but his idea of a specific internal secretion associated with the testis prompted further research on internal secretions. With the assistance of vaudeville comedians in that prudish and prurient era, his demonstration also produced for posterity the monkey-gland legend of geriatric lechery that still insidiously negates the concept of psychoendocrine sexology as science.

Early in the twentieth century, the physiologist, Eugen Steinach (Benjamin 1945) in Vienna, continued to apply the experimental method of internal secretions to sexual psychoendocrinology. In castrated, neonatal guinea pigs, he transplanted heterotypical gonadal tissue, and achieved a dramatic somatic and behavioral masculinization of females, and feminization of males, respectively. Next he turned his attention to the other end of the age scale and the endocrinological possibility of slowing the aging process. Testicular implants or extracts being immunologically unsatisfactory, he developed a hypothesis based on vasoligation, namely, that the testis after vasoligation undergoes tubular degeneration with compensatory Leydig-cell hypertrophy, which in turn increases its hormonal output, which in turn has a rejuvenating effect. The experimental and clinical evidence in support of this hypothesis was equivocal, and a storm of controversy arose around the "Steinach operation" for the mental and physical rejuvenation of aging men, some of them very famous, like Freud (Benjamin 1945). This controversy overshadowed the subsequent, uncontroversial phase of Steinach's work on purification of ovarian hormones, which led to the production of Progynon, the first commercially available estrogen; and on anterior pituitary extracts that activated gonadal secretions. Hitler's invasion of Austria in 1938 forced Steinach into exile in Switzerland where, without laboratory facilities, his research career terminated, just at the time when endocrinology had become firmly established in the biochemistry laboratory.

MULTIVARIATE VERSUS UNIVARIATE DETERMINISM. When the sex hormones were isolated in the 1920s, and synthesized in the 1930s, they were named for estrus (estrogen), for the testis (testosterone), and for gestation (progesterone), thus setting the stage for an oversimplified myth of causality, relating masculinity and femininity of behavior, as well as of morphology and reproductive function, to male and female hormones, respectively.

This oversimplification of hormonal cause and behavioral effect served tolerably well in the 1920s in pioneer psychoendocrine studies like, for example, those of C. P. Stone. But eventually it impeded the progress of psychoendocrinology until mid-century and beyond. Thus it is still fashionable for physicians to prescribe testosterone for impotence, and also for homosexuality in men, both without effect. With the crude measurements available in the 1930s and '40s, some attempts were made to connect homosexuality with androgen deficiency. The attempts failed, but the hypothesis of a causal connection between hormone levels and homosexuality in men persisted, and continues to do so (Chapter 6).

The major thrust of sexual psychoendocrinology in the 1940s was in the pituitary-gonadal regulation of mating behavior, and also of parental behavior. Not too surprisingly, it was in the laboratory that the major advances in basic knowledge were made. From the laboratory also came the needed theoretical reconceptualization. In 1948, in *Hormones and Behavior*, Frank Beach, the noted animal psychoendocrine sexologist, revised the simple formula of hormonal-cause/behavioral-effect into a multivariate formula: species variability can be accounted for only by taking into account the evolutionary status of the brain, and in particular the cerebral cortex. The higher a species in the phyletic scale, the less is its sex-divergent mating behavior enchained to hormonal functioning, and the more is it subject to stimulus perception and developmental learning.

New evidence began accumulating in the 1950s in support of multivariate determinism and completely changed the course of psychoendocrinology by implicating the brain itself as an endocrine organ. The region involved was not the neocortex, the organ of stimulus-perception and learning in Beach's theory, but the hypothalamus. Guillemin and Schally were awarded a Nobel prize in 1977 for discovering the chemical structure of the hypothalamic releasing hormone, LHRH, that governs the pituitary's release of luteinizing hormone. Their success rested on the hormonal radioimmunoassay technology for which Yalow shared the 1977 Nobel prize; and also on the trail-blazing neuroendocrine research in Britain of the late Geoffrey Harris who had demonstrated, contrary to established dogma, that cells in the hypothalamus do indeed secrete hormonal substances that govern the secretions of the neighboring pituitary gland. Harris's research was built on foundations laid in 1936 by Pfeiffer, who had demonstrated in newborn rats that the presence of testicular tissue, even if transplanted into the neck of genetic females, would prevent cyclic functioning of the pituitary and, hence, cyclic functioning of the ovaries. Pfeiffer's experiments antedated the synthesis of the hormone, testosterone, which soon would be identified as the active principle in his testicular implants.

The work of Pfeiffer and Harris showed how to alter female cyclicity of pituitary-gonadal secretions by means of prenatal hormonal intervention, and how to use physiologic measures of outcome. Since cyclicity is manifested not only in the physiology but also in the behavior of mating and reproduction, it was inevitable that, sooner or later, the neuroendocrinology of sex-differentiated behavior would be subject to scientific investigation. Here the trail-blazer was the anatomist, William C. Young.

Young pursued a parenthetical 1938 observation of Dantchakoff (Chapter 3) whose research in France on female guinea pigs made hermaphroditic by treatment with testosterone in utero had been terminated by World War II, namely, that they performed sexually as males. Steinach (Benjamin 1945) earlier had also recorded this same observation. Young and his coworkers used first the guinea pig and then the rhesus monkey as their experimental animals, and showed that prenatal androgenization of females influences not only their anatomy but also their juvenile behavior, in that it tends to be more masculine.

The work of Harris, Young, and many others who have followed them in sex-differentiated neuroendocrinology and behavior necessitates a revision of Beach's early enunciation of the multivariate formula of psychoendocrine causality: a part of the brain, the hypothalamus, is itself a psychoendocrine organ; it can directly influence both the endocrine system and behavior as male or female; under the influence of sex hormones in prenatal development, it can be programed to function dimorphically in either a male or female way; its prenatal programing will affect the way it reacts to the hormones of puberty; its response to the hormones of puberty will influence the dimorphism of sexual behavior in mating.

MULTIVARIATE SEQUENTIAL DETERMINISM. This formula is more than multivariate. It is multivariate and sequential. It means that one cannot predict the influence of sex hormones after puberty without knowing the prenatal hormonal history. Nonetheless, it is incomplete, for the variable, the neocortex, specified by Beach needs to be included. The neocortex signifies learning.

At the present time, it is possible only in limited degree to investigate in animals the role of learning in the expression of sexual psychoendocrine function. Harlow's social isolation studies of rhesus monkeys, for instance, have shown that monkeys isolated from birth, and thus deprived of sexual rehearsal play with other members of their species, are unable, postpubertally, to position themselves for copulation and do not reproduce their species.

Animal experiments, however, just as they have limited applicability to the learning of human language, have, and probably always will have, limited applicability to learning in human G-I/R differentiation, including the differentiation of its erotic/sexual component as it expresses itself in variable imagery as well as variable practice. Experimental manipulation of human lives being ethically inadmissible, it is to the so-called experiments of nature, the spontaneously occurring clinical syndromes, that one must turn for direct information about human psychoendocrine sexology.

Clinical investigation of the psychoendocrine sexology of intersexual conditions has long been associated particularly with the Psychohormonal Research Unit at Johns Hopkins. Studies here, in particular those of matched pairs of hermaphrodites concordant for prenatal biography and diagnosis, but discordant for postnatal biography, case management, and prognosis, have demonstrated that the prenatal neuroendocrine history does not automatically preordain postnatal psychosexual status. Rather it regulates a threshold for sex-shared behavior that is different in male/female prevalence and stimulus sensitivity, but can be assimilated into the postnatal continuation of the differentiation of psychosexual status as either male or female, as influenced by social stimulus and response.

In Figure 3-1 (Chapter 3), now well-known and republished in many books, social input is included among the other multivariate determinants in a sequence that begins with chromosomal sex and ends with adult gender identity/role. The sequence applies not only to the overall status of G-I/R, but to its specific erotic/sexual component as well.

The most recently discovered variable in Figure 3-1 is H-Y antigen, the histocompatibility antigen associated with the Y chromosome, without which gonadal tissues in their undifferentiated embryonic phase will not differentiate as testes and, hence, will fail to provide masculinizing hormonal secretions.

DEVELOPMENT OF CONCEPTS IN NONSEXOLOGICAL HORMONAL BEHAVIOROLOGY. The most highly developed branches of hormonal behaviorology (psychoendocrinology), in addition to the sexual one, are those that pertain to thyroid and IQ, and to pituitary and growth. Yet, in these branches of knowledge, empirical application of the concept of multivariate sequential determinism has barely begun.

Thyroid psychoendocrinology made its appearance early in the twentieth century, when thyroid deficit was recognized as the responsible factor in the extreme impairment of statural and intellectual growth in endemic goitrous cretinism. Nutritional iodine deficiency was pinned down as epidemiologically responsible for thyroid failure in endemic goitrous cretinism in regions isolated from the sea and iodine-rich seafood. Yet, it could not, and still cannot be explained why some members of a birth cohort in an iodine-deficient community would become cretinous, and others would not. The same question remains unanswered today in those areas, like African equatorial Zaire, in which endemic cretinism is a side-effect of a diet heavy with casava, a naturalized New World tuber that has powerful antithyroid properties. The same diet afflicts some children, while leaving some of their own siblings unaffected and normal in both somatic and intellectual growth.

The old, simplistic equation was that congenital hypothyroidism equaled mental retardation. However, in 1978 a 25-year follow-up study at Johns Hopkins (Money, Clarke, and Beck 1978) showed that the equation is not so simple. Given constant replacement thyroid therapy and prolonged opportunity to learn, mentally defective hypothyroid children may, until late in their twenties, gain sufficient catch-up intellectual growth so that the IQ eventually tests at low average or higher. As yet, there is no prognostic screening method whereby IQ elevation can be prophesied. As the IQ improves, the chances of erotosexual life are enhanced.

Development of the pituitary endocrinology of growth and dwarfism depended on the technological problems posed by the complex molecular structure of pituitary peptides. It was in the mid-1950s that human growth hormone (somatotropin), which still has not been synthesized, was first isolated. Extract of human pituitary growth hormone first became available for human clinical trials in the treatment of hypopituitary dwarfism in 1957. Previously, the only treatment available for such patients had been to replace thyroid, cortisol, or sex steroids, if the pituitary tropic hormones that stimulate their secretion were missing or deficient. With purified growth hormone, dwarfism in statural growth could itself be corrected. Postnatal growth hormone deficiency, even when total, does not bring about impairment of intellectual growth. Prenatal deficiency, according to some preliminary animal experimental evidence by Sara, from Australia, may impair brain-cell growth and differentiation. Human patients with an idiopathic deficiency of growth hormone postnatally apparently do not have a history of prenatal deficiency, according to the criterion of their birth size, which is within normal limits.

The behavioral concomitants of hypopituitary dwarfism in childhood, according to the evidence available, are secondary to the social consequences of being infantilized in concordance with physique age, instead of being treated according to chronologic age. After the age of puberty, a more direct effect may emerge, namely, a deficit in pair-bonding. This deficit is currently under investigation in the Johns Hopkins Psychohormonal Research Unit. It may correspond to the deficit in hypothalamic releaser function that induces failure of pituitary hormone secretion, and, if so, may be attributable to a neurotransmitter failure on brain pathways yet to be identified.

Psychohormonal theory in hypopituitary dwarfism underwent a dramatic change in 1967. This was the year in which was published the finding from the Pediatric Endocrine Clinic at Johns Hopkins that growth-hormone failure rectifies itself in a syndrome of reversible hypopituitary dwarfism by a nonendocrine treatment, namely, changing the domicile. The association of child abuse as an etiologic factor in the syndrome was first established by members of the Johns Hopkins Psychohormonal Research Unit. In the domicile of abuse, pituitary hormonal secretion becomes either greatly reduced or completely shutdown. Both statural and intellectual growth become grossly impaired. A change from the traumatizing domicile of abuse and neglect to a benign one restores the pituitary to normal function and statural and intellectual growth resume. Sleep deprivation and nutritional deprivation both may be implicated. The next installment of information on how statural and intellectual growth failure are mediated awaits new knowledge of the brain and its neurotransmitters.

Within the last ten years, increasing experimental attention has been directed toward the peptide hormones as neurotransmitters, especially at the Institute of Pharmacology under David de Wied, at Utrecht. ACTH (adrenocorticotropic hormone), or rather a short chain of amino acids from its molecule, has, in addition to regulating stress responses, been implicated as an active principle in conditional reflex learning and extinction. Much remains to be discovered about neuropeptides and learning.

Neurotransmitters probably will prove to be the key essential to the formulation of an empirically acceptable theory to explain both the association of psychopathology with endocrine pathology, and the unpredictability of its occurrence, severity, specificity, and reversibility. The only theory extant is Manfred Bleuler's 1954 theory of a general and nonspecific endocrine psychosyndrome. Nonspecificity, however, contradicts the specificity of depression (which includes hyposexualism) and hypothyroidism in myxedematous psychosis; of agitated or manic excitement (which may include hypersexualism), or, paradoxically and more rarely, apathy, in hyperthyroidism; of paranoid ideation in hyperparathyroidism; of gross memory and learning impairment in hypoparathyroidism; of arbitrary or bizarre behavior in the hyperadrenocorticism of Cushing's syndrome; and the toxic, hallucinatory or schizophreniclike reactions to unphysiologic, therapeutic doses of ACTH or of cortisol itself. In the present state of knowledge, the sex hormones are not known to be associated with symptoms or syndromes of psychopathology, unless, maybe, progesterone should prove related to post partum psychosis. Likewise, the hormones of the pituitary gland appear not to be specifically related to psychopathology.

TOMORROW'S PHYSIOCHEMICAL SEXOLOGY OF THE BRAIN. As for the neurohormones of the hypothalamus, it is too early to know how much they might contribute to the etiology of psychopathology, whether nonsexological or sexological. The same can be said of the biogenic amines, especially the indolamine, serotonin and the catecholamine, dopamine. Though only in a preliminary way, both of these neurotransmitters are known to have a sexological function in the brain, as well as a far more general one. The sexological function, if any, of the very recently discovered morphine-like neurotransmitters in the brain, the endorphins or enkephalins, and beta-lipotropin in the pituitary gland, remains to be discovered.

If the expansion of knowledge of the brain and its neurochemicals continues at its present rate of growth, then one may expect in the early twenty-first century an entirely new sexology of the brain in health and pathology. Even in science fiction, one cannot yet begin to predict its phenomenology and principles.

Sexual Democracy,
Sexual Dictatorship,
Sexual Dissidence

WRONG DEEDS AND WRONG IDEAS. It is not illegal to publish pictures or stories of actual acts of murder, nor to depict murders on stage, in films, or in television dramas, nor to narrate explicit murder scenes in books or magazine stories. A person must specifically substantiate a murder threat or actually commit the act before being arrested, accused, and tried for murder. The law deals primarily with deeds and misdeeds and only secondarily with the mental state that engendered them. In fact, the law does not have good criteria for dealing with such mental states as knowing right from wrong, irresistible impulse, and planned intention versus fortuitous or provoked response. The law also lacks good criteria for dealing with treason and heresy, in both of which not deed but ideology goes on trial.

Treason applies to the secular authority or political system, and heresy to the ecclesiastical authority or theological system. The two terms are not much used with contemporary reference, but what they stand for is by no means extinct in the running of society.

Today the Iron Curtain synonym for treason is capitalism. In the west, the synonym for treason is communism, though in the United States it carries much less force now than it did in the 1950s, the era of Senator Joe McCarthy. Treason means to contravene the authority of the governing power by endorsing an opposing ideology, especially that of an enemy power.

The synonym for heresy in today's pluralistic and ecumenical theology is sex. In the church, heresy pertains to masturbation, contraception, abortion, legal prostitution, homosexuality, children's sexuality, women priests, and married clergy.

SECULARIZATION OF SEXUAL HERESY. In contemporary democratic states, the church's ecclesiastical authority to enforce doctrinal obedience and punish sexual heresy is limited by the secular authority of the judiciary. However, where ecclesiastical authority fails, secular authority succeeds. The law steps into the shoes vacated by the church and, wearing them, pursues with Inquisitorial zeal the eradication of sexual heresy. The charges are the same and the indictment does not change. The only alteration is the secularization of the prosecuting authority. Defying redefinition, sexual heresy has survived the transfer of antiheretical authority and power of enforcement from church to state.

One's first impulse is to marvel that this astonishing sociological phenomenon could indeed have occurred. Pragmatically, it is not so astonishing, however, insofar as legal heresy hunters receive only their authority from the state, not their personal faith as to what moral sexosophy is dogma and what is heresy. Their faith is a direct legacy from the church transmitted through the common law, statutory law, case law, and, above all, in the rearing of children, folk adherence to sexual doctrine and taboo that is still the official teaching of the church.

Sociologically, there is an additional explanation of how the definition of sexual heresy has survived the transfer of antiheretical authority and power of enforcement from church to state. To an unknown degree, the church utilizes the methods of espionage as employed internationally by nation states and terrorist groups, and domestically by guerrilla movements and crime syndicates. That is to say, the church brings covert pressure to bear on its own members employed in positions of secular power, or educates its students to become superior candidates for appointment to positions of secular power. In Customs, for example, or Justice, or the Post Office, a high-ranking official who understands the will of the church is able to assign priorities to what to investigate, what to seize, and what to prosecute.

So it is that the secular authority performs the Inquisitional function of suppressing sexual heresy, and of dictating and censoring what the people should and should not know or do sexually. When a secular authority dictates, it becomes a dictatorship. We live today in a sexual dictatorship that restricts not only what people may do sexually but also what they may read, see, hear, or otherwise have existing in their minds. Any deviation qualifies as secular heresy.

LEGAL DEFINITION OF SEXUAL HERESY. In a democracy, it is actually an embarrassment to the judiciary to have to arbitrate on what is sexually the secular equivalent of heresy and what is not. To do so infringes on the right of freedom of conscience and freedom of speech, and comes dangerously close to abrogating the principle of separation of church and state. In what follows, I use the United States as my example, simply because I know its system best. Unless you come from a juridically liberated country like Denmark, you may substitute the name of your own country and you will not, for the most part, be wrong. In the United States, the Supreme Court has circumvented the basic constitutional issue of whether the federal judiciary may justifiably address itself to defining and regulating secular heresy with respect to sex. Instead, it has acted on a principle of decentralization that identifies sexual heresy as a local phenomenon, locally defined and locally regulated. Abortion, for example, is now, in 1979, a heresy, though only for poor people who have no money to pay for it, since local or regional authorities have the right to disqualify the use of public funds to pay for it. Likewise, the demand of civil rights for homosexuals must be argued locally, for the Supreme Court has, to date, declined to accept appeals from lower courts. The heresy of explicit erotica, otherwise known as obscenity and pornography, also clearly illustrates the Supreme Court's policy of sexual decentralization, as is evident in what follows.

According to what is now known as the Miller decision, the Supreme Court of the United States in 1973 updated its criteria of the obscene or pornographic in sex. The arbiter is the average man or woman in the role of member of the jury. The standard is that of the contemporary community, with no regional limits stated. The material to be decided upon is to be evaluated as a whole.

To qualify as obscene or pornographic, material should (1) appeal to the prurient interest; (2) depict or describe sexual conduct in a patently offensive way; (3) lack serious literary, artistic, political, or scientific merit.

Etymologically, prurient means itching, and also to have a longing for something. In contemporary usage, when the connotation of the longing is sexual, it is immoral or indecent. Webster's dictionary defines prurient not as amative, romantic, or erotic, but as lustful, lewd, or lascivious. Here the law is blatantly tautological, for it connotes as indecent that which has prurient appeal, and prurience has the connotation of indecent appeal. To escape this logical trap, the courts have extended the definition of prurient to mean shameful and morbid appeal. This escape is illusory, because average people, including heterosexual jury members, do not consider the kind of sex that appeals to them to be shameful and morbid, but normal and healthy. Average people are heterosexual. Therefore, heterosexual intercourse cannot be judged shameful and morbid, and hence as having prurient appeal. Paradoxically, it is erotic material that does not appeal to them, and perhaps even disgusts them, that average people are likely to classify as shameful and morbid. To whose pruriency, then, does such material appeal? The courts have answered this question by defining a shameful and morbid appeal in terms of the presumptive target audience or readership to whom a given type of material is addressed. Homosexuals, for example, are in many courts defined as having a shameful and morbid interest in homosexual erotic materials. Homosexuality is thus, in effect, given the status of secular heresy, as is any other form of sexual expression that does not conform to the ideology officially espoused, though not necessarily privately practiced, by the members of the average jury.

Once erotic material has been declared shameful and morbid because of the special group, the heretics, to whom it appeals, it is a foregone conclusion that, applying contemporary community standards, it will also be declared as patently offensive to the average person.

In Hitler's Germany, Jews, dwarfs, and homosexuals were declared patently offensive to the average person, applying Hitler's contemporary German community standards, and the average German condoned the extermination of millions of them. In an earlier era, average persons in Christian Europe had condoned the extermination of entire villages for the heresy of witchcraft. The average person all too often is wrong—just plain wrong!

Material that is adjudged shameful, morbid, and patently offensive surely, it would seem, must lack serious literary, artistic, political, or scientific value. But such is not the case. All materials have scientific value for the scientists into whose specialty they fall. Thus, all sexual materials are of scientific value to the science of sexology. Likewise, their literary, artistic, or political value cannot be measured against absolute standards, for there are none. These values, like scientific values, are relative to the appraiser. Like beauty, which resides in the eye of the beholder, and like color-blindness, which is in the eye of the viewer and not in the view, all values are intensely subjective and privately engendered. Values may be highly idiosyncratic or unusual without being debased.

JURY DEFINITION OF OBSCENITY. There is no way in which the Supreme Court's attempt to define obscenity and pornography can be salvaged. It is flawed irreparably by the transcendental fallacy of defining good and bad not in terms of deeds performed, or their outcome, but in terms of mental states that have no exact definition and no dimensions by which to be measured—arousal of prurient interest, a feeling of offensiveness, and a judgment of literary, artistic, political, or scientific merit.

Normally a jury is required to weigh evidence as to whether an act was or was not committed, and under what circumstances. Not so in a por-

nography trial. There, in no more than a few days, and without preliminary study and preparation, a jury is bombarded with information from
expert witnesses that a graduate student would spend an entire semester
digesting. Then, without a public-opinion poll as a guide to community
standards, the jury must believe that its own subjective reactions are
typical of the community at large.

What in fact the jury does do in defining obscenity and pornography is
what all people do: it judges erotic material as obscene or pornographic
if to read, hear, or see it breaks a taboo or prohibition formerly intensively inculcated, especially in childhood, and so creates a feeling of
being sneaky and of doing something wrong (Chapter 5). This judgment
is made irrespective of the content of the tabooed and prohibited material. The fact that the prohibition was insistently inculcated early in life is
what counts. The sexual taboo in our society is enormously pervasive
and broad in the scope of what it prohibits. It allows only a narrow range
of human sexual expression that is doctrinally correct. All the rest is
heresy. A jury usually has no difficulty, therefore, in bringing in a guilty
verdict. With few exceptions, its verdict in effect brands all erotic materials as heresy.

SEXUAL AND POLITICAL DISSIDENCE: PARALLELISM. In a
political dictatorship, the name of heresy is dissidence. Dissident writings, graphics, or speeches may be defined as those that promulgate
ideas which, taken as a whole, are adjudged by the average person,
applying contemporary community standards, to have shameful and
morbid appeal, to be patently offensive, and to lack serious literary,
artistic, political, and scientific merit. You perceive, of course, that this
definition is identical with the definition of obscenity and pornography
in the Supreme Court of the United States. It demonstrates an extraordinary parallelism between the United States and, for example, Russia,
regarding ideological nonconformity. It is a parallelism of which, I suspect, neither side is aware. The sexual dissident in the United States is
the counterpart of the political dissident in Russia. Epidemiologically,
both are considered infected with contagious ideas that threaten the
health of society. Both are kept under police surveillance, and are subject to police harassment and entrapment. Both are arrested and
brought to trial at enormous expense to the taxpayer. Both are subject to
sanity tests and both may be sentenced to custody in either a psychiatric
institution or a prison. Both are professionally dispossessed and cannot return to their former occupations. Both have their families economically ruined and morally traumatized. Both are defined as Prisoners of Conscience by Amnesty International insofar as, in 1977, the
International Council of Amnesty International resolved that Prisoners

of Conscience include persons detained or imprisoned because of sexual orientation or behavior, provided that those persons have not infringed the human rights of any other person. The reference to sexual orientation is in particular to homosexuality.

A further similarity between both types of dissident is that the materials they produce and publish do not disappear. They achieve subversive fame and circulate on an underground or black market. In some instances, especially regarding sexual materials, the black market may produce great wealth, and with it corrupt political power for the bootleggers of the crime syndicate that exploits it. Thus does society's persecution of the dissident boomerang disastrously upon itself, insofar as black-marketing inflates prices and encourages blackmail, extortion, murder, and corruption of politicians and law enforcement officers. It also robs from the public purse billions of dollars in untaxable black-market revenue (Chapter 5).

HARMFULNESS VERSUS WRONGFULNESS. The prohibition of dissidence is often defended with arguments that amount to a belief in the social contagion of sinfulness. Monkey see, monkey do! This is the maxim of how wrong is perpetuated, always at the expense of righteousness. Belief in the social contagion of sinful sex is the residual survival of its Inquisitional predecessor, belief in demonic possession. As a belief, and despite a total absence of empirical support, the contagiousness myth has exhibited extraordinary survival and power. The most likely reason is that any explanation is better than none, when people are afraid—and they are afraid of difference, especially in those who differ sexually from themselves. Intolerance and persecution of nonconformity or difference, irrespective of its origin, is widespread in the animal kingdom. Both are overinclusive rather than individually discriminative. The harmless suffer with the harmful.

Harmfulness is a covert component of the idea of wrongfulness that people attribute to sexual nonconformity. Here again overinclusiveness characterizes the way people think. Society overreacts and labels too much as harmful, without checking the facts. Nonetheless, harmfulness cannot be dismissed altogether. Quite to the contrary! The concept of harm can be used to establish the dividing line between what society should and should not tolerate in the way of individual sexual nonconformity.

SEXUAL HARMFULNESS DEFINED. Harmful sexuality can be defined as nonconsensual, imposed or enforced. It infringes upon the personal inviolacy of the partner. Spelled out in operational terms, an infringement of personal inviolacy means that the partner is unable to enter into a consensual relationship because the terms of the contract are not fully specified. The beginning does not predicate the end.

The principle of noninfringement of personal inviolacy is, like any statute or law, a broad generalization that needs to be applied and tested, case by case, in order to establish examples and precedents. Some infringements are categorically intolerable—violent assault or mutilation, for example. The violator will always be subjected to detention and/or to therapy, if therapy is available. Combined antiandrogen-plus-counseling therapy for crimes of violent sex is one possibility (see Appendix).

In violent sexual assault or mutilation, the victim does not predicate his or her injury or death as the culmination of the sexual encounter. Logically, an exception may be argued in the case of a masochist who stage-manages his own mutilation and death at the hands of a sadistic lust-murderer who stage-manages the uncertainty of whether he will be caught or not. Such a case represents a rare and extreme type of reciprocal terminal sadomasochism. Perfectly reciprocal matching of a couple in a pact of mutilation, suicide, or murder of one or both partners is statistically difficult to achieve, and so it seldom challenges society. So long as the couple maintain total privacy, society is none the wiser. Society is alerted only when privacy is not maintained, either because the relationship is not perfectly reciprocal and one of the partners complains, or because a third party becomes a witness or accessory and fails to complain. If a hypothetical third party should make a movie of consensual sadomasochistic mutilation, suicide, or murder, then paradoxically, according to today's law, it would qualify as illegal, not because it depicted mutilation and killing, but because it depicted exposed genitalia in action.

PARAPHILIA AND OBSCENITY. All of today's erotic movies that qualify as obscene and illegal earn that qualification because they depict the exposed genitals being used erotically. Normal heterosexual intercourse in a movie is condemned as obscene, but with less vehemence than if the movie also depicts a paraphilic theme. In the vernacular, a paraphilia is known as bizarre or kinky sex. For many people, paraphilic imagery seems not only wierd but also so repulsive that they want to get rid of it. They define it as socially dangerous and believe that it spreads by social contagion.

As a test case, consider urophilia, a paraphilia that dictates that a person, almost invariably a man, will be able to get erotically aroused and be able to perform sexually to orgasm, only if his partner urinates on him and in his mouth. To its critics, this ritual seems filthy and disease-infecting, as well as repugnant. Repugnance and infection are not, however, the same thing. In actual fact, in healthy beings, urine is a sterile fluid. Many animals keep their babies clean by licking up their excreta. In Kenya, among the Masai, a major source of nourishment is a mixture of the milk, blood and urine of cows. In India, Moraji Desai, the prime minister, drank some of his own urine each morning for medicinal purposes. Reading this information about ingestion of urine is by itself alone powerless to turn you into a urine drinker, even if you read or hear it hundreds of times. Likewise, hundreds upon hundreds of exposures to urophilic narratives, pictures, or movies will not convert a single person into being a urophiliac. None of the paraphilias is transmitted by social infection. Each paraphilia appeals only to a person who already has that same paraphilia. All the paraphilias have their origin in early childhood development, before puberty. A paraphilia is a developmental dissidence, and the prime suspect in the etiology of all paraphilias is excessive restriction of normal infantile and childhood sexual rehearsal play, plus excessive punishment for being caught at it (Chapter 4). Restriction and punishment produce a sexual dissidence, which is then subject to more restriction and further punishment. The formula is repeated on the next generation, and so our ancient heritage of sexual taboo perpetuates itself with incredible tenacity.

SEXUAL DICTATORSHIP, TABOO, AND PROTEST. A taboo by its very nature always restricts something, like eating or sex, that human beings ordinarily do, and it is inculcated into the members of a society in early childhood, according to the principle of avoidance or punishment learning (Chapter 6). Infringement brings retribution and establishes shame and guilt, which enables the taboo to maintain itself throughout life and to be transmitted to the next generation.

Most politicians endorse the sexual taboo in our society. For example, when the Report of the Commission on Obscenity and Pornography came before the U.S. Senate, the vote was 60:5 to reject it on the basis of a forewarning that it was not sufficiently condemnatory of explicit erotica. Inchoately, politicians like parents and priests realize their advantage in being able to manipulate in others the lever of guilt and shame in order to obtain conformity. Thus, they are loath to remove the last great barrier to full democratic freedom, the barrier against sexual democracy.

Democratic freedom is not, of course, equivalent to license. It does not mean that anything goes. It means that sexual freedom is your birthright and mine, so long as it does not cross the dividing line of infringing on the personal inviolacy of the partner. Across that dividing line, the violator may in some cases be tolerated as an eccentric. In other cases, he may be offered whatever medicine has to offer by way of its expanding therapeutics and rehabilitation. In only rare cases will the violation be so dangerous and the violator so unresponsive to nonincarcerative treatment that prolonged detention will be the only resort.

Today's politicians, attorneys, law-enforcement officials, news reporters, health professionals, and researchers all in their various ways take advantage of sexual dictatorship and the suppression of sexual democracy. They thereby gain various combinations of notoriety, power, profit, and career advancement, unendangered by retaliation or reprisal. The public, if it does not overtly condone, apathetically bows under the yoke of the system; it lacks the factual knowledge with which to protest. Sexologists either have this knowledge, or else the skills with which to obtain it. With them rests the responsibility of transmitting this knowledge first to their fellow educators and clinical professionals, then to the news media, the law, and the policy-makers in politics and the church, until finally it filters down to people everywhere.

To protest the status quo is to become a dissident oneself, victimized by the immense power of the social machinery of taboo maintenance. For many people the status of protester is too demanding. Like the victims of child abuse, these nonprotesters endorse their persecution and do not complain as they perpetuate things as they are. They are the antithesis of those for whom the challenge of a too-heavy taboo is an incitement to protest. The destiny of these protesters is to turn the words of the Sexual Revolution into deeds. If they succeed, they will in the twenty-first century bring into being a genuine sexual democracy for the greater betterment of us all, young and old of both sexes, pair-bonded and not pair-bonded.

Antiandrogenic and Counseling Therapy of Sex Offenders

Rationale for Depo-Provera Treatment of Sex Offenders (Paraphiliacs).
Studies begun at Johns Hopkins in 1966 have shown that sex offenders
or paraphiliacs, for example, pedophiliacs, treated with the antiandrogenic hormone, Depo-Provera, plus counseling have gained in self-
regulation of sexual behavior. Depo-Provera suppresses or lessens the
frequency of erection and ejaculation and also lessens the feeling of
libido and the mental imagery of sexual arousal. For the pedophiliac, for
example, there will be decreased erotic "turn-on" to children. Metaphorically, the sex offender has "a vacation" from his sex drive, during which
time conjunctive counseling therapy can be effective.

Antiandrogenic Effect of Depo-Provera. Depo-Provera, a long-acting,
injectable form of medroxyprogesterone acetate manufactured by Up-
john, is a synthetic progestin that is classified pharmacologically as an
antiandrogen. Antiandrogen inhibits the release of androgen, the so-
called male hormone, from the testicles. Some progestinic hormone is
normally present in the male body, but at a very low level. Increasing the
level allows progestin to compete with androgen and to take over. Androgen is a sexual activator. Progestin in the male is sexually inert. It
therefore induces a period of sexual quiescence in which the sex drive is
at rest.

Mode of Endocrine Action. In terms used by endocrinologists, Depo-
Provera inhibits, through its effect upon neural pathways in the sexual
system of the brain, the release of luteinizing hormone (LH) from the
pituitary gland. LH is the chemical messenger that normally stimulates

the testicles to produce androgen. Hence, the ultimate effect of Depo-Provera is to reduce the level of androgen, especially testosterone, in the blood stream. Typically, in the adult male, Depo-Provera reduces the blood level of testosterone to that of a normal prepubertal boy (from approximately 575 nanograms/100 milliliters to 125 nanograms/100 milliliters).

Brain Effect. In addition to lowering the level of testosterone, Depo-Provera, like all progestinic hormones, acts on the brain as an anesthetic if given in huge doses. In small doses, as in the treatment of sex offenders, the influence on sexual pathways in the brain, though mild, has the great advantage of being sexually calming or tranquilizing. The patient feels relief from an urge that was formerly insistent, commanding, and not subject to voluntary control.

Peripheral Physiological Effects. Depo-Provera, through decreasing the testosterone level, temporarily decreases penile erection and ejaculation and the production of sperm (spermatogenesis). In addition, the sexual accessory organs, the prostate and seminal vesicles, temporarily shrink. Occasionally, increased drowsiness, and weight gain have been reported as minor side effects.

Reversibility of Changes. All of the changes attributed to the medication are reversible upon cessation of treatment; within 7–10 days erectile and ejaculatory capacity begin to return, along with the subjective experience of more sexual drive.

Dosage Level. Tailored for the specific patient, intramuscular injections of Depo-Provera range from 100 milligrams to 500 milligrans (1.0 to 5.0 milliliters) every 7 days. The typical weekly maintenance dosage of Depo-Provera for sex offenders is 300 milligrams. For taller, heavier patients, the maintenance dosage may be as high as 500 milligrams, and the highest dosage used is 600 milligrams per week.

Hormonal Monitoring. Hormonal measures of testosterone and LH (luteinizing hormone) initially can be monitored monthly or bimonthly, and later quarterly, to gauge the effectiveness of the dosage. The recent application of radioimmunological techniques to the assay of testosterone and LH has made such endocrine monitoring precise, reliable, rapid, and relatively inexpensive, as compared to prior methods.

No Increased Tolerance. The patient does not require a progressively increasing dosage, because there is no tolerance build-up to Depo-Provera.

Comparison with Surgical Castration. Prior to the discovery, manufacture, and medical use of antiandrogen, the method of reducing the level of testosterone in men was surgical castration. Used in many societies throughout history, castration is disfavored in contemporary American legal-medical management of sex offenders. Obviously, surgical castration is irreversible. It is also less effective than hormonal antiandrogenic therapy.

Behavioral Effects of Depo-Provera Treatment. In many cases, it is possible for patients to be weaned off Depo-Provera. Since the weaning is a step-by-step lowering of the hormone dosage, it is possible for the patient to discover how completely he has become relieved of the tendency to engage in the sex offending behavior, both in actuality and imagination. In many cases, there is long-lasting remission, so that the patient is no longer compelled to commit sex offenses, but is enabled to have a sex life with a socially suitable consenting partner instead. Some patients prefer to continue on a low, maintenance dosage of the medication so as to ensure a maximal guarantee of no relapse. Those patients who establish a strongly pair-bonded relationship with a permanent partner appear to be additionally guaranteed against relapse. The counseling component of treatment facilitates this achievement and is essential.

Compliance. Some patients, as in all specialties of medicine, are more faithful than others in adhering to medication schedules. Some overly confident patients drift into noncompliance. Other patients neglect specific instructions about their medication schedule. For this reason, it is advisable that as a condition of probation or parole, supervision be legally required so as to ensure strict compliance in adhering to the treatment schedule.

Statistical Assessment. Sex offenders treated with Depo-Provera at Johns Hopkins are kept in long-term follow-up. A dozen have now been followed for between 5 and 13 years. Of this group, 9 have proved able to self-regulate their sexual behavior, and 3 have had relapses correlated with noncompliance. Improvement follows resumption of treatment.

Counseling Therapy. Counseling sessions are provided weekly, at first, and then spaced to once a month. These sessions enable the patient to establish a new life-style. The fundamental impairment in paraphilia (sex-offending) is not of sexual function, but of love, attraction, and pair-bonding. It is this impairment that responds to counseling therapy. In true homosexual pair-bonding, the defining characteristic is unyielding inability to fall in love with an opposite, but not same sex partner.

Glossary

abuse-dwarfism: retardation of growth in body and mind secondary to child abuse and neglect.

acceptive phase: in an erotic/sexual relationship, the second or middle phase, the one in which the two bodies, and specifically the sex organs, accept one another; *see also* **proceptive** and **conceptive phases.**

acrotomophilia: the condition of being dependent on the appearance or fantasy of one's partner as an amputee in order to obtain erotic arousal and facilitate or achieve orgasm.

ACTH: adrenocorticotropic hormone. A pituitary peptide hormone named for its role in stimulating the release of adrenocortical hormones.

Adam principle: in fetal life, the differentiation of a male requires that something be added, in particular MIS and testosterone. Partial or complete differentiation otherwise takes place, regardless of chromosomal sex; *see also* **Eve principle.**

adolescence: the developmental period of maturation, predominantly during teenage, from puberty to young adulthood.

adrenal cortex: the outer three layers of the adrenal gland, as contrasted with the innermost part, the medulla. The cortex produces steroidal hormones, among them the glucocorticoid, cortisol, and nonpotent sex hormones; *see also* **adrenal gland; cortex.**

adrenal gland: an endocrine gland located immediately above the kidney. It consists of two portions: a cortex, and a medulla. The cortex produces and secretes steroidal hormones, among them cortisol (a glucocorticoid), and weakly active sex hormones. The medulla produces adrenalin (epinephrine), a catecholamine.

adrenogenital syndrome: a condition produced by a genetically transmitted enzymatic defect in the functioning of the adrenal cortices of males or females that induces varying degrees of insufficiency of cortisol and aldosterone and excesses of adrenal androgen and pituitary adrenocorticotropin. Abnormal function of the adrenal cortex starts in fetal life and, unless treated, continues chronically after birth. Females born with the syndrome have ambiguous genitalia and, if they survive without salt loss and dehydration, undergo severe virilization. Males are usually not recognized at birth, but if they survive, will prematurely develop sexually during the first years of life. In the severe form of the disease, untreated, mortality rate is almost 100 percent for both sexes. Treatment with glucocorticoids, and in some cases also with salt-retaining hormone, is life-saving and prevents postnatal virilization. Plastic surgery is needed on the female genitalia. With appropriate therapy, prognosis for survival and good physical and mental health is excellent.

adventive: adventitious, or happening in one's life history in a unique way and not according to a universal system; *see also* **imperative.**

209

age-avoidancy: a socially dictated constraint on personal disclosure to people of a different age group than oneself. It affects erotic/sexual behavior and communication; *see also* **allosex-avoidancy** and **intimacy-avoidancy.**

agenesis (*adjective,* **agenetic**): partial or complete failure of an organ or part of the body to form or develop.

allosex-avoidancy: a socially dictated constraint on personal disclosure to members of the other, but not one's own, sex. It affects both behavior (as in locker-room nudity, for example) and communication, as in sexual joking; *see also* **age-avoidancy** and **intimacy-avoidancy.**

ambiguous: having more than one possible meaning; equivocal.

ambivalent: going both ways or leaning in both directions at once, especially with respect to loyalty or allegiance to a person or idea.

amelotasis: the condition of having an erotic inclination toward the stump of an extremity missing either congenitally or as a result of amputation; *see also* **acrotomophilia; apotemnophilia.**

amenorrhea: absence or failure of the menstrual periods.

amygdala: a part of the brain situated in the temporal lobe. It belongs to the "old brain" or limbic system.

anachronism: a historical error, placing a person, thing, or event either before its time or after it has become outdated.

androgen: male sex hormone, produced chiefly by the testis, but also by the adrenal cortex and, in small amounts, by the ovary. In biochemical structure, there are several different but related steroid hormones that qualify as androgens. They differ in biological strength and effectiveness.

androgen-insensitivity syndrome (*also called* **testicular-feminizing syndrome**): a congenital condition identified by a 46,XY sex karyotype in girls or women who appear externally to be not sexually different from normal females, except in some cases for a swelling or lump in each groin, or for the absence of pubic hair after puberty. The cells of the body are unable to respond to the male sex hormone, which is made in the testes in normal amounts for a male. They respond instead to the small amount of female sex hormone, estrogen, which is normally made in the testes. The effect before birth is that masculine internal development commences but is not completed. It goes far enough, however, to prevent internal female development. Externally, the genitalia differentiate as female, except for a blind vagina, which is usually not deep enough for satisfactory intercourse and needs either dilatation or surgical lengthening in or after middle teenage. There is no menstruation and no fertility. Breasts develop normally.

androgeny: the condition of showing some characteristics of both sexes in body, mind, or behavior.

androgynophilia: erotosexual pairing with a man and a woman serially or simultaneously by a member of either sex. It includes falling in love. *See also* **bisexuality.**

andromimetic: a girl or woman being a person manifesting the features or qualities of a male in bodily appearance, dress and behavior. There is no fixed vernacular synonym except, maybe, a bull dyke, that is a female homosexual who lives in the role of a man. She may request breast removal, but not genital surgery, and usually not hormones to masculinize the voice, beard and body hair. *See also* **gynecomimetic.**

androphilia: erotosexual pairing with a man by a woman (female androphilia) or a man (male androphilia). It includes falling in love. *See also* **heterosexuality; homosexuality.**

anesthesia, penile: diminution of erotic/sexual feeling in the penis and its replacement to some degree with a feeling of numbness.

anesthesia, vulval: diminution of erotic/sexual feeling in the sex organs of the female, and its replacement to some degree with a feeling of numbness.

anhedonia: lack of pleasure in doing or experiencing something, or doing it only as an obligation, duty, or drudgery.

anlage (*plural,* **anlagen**): in embryology, the initial element or structure that develops and differentiates into a more complex structure.

anorgasmia: failure to attain a sexual climax or orgasm during the acceptive phase of an erotic/sexual episode. It is also known, in men, as ejaculatory delay or incompetence. In women it is confused with frigidity.

anovulatory: without ovulation, as when an estrous or menstrual cycle occurs without the release of an egg from the ovary. Anovulatory cycles are infertile cycles. Until ovulation resumes, a female is said to manifest anovulatory sterility.

antigen: a substance which, when present in animal tissue, stimulates the production of antibodies.

apathy, erotic: inertia, lack of arousal, and lack of interest in having sexual relations.

apotemnophilia: the condition of being dependent on being an amputee, or fantasying oneself as an amputee, in order to obtain erotic arousal and facilitate or achieve orgasm. It is accompanied by obsessional scheming to get one or more limbs amputated.

areola (*plural,* **areolae**): the area of pigmented skin immediately surrounding the nipple of the breast.

asphyxiophilia: *see* **erotic self-strangulation.**

atrophy (*adjective,* **atrophied, atrophic**): a defect or failure of cell nutrition manifested as decrease in size and healthiness of an organ or tissue; *see also* **dystrophy.**

autoassassinatophilia: the condition of being dependent on the masochistic staging of one's own murder in order to obtain erotosexual arousal and facilitate or achieve orgasm.

azoospermia: absence of sperm in the semen, with resultant infertility.

Barr body: the color-staining spot (the sex chromatin) located at the edge of the nucleus of cells taken from individuals with more than one X chromosome. It is normally found in female cells, and so is used as a sign of female genetic sex. It is also found in men with the 47,XXY (Klinefelter's) syndrome. It is missing in girls with the 45,X (Turner's) syndrome. The Barr-body test is rapid and inexpensive as compared with actual chromosome counting, and so is used as a method of preliminary X-chromosome screening.

beta-lipotropin: the biochemical precursor substance from which the body synthesizes endorphins. It is related to ACTH. *See also* **ACTH; endorphins.**

biogenic amine: a biologically synthesized substance, fundamentally a nitrogen compound, widely dispersed in the body. Some hormones, such as adrenalin (epinephrine) are compounds containing an amine. *See also* **catecholamine; indolamine.**

bisexuality: erotic pairing with partners of either genital morphology, usually serially, but possibly simultaneously.

catecholamine: one of the biogenic amines, including epinephrine, which is both a hormone (adrenalin) and a neurotransmitter; and dopamine, a neurotransmitter. *See also* **biogenic amine; indolamine; dopamine.**

cerebral cortex: the external gray layer of the brain, the neocortex; *see also* **limbic system.**

cervix (*adjective,* **cervical**): the neck or neck-like part of an organ. The cervix of the uterus is at its lower end, where the uterus and the vagina meet.

circadian: fluctuating regularly on a 24-hour basis.

climacteric: in women, the menopause; in men, the life changes that may or may not occur as the counterpart of the menopause in women.

clitoris: the small, hooded organ at the top of the cleft of the female sex organs, which is the counterpart of the penis in the male. In the rat, mouse, and hamster, the clitoris is not hooded, but its covering is fused as in the male's penis to form a urinary tube.

coital aninsertia: inability in the female to have the penis inserted into the vagina, or in the male to insert the penis. It may be associated with neglect or denial of one's own penis or vagina (as in many unoperated transexuals) or, more commonly, with phobic anxiety or panic and avoidance of penetration of one's own vagina, or of inserting one's own penis.

coital fantasy: imagery of erotically stimulating content that accompanies sexual intercourse and may precede it and be essential to the attainment of orgasm. It may or may not be related to the actual partner and activity going on, and may in fact be an intrusion that cannot be voluntarily controlled. Alternatively, it may disappear as sexual excitement builds up, as the person becomes totally immersed in body sensations. *Synonyms:* **copulation fantasy; intercourse fantasy.** *See also* **masturbation fantasy.**

coitus *or* **coition:** the sexual act, specifically the taking of the penis into the vagina, or the penetrating of the vagina with the penis; but more generally the complete interaction between two sexual partners; *see also* **copulate; intercourse; mount.**

complementation: reciprocation; the converse of identification.

conceptive phase: in an erotic/sexual relationship, the third and final phase which, if it occurs, is characterized by conception, pregnancy, and parenthood; *see also* **proceptive** and **acceptive phases.**

coprophilia (*adjective,* **coprophilic**): the condition of being responsive to, or dependent on, the smell or taste of feces for erotic arousal and the facilitation or achievement of orgasm. From the point of view of the species, it probably has its origins in mammalian hygiene whereby infants are licked clean. In individual biography, the correlation between feces and eroticism is varied in origin. It may be related to masochism and self-deprecation. Coprophilia may involve also the sight and sound of a person defecating.

copulate (*noun,* **copulation**): to couple, join, or unite as in sexual interaction; *see also* **coitus; intercourse; mount.**

core gender identity: a term newly introduced into psychoanalytic theory to refer to an infant's developing sense of self as a boy or girl in the second year of life, well in advance of the classic oedipal phase to which the origin of differences in the psychology of sex is attributed in traditional theory.

corpora cavernosa: the pair of "cavernous" or spongy columns of erectile tissue in the penis below which is the urethra and corpus spongiosum. Pumped full of blood, these spongy bodies hold the penis erect.

corpus luteum (*plural,* **corpora lutea**): "yellow body;" a yellow mass in the ovary formed from the graafian follicle after the egg is released. It produces progesterone, the pregnancy hormone, and grows and lasts for several months if the egg is fertilized and pregnancy occurs.

cortex (*plural,* **cortices**): literally, the bark or outer layer; in anatomy, the outer layer or section of an organ, as the cortex of the brain and the cortex of the adrenal gland; *see also* **adrenal cortex; neocortex.**

cortisol: the main glucocorticoid hormone in man produced by the adrenal cortices; also known as hydrocortisone. It is essential to the maintenance of life. It is available in synthetic form.

cortisone: one of the glucocorticoid hormones, a metabolite of cortisol. In synthetic form, it is used therapeutically and converted in the body into the biologically more potent hormone, cortisol. Historically, the term "cortisone" has also been used generically to refer to all the synthetic glucocorticoids used therapeutically.

cryptorchidism: the condition of having one testis (unilateral) or both (bilateral) undescended into the scrotum.

culturistic: developmentally induced according to the dictates of society or culture; the converse of nativistic.

cunnilingus: erotic stimulation of the female sex organs with the tongue and mouth by partner of either sex. It is considered a normal part of love play.

cunnus: the Latin term for the female external genitals.

Cushing's syndrome: a disorder of overproduction of cortisol hormone from the adrenocortical glands, usually involving malfunction of the pituitary gland, and likely to lead to symptoms of psychopathology as well as severe somatic pathology.

cyproterone: a synthetic, hormonal steroid substance, related to progesterone, which is potent as an antiandrogen. A variant form is cyproterone acetate, which is more powerful in its antiandrogenic effect.

cytogenetic syndromes: those conditions of development marked by various bodily and behavioral symptoms that stem from a deficiency, excess, or other gross defect in the number, size, and shape of the chromosomes in each of the body's cells. For example, in most girls with Turner's syndrome, one sex chromosome is missing (45,X); in most boys with Klinefelter's syndrome, the male's one X chromosome is duplicated (47,XXY); and in most boys with the YY syndrome, the male's Y chromosome is duplicated (47,XYY).

cytogenetics (*adjective,* **cytogenetic**): that branch of the science of heredity that deals with the chromosomes and genes (carriers of the genetic code) within the cell nucleus.

DES: diethylstilbestrol. A synthetic drug that acts as a female sex hormone. Structural variants include dipropionate, dilaurate, and dibutyrate esters, and C^{14}-diethylstilbestrol dibutyrate, the radioactive form used only for special investigative procedures.

dimorphism: having two forms or manifestations, though of the same species, as in a juvenile and adult form, or a male and a female form. Though usually used to refer to bodily form and appearance, in this book the meaning of the term is extended by analogy to apply to sex differences in behavior and language.

dirty joke: a sexual example of what in anthropology is known as a joking relationship, that is a socially permissible manner of communication between people who are otherwise socially forbidden to talk together, either in general or on a specific topic, like sex.

diurnal: recurring daily, or in the daytime.

dopamine: a catecholamine that is active as a neurotransmitter in the brain. On sexual pathways it acts as an arouser. *See also* **serotonin; catecholamine; indolamine; biogenic amine.**

dyspareunia: the experience of pain, especially in the sex organs or within the pelvis, during sexual intercourse. It may also include coital migraine headache. It may occur in either sex, but traditionally has been named dyspareunia in women and coital pain in men.

dystrophy (*adjective,* **dystrophic**): partial atrophy of tissue or an organ as a result of imperfect cell nutrition; *see also* **atrophy.**

endocrine gland: one of the body's ductless glands from which a hormone is secreted directly into the bloodstream.

endometrium: the lining of the uterus or womb. Structurally, it is mucous membrane.

endorphins (*singular,* **endorphin**): the general term to refer to all of the body's own endogenous morphine-like substances. In chemical structure, they are neuropeptides. They are active as neurotransmitters. *See also* **neuropeptide; neurotransmitter; enkephalin.**

enkephalin: one of the endorphins, and the one that predominates in the brain. There are two basic types, methionine and leucine enkephalin. *See also* **endorphins.**

ephebophilia (*adjective,* **ephebophilic**): the condition in which an adult is responsive to and dependent on the actuality or imagery of erotic/sexual activity with an adolescent boy or girl in order to obtain erotic arousal and facilitate or achieve orgasm. An ephebophiliac may be of either sex. Ephebophilic activity may be replayed in fantasy during masturbation or copulation with an older partner.

ephemera (*plural,* **ephemerae**): something that is short-lived or of transient existence.

epistemology: the branch of philosophy that investigates the origin, nature, methods, and limits of human knowing.

eroticism (*adjective,* **erotic**): the personal experience and manifest expression of one's genital arousal and functioning as male or female, either alone or with a partner, and particularly with reference to the sensory stimuli of arousal. *See also* **sexuality.**

erotic self-strangulation (**asphyxiophilia**): the rare condition in which a person, usually an adolescent male, is dependent on partial asphyxiation, as by hanging, or by restaging of it in fantasy, in order to obtain erotic arousal and facilitate or achieve orgasm. Death may inadvertently result. Some victims have been found cross-dressed.

erotic/sexual: simultaneously erotic and sexual. One can be sexual without being erotic, as in donor insemination. Conversely, being erotic does not necessarily entail being sexual, especially in the sense of copulation, fertility or reproduction. *See also* **eroticism, sexuality;** *synonym,* **erotosexual.**

erotography: explicit erotic writings and pictures.

erotosexual: *see* **erotic/sexual.**

estradiol: the most biologically potent of the naturally occurring estrogens. It is produced chiefly by the ovary. Commercially it is prepared in various compounds, such as estradiol benzoate and ethinyl estradiol.

estrogen: female sex hormone, produced chiefly by the ovary, but also by the adrenal cortex and, in some amount, by the testis. Named so because, in lower animals, it brings the female into estrus (heat). In biochemical structure, there are several different but related steroid hormones that qualify as estrogens. They differ in biological strength and effectiveness; *see also* **progesterone.**

estrus (*adjective,* **estrous**): the phenomenon of being sexually receptive, or in heat, as found in the sexual cycle of the females of some species. A condition or syndrome of persistent estrus can be produced in some animals (for example, the rat) by hormonal injection of the newborn, notably with androgen; *see also* **TSR.**

Eve principle: in fetal life the differentiation of a female always occurs in the absence of fetal testicular secretions (MIS and testosterone), regardless of chromosomal sex. If in the differentiation of a female testosterone is added, differentiation thenceforth proceeds as male; *see also* **Adam principle.**

excitement phase: the first of the four sexual phases delineated by Masters and Johnson; *see also* **plateau, orgasmic,** and **resolution phases.**

exhibitionism (*noun,* **exhibitionist**): the condition of being responsive to, or dependent on the surprise, debasement, shock, or outcry of a stranger (usually female), unexpectedly exposed to the sight of the penis, in order to obtain one's erotic arousal and facilitate or achieve orgasm. The actual event may be replayed in a masturbation or coital fantasy.

falling in love: the personal experience and manifest expression of becoming intensely, and possibly suddenly, attached or bonded to another person. It may be reciprocal and a source of great ecstasy, or one-sided and a source of great agony. Usually it is erotosexual.

fallopian tubes: the left and right tubes of the uterus that connect the uppermost part of the uterine cavity bilaterally with the ovaries. They are so positioned as to be able to transport the egg released from the ovary to the uterine cavity for implanting. They are named for the Italian anatomist Gabriello Fallopius (1523–62).

fantasy (*verb,* **to fantasy**): imagery in the mind that is fictive rather than perceptual, and that tells a story in either pictures or words. A fantasy, like a dream, may be a program of expectations for the future, or a replay of past happenings, or a combination of both.

fellatio: stimulation of the penis by taking it into the mouth, possibly to the point of orgasm. The partner may be of either sex. It is considered a normal part of love play.

fetish: an object, substance or part of the body that has a unique power of sexual arousal specific to the person who responds to it.

fetishism: the condition in which a person is dependent on a talisman or fetish object, substance, or part of the body in order to obtain erotic arousal and facilitate or achieve orgasm.

fictive image: an image in the mind that is not perceived through the senses, but construed in the imagination on the basis of past perceptions retrieved from memory and reconstituted; *see also* **perceptual image.**

follicle: a small cavity, sac, or gland, such as a hair follicle or ovarian follicle. The latter secretes hormones, estrogen and progestin, that regulate the menstrual cycle. *See also* **graafian follicle.**

foreplay: the traditional term for erotic/sexual activity during the proceptive phase in which manual, oral, and other skin and body contact ensure erection of the penis, lubrication of the vagina, and an urgency of being ready for orgasm, usually penovaginally induced.

frigidity: in sex, the failure to become sexually aroused or passionate. Traditionally, it has been applied chiefly to women, but now is considered too imprecise and in need of subdivision, as in Table 5–4 in the text.

frotteurism: the condition in which a person (a frotteur) is dependent on rubbing against and feeling the genital or other region of the body of a stranger, especially in a tightly packed crowd, in order to obtain erotic arousal and facilitate or achieve orgasm.

FSH: follicle-stimulating hormone. It is produced by the pituitary gland and stimulates the formation of the ovarian follicle on the ovary and the production of estrogen. When the follicle ripens, luteinizing hormone takes over, and the progestinic phase of the menstrual cycle appears; *see also* **LHRH; ICSH.**

fuck (*noun; verb*): the Anglo-Saxon synonym for sexual intercourse, coition or copulation (all Latin-derived). To copulate and to fuck are the only one-word verbs for mutual genital intercourse. The former is too stilted for vernacular use. The latter, being tabooed as dirty, is often replaced by euphemisms like to screw or to ball.

gay (*adjective; noun*): the name that, in the twentieth century, homosexual people popularized as a term of self-reference that carries no moral or legal stigma.

gender: one's personal, social and legal status as male or female, or mixed, on the basis of somatic and behavioral criteria more inclusive than the genital criterion alone; *see also* **gender-identity/role.**

gender identity/role (G-I/R): gender identity is the private experience of gender role, and gender role is public manifestation of gender identity. Gender identity is the sameness, unity, and persistence of one's individuality as male, female, or ambivalent, in greater or lesser degree, especially as it is experienced in self-awareness and behavior. Gender role is everything that a person says and does to indicate to others or to the self the degree that one is either male or female, or ambivalent; it includes but is not restricted to sexual arousal and response.

genital: having to do with the sex organs; *see also* **eroticism; sex; sexuality.**

genitalia: the sex organs, internal and external. The word is often used to refer to the external organs only; *synonym,* **genitals.**

genotype: the genetic constitution of an individual; *see also* **phenotype.**

gerontology: the science of aging and age-related phenomena.

gerontophilia (*adjective,* **gerontophilic**): the condition in which a young adult is responsive to and dependent on erotic/sexual activity with a much older partner in order to obtain erotic arousal and facilitate or achieve orgasm.

gestagen: *see* **progestin.**

G-I/R: *see* **gender identity/role.**

gonadostat: the term, formed by analogy with thermostat, for the hypothetical mechanism whereby the hormonal secretions of the gonad (ovary or testis) regulate the secretions of pituitary and hypothalamic cells.

gonadotropin: one of the hormones released by the anterior lobe of the pituitary gland, which programs the activity of the ovary in the female and the testis in the male.

graafian follicle: the follicle on the ovary in which the egg grows. After the egg is released, the graafian follicle becomes the corpus luteum. Named for R. de Graaf, Dutch anatomist (1641–73).

gynandromorphy: a term of Greek etymology meaning woman-man-shape. Thus, literally, the term means having some of the body morphology and measurements of an average woman and some of an average man, or being at neither extreme.

gynecomastia: the development of breasts on a male, spontaneously or as a result of hormonal treatment.

gynecomimetic: a boy or man being a person manifesting the features or qualities of a female in bodily appearance, dress, and behavior. Specifically, a drag queen, which is the vernacular term for a male homosexual who lives in the role of a woman. He retains his male genitalia, even though he may take hormones to grow breasts; *see also* **andromimetic.**

gynophilia: love of a woman by a man (male gynophilia) or a woman (female gynophilia). It includes falling in love. *See also* **heterosexuality; homosexuality; lesbian.**

haptic: having to do with touch and the sense of touch.

hermaphroditism: a congential condition of ambiguity of the reproductive structures so that the sex of the individual at birth is not clearly defined as exclusively male or exclusively female. The condition is named for Hermes and Aphrodite, the Greek god and goddess of love.

heterosexuality: erotosexual pairing with a partner of the complementary genital morphology. Its full manifestation includes falling in love; *see also* **homosexuality.**

histocompatibility: compatibility between different tissues, as in skin grafting or organ transplants, so that the immune mechanism of the host does not bring about the rejection of the graft or transplant. Histocompatibility in the case of H-Y antigen means that the Y-chromosome-associated histocompatibility antigen is expressed on male cells only, so that male cells may be recognized as foreign by the female immune system, if transplanted to a female.

hippocampus: a structure of the limbic system of the brain named for the resemblance of its curved shape to a sea horse. It is situated in the region of the temporal lobe of the cerebral cortex and is important, among other things, in the processing of short-term memory. *Synonym,* **Ammon's horn.**

homicidophilia: *see* **lust murderism.**

homosexuality: erotosexual pairing with a partner of the same genital morphology. Its full manifestation includes falling in love; *see also* **heterosexuality.**

hormone: a body chemical secreted from specialized glandular cells, especially in the endocrine glands, and carried in the bloodstream for use in other parts and cells of the body.

Huntington's chorea: a chronic and progressive disease of the central nervous system characterized by irregular body movements, disturbance of speech, and gradually increasing mental deterioration. It is hereditary in origin and is transmitted as a genetic dominant.

H-Y antigen: Y-chromosome-induced histocompatibility antigen. It is believed to adhere to the surface of all male mammalian cells, including the Y-bearing sperm of fertilization. In the course of normal embryogenesis, it is held responsible for programing the cells of the undifferentiated gonadal anlage into a testis.

hyperparathyroidism: excessive secretion of parathyroid hormone from the parathyroid glands, which are situated alongside the thyroid gland in the throat, and which play a role in regulating the amount of calcium in blood and body tissues.

hyperphilia: supranormal in sexual and genital responsiveness or frequency.

hypertrophy (*adjective,* **hypertrophied, hypertrophic**): over-development in size of an organ or of its constituent cells; *synonym,* **hyperplasia;** *antonym,* **atrophy.**

hypophilia: impaired or deficient in sexual and genital responsiveness or frequency. For examples, see Table 5-4 in text.

hypopituitarism: a generalized endocrine deficiency condition produced by failure, either partial or complete, of the pituitary gland to secrete its proper hormones. Failure after surgery for a pituitary tumor is usually complete. Idiopathic failure may be either complete or partial. In some instances, partial failure may involve chiefly the secretion of pituitary gonadotropins, the hormones that stimulate the ovaries or the testes to produce their own hormones.

hypospadias (*adjective,* **hypospadiac**): a birth defect in the positioning of the urinary opening on the penis. In mild hypospadias, the opening is only slightly removed from the tip of the penis. In severe hypospadias, the opening is in the female position, and the penis has an open gutter on its underside, instead of a covered urinary canal. A hypospadiac penis may be normal-sized or small; *see* **microphallus.** A small penis with a severe degree of hypospadias is identical in appearance with an enlarged clitoris below which is a single opening or urogenital sinus leading to both the urethra and the vagina; *see* **hermaphroditism.**

hypothalamus: a structure of the diencephalon; a portion of the brain of special importance in regulating vital functions, including sex, by means of the release of neurohumoral substances from nerve cells. These substances in turn regulate the nearby pituitary gland.

hypothyroidism: deficiency of thyroid hormone; the opposite of hyperthyroidism. The thyroid gland is in the throat, near the larynx or Adam's apple.

ICSH: interstitial cell stimulating hormone, stimulates testosterone secretion from the testes. *Synonym,* **LH** (luteinizing hormone).

identification: the process of becoming like someone secondary to copying and imitation.

ideogogic (*noun,* **ideogogy**): in sex therapy, treatment that involves discussion of ideas and the meaning of one's behavior to other people who are affected by it; *see also* **somesthetic.**

idiographic: specific to the self and unique to one's own biography.

idiopathic: of unexplained origin, as in the development of a symptom or syndrome.

imperative: the converse of adventive, in the sense of being obligatory in the development of all members of a species; *see also* **adventive.**

impotence: recurrent premature loss of erection of the penis, or its failure to become erect, during the acceptive phase of an erotic/sexual episode.

imprinting: developmental learning of a type first brought to scientific attention in studies of animal behavior by ethologists. Imprinting takes place in a given species when behavior programed into the nervous system of that species requires a matching social-environmental stimulus to release it, when the matching must take place during a critical or sensitive developmental period (not before or after), and when, having occurred, the resultant behavioral pattern is unusually resistant to extinction. In human beings, language learning is a manifestation of imprinting.

incest: sexual intercourse between persons to whom it is locally forbidden by law or custom because of their relatedness as kinsfolk or totemic clanfolk. The degree of relatedness varies among societies, and the relationship need not be genealogical.

indolamine: one of a subgroup of biogenic amines; it functions as one of the brain's neurotransmitters. Serotonin is the best known indolamine. *See also* **biogenic amine; catecholamine; serotonin.**

inertia: in erotic/sexual usage inertia is apathy or lack of responsiveness or arousal at the proceptive phase. It typically involves also the acceptive phase. It is experienced subjectively as lack of desire or drive. *Antonym,* **ultraertia.**

intercourse: connection or interaction between people. In sexual intercourse, the connection is usually defined as being between two people. It is erroneously defined as putting the penis into the vagina (penovaginal intercourse), for the entire sexual interaction between the partners constitutes sexual intercourse; *see also* **coitus; copulate; mount.**

intersexuality: an alternative term for hermaphroditism. In past usage, a genetic etiology was sometimes assumed for intersexuality, and a hormonal etiology for hermaphroditism, but the distinction is now known to be untenable.

intimacy-avoidancy: a socially dictated constraint on personal disclosure to specified individuals or groups, or on a specified topic. It affects erotic/sexual behavior and communication. It may affect only intimate communication, but not behavior with one's sexual partner; *see also* **age-avoidancy** and **allosex-avoidancy.**

kleptophilia (*adjective,* **kleptophilic**): the condition in which a person is dependent on carrying out or fantasying the stealing of something in order to obtain erotic arousal and facilitate or achieve orgasm.

Klinefelter's syndrome: a condition identified by a chromosomal anomaly in morphologic males with the pathognomonic symptoms of a small penis, small testes, and sterility. The basic genetic defect is an extra sex chromosome with a total count of 47,XXY. Variants of the syndrome are characterized by more than one extra X chromosome, e.g., 48,XXXY. The secondary sex characteristics are usually weakly developed and do not respond well to treatment with male sex hormone.

klismaphilia (*adjective,* **klismaphilic**): the condition in which a person is dependent on being given an enema, or on the restaging of it in fantasy, in order to obtain erotic arousal and facilitate or achieve orgasm.

lactogenic hormone: the pituitary hormone that stimulates the production of milk from the mammary glands; *synonym,* **prolactin.**

lekking: a mating ritual, relatively rare among species, in which at the beginning of the mating season males assemble on the mating ground or lek and wait until they are visited by females and selected for mating; *see also* **proceptive phase.**

lesbian (*adjective,* **lesbian**): female homosexual; named after the Aegean island, Lesbos, whence came the homosexual woman poet, Sappho, of ancient Greece. There is no corresponding word for a male homosexual.

Leydig cells: the interstitial cells in the testes that produce testosterone; they are packed between the seminiferous tubules in which the sperms grow.

LHRH: luteinizing hormone releasing hormone from the hypothalamus. It releases the pituitary gonadotropins, LH and FSH. LH frees the ovum and changes its graafian follicle into the corpus luteum. LHRH, LRH, LRF (F=factor) and GnRH (Gn=gonadotropin) are synonymous; *see also* **FSH, ICSH.**

libido: sexual drive, subjectively experienced and reported. Hypothetically, in psychoanalytic doctrine, it also means the positive life force of Eros as compared with Thanatos, the death force.

limbic system: the old cortex or paleocortex, as contrasted with the neocortex, of the brain. Its functions pertain to those aspects of the human mind and behavior that are shared by lower species.

limerence (*adjective,* **limerent**): the state of having fallen in love and being love-smitten.

love (*verb,* **to love**): the personal experience and manifest expression of being attached or bonded to another person. There is sacred and profane love, and affectional and erotic love. The word is also used in the vernacular as a synonym for like. *See also* **eroticism; falling in love.**

lovesickness: the personal experience and manifest expression of agony when the partner with whom one has fallen in love is a total mismatch whose response is indifference, or a partial mismatch whose reciprocity is incomplete, deficient, anomalous, or otherwise unsatisfactory.

lust murderism (homicidophilia): the very rare condition in which a person is dependent on sadistic homicide of the partner, or the restaging of it in fantasy, in order to obtain erotic arousal and facilitate or achieve orgasm. Recorded cases are either heterosexual or homosexual, but not bisexual. The converse condition is the masochistic staging of one's own murder (autoassassinatophilia).

masochism (*adjective,* **masochistic**): the condition of being responsive to or dependent on being the recipient of punishment and humiliation in order to obtain erotic arousal and facilitate or achieve orgasm. As the partner of a sadist, a person may impersonate a masochist for commercial gain, within the limits set by the pain threshold.

masturbation: etymologically, hand-rape, the manual practice of erotic self-stimulation, formerly stigmatized as a crime against nature. Today it is considered normal and healthy and is not limited to either the hands or the self. It includes digital stimulation of the genitalia of a partner as well as of oneself.

masturbation fantasy: imagery of erotically stimulating content that accompanies, and may precede, an episode of masturbation. Like the imagery of a sleeping dream, its content has a high degree of autonomy and is not voluntarily chosen; *see also* **coital fantasy.**

medroxyprogesterone acetate: a pharmaceutical hormonal product marketed under the name of Provera or Depo-Provera.® It has many of the physiological properties of progesterone, and so is known as a synthetic progestin, though in chemical structure it is actually an androgen, like testosterone, which is closely related to progesterone. Therapeutically, medroxyprogesterone acetate has varied uses: to suppress ovulation (in the birth-control pill); to prevent spermatogenesis (as a male contraceptive); and as an antiandrogen to suppress androgen release and libido, reversibly, in male sex offenders.

menopause: in a female, the so-called change of life marked by the cessation of menstrual functioning. It does not bring about cessation of sex life.

microcannula: a hair-thin glass tube so small that it can penetrate a single cell and deliver a minute drop of a liquid substance into the cell.

microelectrode: an electrode made of a filament so hair-thin that it can penetrate a single cell, such as a nerve cell, and deliver to or receive from the cell a minute amount of electrical current.

micropenis: an exceptionally small penis that resembles the clitoris in size. A micropenis may carry the urethral tube or may be hypospadiac. Typically, it is formed mostly of skin, the body (corpora cavernosa) of the penis being hypoplastic. The condition is also known as microphallus or penile agenesis.

microphallus: *see* **micropenis.**

MIS: mullerian inhibiting substance. It is produced by the fetal testis, and its function is to vestigiate the primordial mullerian ducts, thus preventing the development of a uterus and fallopian tubes in the male.

mount: together with thrusting, the penovaginal part of sexual intercourse. In human beings, either sex may get in position to mount the other, whereas in most other animals the female presents, and the male mounts; *see also* **coitus; copulate; intercourse.**

mullerian ducts: the structures in the fetus that will, in the female, develop into the uterus and fallopian tubes; named for Johannes P. Müller, German physiologist (1801–48); *see also* **wolffian ducts.**

multiphilia: the compulsive condition of recurrent limerence or falling in love and pair-bonding with a new partner for a period of limited duration. It is one of the manifestations of ultraertia. The degree of pair-bondedness with the partner, despite its brevity, distinguishes multiphilia from nymphomania and satyriasis (Don Juanism).

mysophilia (*adjective,* **mysophilic**): the condition in which a person is dependent on something soiled or filthy, for example, sweaty underwear or used menstrual pads, in order to obtain erotic arousal and facilitate or achieve orgasm.

myxedematous psychosis: a severe mental illness characterized by depression and watery swelling of the body's tissues brought on by failure of the thyroid gland, which is in the throat near the larynx, to secrete its thyroid hormone.

narratophilia (*adjective*, **narratophilic**): the condition of being responsive to, or dependent on reading or listening to erotic narratives in order to obtain erotic arousal and facilitate or achieve orgasm.

nativistic: native to the organism; the converse of acquired or culturally induced; *see also* **culturistic.**

necrophilia (*adjective*, **necrophilic**): the condition of being responsive to or dependent on sexual activity with a cadaver in order to obtain erotic arousal and facilitate or achieve orgasm. In necrophilia, there is an obsession with death, not as there is in sexual homicide with killing.

neocortex: the outermost layer or cortex of the brain, which in the evolutionary sense is new and is most highly developed in man. It is contrasted with the paleocortex (the old cortex or limbic system) that it encapsulates.

neuropeptide: a class of biochemical substances, related to peptide hormones, that are active in the brain and nervous system, for example, as neurotransmitters; *see also* **peptide hormones; neurotransmitter; endorphins.**

neurotransmitter: one of many different body chemicals released by brain and nerve cells, that carry messages from cell to cell across neuronal junctions.

nymphomania: the compulsive condition in a female of recurrent sexual intercourse with different male partners, promiscuously and without falling in love, but not as a paid prostitute or call girl. *Antonym*, **satyriasis; Don Juanism.**

obscenity: pornography; also sexual actions or utterances that are traditionally classified as forbidden.

olfaction (*adjective*, **olfactory**): the function of smelling.

orgasmic phase: the third of four sexual phases delineated by Masters and Johnson; *see also* **excitement, plateau,** and **resolution phases.**

ovariectomy: surgical removal of the ovaries; female castration.

pair-bond: a strong and long-lasting closeness between two people such as exists between lovers, and between parent and child.

paranoid (*noun*, **paranoia**): characterized by thinking that is delusional and, maybe, hallucinatory. It is incorrectly used as a synonymn for suspicious.

paraphilia (adjective, **paraphilic**): an erotosexual condition of being recurrently responsive to, and obsessively dependent on, an unusual or unacceptable stimulus, perceptual or in fantasy, in order to have a state of erotic arousal initiated or maintained, and in order to achieve or facilitate orgasm. The majority of paraphilias are believed to occur significantly more frequently in males than females. For examples, see Table 5-2 in the text.

paraphiliac: a person with a paraphilia.

paraplegia: paralysis with numbness and total loss of sensation and control of voluntary movement in the legs and lower body. It follows spinal cord injury or disease that disconnects the brain from its nerve supply to and from the body below.

pederasty: literally, boy love; *see* **pedophilia.** Pederasty is usually used in the restricted sense to refer to anal intercourse performed by an older youth or man on a prepubertal or early pubertal boy. It is not applied to the relationship between an older woman and a boy.

pedophilia (*adjective*, **pedophilic**): the condition in which an adult is responsive to or dependent on the imagery or actuality of erotic/sexual activity with a prepubertal or early pubertal boy or girl, in order to obtain erotic arousal and facilitate or achieve orgasm. A pedophiliac may be a male or a female. Pedophilic activity may be replayed in fantasy during masturbation or copulation with an older partner.

peeping Tom: voyeur.

peptide hormones: a class of hormone biochemically constructed of the same components of which proteins are made. They include several of the hormones secreted by the pituitary gland, e.g., growth hormone; *see also* **steroid hormones.**

perceptual image: an image in the mind as presently being perceived through one or more of the senses; *see also* **fictive image.**

phallus: a synonym for penis, which is also used to refer to the enlarged clitoris or penis-like structure of a female hermaphrodite.

phenotype: the observable traits that characterize the morphology, function, or behavior of the members of a genotype. The phenotype may be many steps removed from the genotype; *see also* **genotype.**

pheromone: an odoriferous substance that acts as a chemical messenger between individuals. By contrast, a hormone acts as a chemical messenger within the bloodstream of a single individual. In mammals, pheromones serve as foe repellants, boundary markers, child-parent attractants, and sex attractants.

phlogiston: a hypothetical substance which, prior to the discovery of oxygen, was thought to produce fire.

phyletic: of or pertaining to a race. Phyletic components or aspects of behavior in human beings are those shared by all members of the human race, as compared with behavior which is individual and biographically idiosyncratic. Phyletic behavior is the product of both prenatal and postnatal determinants, as is personal biographic behavior. Both are the end product of both innate and experiential determinants.

pictophilia (*adjective,* **pictophilic**): the condition of being responsive to or dependent on erotic pictures in order to obtain erotic arousal and facilitate or achieve orgasm.

pituitary gland: an endocrine gland situated deep in the brain in the midline behind the eyes, and directly below the hypothalamus. The hormones of the anterior pituitary regulate many functions of the other endocrine glands of the body. The pituitary is also known as the hypophysis.

plateau phase: the second of the four sexual phases delineated by Masters and Johnson; *see also* **excitement, orgasmic,** and **resolution phases.**

polyandry: the practice or the condition whereby a woman has more than one established erotic/sexual female partner; *see also* **polygyny.**

polygamy: the practice of having more than one marriage.

polygyny: the practice or the condition whereby a man has more than one established erotic/sexual female partner; *see also* **polyandry.**

polyiterophilia: a form of hyperphilia in which a person's own erotosexual responsiveness is built up toward orgasm by reiterating the same activity (manual, oral, anal, vaginal, or penile) many times with many partners.

pornography: explicit erotic writings and especially pictures that are legally or by custom classified as forbidden.

praxic: related to hand-eye coordination in making things and in figuring out the logic of how shapes fit together.

premature ejaculation: orgasm recurrently attained too soon before or at the acceptive phase of an erotic/sexual episode.

present (*pronounce* prē zent′): in animal mating, the position assumed by the female to allow the male to mount and thrust. For the penovaginal part of human sexual intercourse, either sex may present to the other; *see also* **coitus; copulate; intercourse.**

priapism: persistent abnormal and painful erection of the penis, usually without sexual desire. The cause is often unknown. It almost always results in destruction of the spongy tissues of the penis as a result of coagulation of blood in them, with resultant chronic impotence.

Priapus: in Greek and Roman mythology, the male god of generation, often represented with an erect penis.

proceptive phase: in an erotic/sexual relationship, the initial phase in which the two partners both woo in a ritual of solicitation, attracting, responding, and courtship. The signals are chiefly odors, motions, or visual signs, or mixed; *see also* **acceptive** and **conceptive phases.**

progesterone: pregnancy hormone, one of the two sex hormones chiefly characteristic of the female. It is produced by the ovary in the corpus luteum, following ovulation, and also by the placenta during pregnancy. The metabolic pathway of hormone production in the body leads from progesterone to androgen to estrogen.

progestin: any one of the class of synthetic sex-hormonal steroids that has a physiologic action resembling progesterone; also known as gestagen.

prolactin: the milk-stimulating hormone secreted from the pituitary gland.

prostaglandins: a group of chemical compounds found in body tissues that belong to the class, fatty acids, and so named because they were first found in the prostate gland. Among other things, they induce uterine contractions and lower blood pressure.

pseudohermaphroditism: hermaphroditism. The prefix was once used to denote the fact that the gonads were not hermaphroditically mixed (ovarian plus testicular tissue) as in true hermaphroditism, but were either testicular (male pseudohermaphroditism) or ovarian (female pseudohermaphroditism). In modern usage, the preferred terms are male, female, and true hermaphroditism. Agonadal hermaphroditism is a fourth form.

psychosocial dwarfism: abuse-dwarfism; *see also* **reversible hyposomatotropic dwarfism.**

puberty: the developmental period of transition under the governance of hormones, especially sex hormones, from being a juvenile to an adolescent.

radioimmunoassay: a procedure for assaying or quantifying minute amounts of target substances such as hormones, neurotransmitters, or drugs in blood or other tissue fluid. It is based on the action of the target substance to bind onto another substance, an antibody, for which it is known to have a special affinity. A measured amount of the target substance is labeled with a radioactive label. It is then mixed with the unlabeled target substance that circulates in unknown quantity in a sample of blood or other fluid, and to the mixture some of the antibody is added. The labeled and unlabeled substances compete to bind on to the antibody. The amount of unlabeled target substance present can then be quantified, because it varies according to how much of its radioactive rival becomes antibody-bound, and the latter can be measured with a radioactivity counter. This is the classical method of antigen competition.

rape: an act of rapism.

rape or rapism: the condition in which a person is dependent on the terrified resistance of a nonconsenting stranger, under conditions of unexpected assault and threats of further violence, in order to obtain erotic arousal and facilitate and achieve orgasm. The rape may be replayed in fantasy while masturbating or copulating. True rape is not the same as the coercive imposition of coitus on an acquaintance or spouse; *synonym*, **raptophilia.**

raptophilia: *see* **rapism.**

reciprocation: the mutual process of adaptation, one to the other, as when the behavior of a person of one sex adapts itself to the behavior of the other; *synonym*, **complementation.**

resolution phase: the fourth of four sexual phases delineated by Masters and Johnson; *see also* **excitement, plateau,** and **orgasmic phases.**

reversible hyposomatotropic dwarfism: abuse-dwarfism; *see also* **psychosocial dwarfism.**

RH: releasing hormone, also known as releasing factor. One of the newly discovered peptide hormones secreted by cells in the hypothalamus of the brain. They release other hormones, especially from the nearby pituitary gland.

romantic (*noun,* **romance**): having a wondrous or story-book quality, visionary and idealized. Romantic love belongs to the proceptive phase of a relationship, especially at its onset. Historically, romantic love stopped short of the acceptive phase of sexual intercourse and marriage, but today there is no strict dividing line.

sadism (*adjective,* **sadistic**): the condition of being responsive to or dependent on punishing or humiliating one's partner in order to obtain erotic arousal and facilitate orgasm. A person, especially a woman, may impersonate a sadist to oblige masochistic partners for commercial gain.

satyriasis: the compulsive condition in a male of recurrent sexual intercourse with different female partners, promiscuously and without falling in love, but not as a paid gigolo, hustler, or call boy. *Synonym,* **Don Juanism.** *Antonym,* **nymphomania.**

scatology (*adjective,* **scatological**): literally the study of excrement; metaphorically, the study of verbal or graphic material legally defined as filthy or obscene and pertaining to sexual rather than excremental activity. A scatophilic telephone caller talks sexually in a manner that he expects will be offensive or shocking to a female listener who does not know him. He is dependent on this maneuver to obtain erotic arousal and facilitate or achieve orgasm.

scoptophilia or **scopophilia** (*adjective,* **scoptophilic**): the condition in which a person is dependent on looking at sexual organs and watching their coital performance in order to obtain erotic arousal and facilitate and achieve orgasm. It is not surreptitious, as in voyeurism.

sensate focus: a term introduced by Masters and Johnson to refer to the procedure in sex therapy whereby each partner in turn explores the sensory responsivity of the other, especially through the sense of touch, as in fondling, and stopping short of penovaginal intercourse.

serotonin: an indolamine that is active as a neurotransmitter in the brain. On sexual pathways it acts as an inhibitor. *See also* **dopamine; indolamine; catecholamine; biogenic amine.**

sex (*noun*): one's personal and reproductive status as male or female, or uncertain, as declared on the basis of the genitalia. Also, a vernacular synonym for genital interaction, as in the expression, to have sex.

sexology: the body of knowledge that comprises the science of sex, or, more precisely, of the differentiation and dimorphism of sex and of the erotic/sexual pair-bonding of partners. Its primary data are behavioral-psychological and somatic, and its primary organs are the genitalia, the skin, and the brain. The scientific subdivisions of sexology are: genetic, morphologic, hormonal, neurohormonal, neuroanatomical, neurochemical, pharmacologic, behavioral, sociocultural, conceptive-contraceptive, gestational-parturitional, and parental sexology. The life-cycle subdivisions of sexology are: embryonal-fetal, infantile, child, pubertal, adolescent, adult, and geriatric sexology. *See also* **sexosophy.**

sexosophy: the body of knowledge that comprises the philosophy, principles, and knowledge that people have about their own personally experienced erotic sexuality and that of other people, singly and collectively. It includes values, personal and shared, and it encompasses culturally transmitted value systems. Its subdivisions are historical, regional, ethnic, religious, and developmental or life-span. *See also* **sexology.**

sex roles: patterns of behavior and thought that are traditionally classified or coded as typical of, or specially suited to, either one sex or the other. Some sex roles are related to procreation, and some are not.

sexual drive: the personal and subjective desire or feeling of readiness to have an erotosexual experience. It cannot be measured directly.

sexuality (*adjective,* **sexual**): the personal experience and manifest expression of one's status as male or female, especially as it relates to the genital organs, pair-bondedness, and reproduction; *see also* **eroticism.**

solipsism (*adjective,* **solipsistic**): the concept that the self is the only verifiable knowledge, or that knowing exists in private. Thus a color-seeing person never knows what it is like to see the world as a color-blind person sees it.

somatotropin: growth hormone; it is secreted by the pituitary gland.

somesthetic (*noun,* **somesthetics**): in sex therapy, treatment that involves the skin senses as in touch, pressure (massage), hot/cold, wet/day, and sensuous body-contact grooming.

somnophilia (*adjective,* **somnophilic**): the condition in which a person is dependent on intruding upon and fondling a partner who is a stranger asleep, or fantasying doing so, in order to obtain erotic arousal and facilitate or achieve orgasm.

STD: sexually transmitted disease, including but not limited to contagious genital infections.

steroid hormones: a class of hormone biochemically constructed of the same components of which fats (lipids) are made. They include the hormones of the testis, ovary, and adrenal cortex. *See also* **peptide hormones.**

steroids (*singular,* **steroid**): the general or generic name for the compounds comprising the sex hormones, adrenocortical hormones, and other body chemistries.

taboo (*also,* **tabu,** and in Polynesia, **tapu,** sacred and forbidden): forbidden by tradition or social usage or other authority. A taboo generates fear, shame, and guilt in those who disobey it, thus enabling those in authority to wield power over those under them.

tactile: pertaining to the sense of touch.

teleology: in philosophy, the doctrine that nature or natural processes are shaped by a purpose and directed toward an end or goal by a driving force or power; *antonym,* **mechanism.**

telephone scatophilia: *see* **scatology.**

template: a pattern or mold that regulates the shape or appearance of a construction or idea.

temporal lobe: in the brain, the part of each cerebral hemisphere that is named for its location internal to the temple.

testosterone: the most biologically potent of the naturally occurring androgens, measurable in blood plasma and in urine. It is produced chiefly by the testis.

toxin: a poison. It may be produced by a virus, bacteria, plant or animal. During pregnancy, a toxin may pass through the placenta from the mother to the fetus.

transexual: (*adjective,* **transexual**): a person manifesting the phenomena of transexualism.

transexualism: behaviorally, the act of living and passing in the role of the opposite sex, before or after having attained hormonal, surgical, and legal sex reassignment; psychically, the condition of people who have the conviction that they belong to the opposite sex and are driven by a compulsion to have the body, appearance, and social status of the opposite sex.

transpositions, gender-identity/role: the interchange of masculine and feminine expectancies and sterotypes in behavior and appearance; see categories in Table 5–3 of text.

transsexual: transexual.

transvestism (*adjective,* **transvestic, transvestitic**): behaviorally, the act of dressing in the clothes of the opposite sex; psychically, the condition of feeling compelled to cross-dress, often in relation to sexual arousal and attainment of orgasm.

transvestite: a person episodically affected with a compulsion to dress as a member of the other sex. In men, the compulsion is commonly essential to the maintenance of erection and achievement of orgasm. It usually is life-long. Rarely, a transvestite may change into a transexual.

troilism (*adjective,* **troilistic**): the condition in which a person is dependent on being the third member of a sexual partnership, or on fantasying being so, in order to obtain erotic arousal and facilitate or achieve orgasm. Typically, a husband arranges that his wife has another male partner, so that he can fantasy her in the role of a whore, without which he cannot become aroused.

TSR: an acronym from the words Testosterone Sterilized (female) Rat. A TSR manifests the persistent estrus syndrome. Lacking ovulatory estrous cycles, she is sterile. The condition is induced experimentally by injections of testosterone prior to the age of eleven days. The first five days of life are the most sensitive or critical ones. Smaller doses are then effective. The effect is life-long.

Turner's syndrome: a condition marked by a chromosomal anomaly in phenotypic females with the chief pathognomonic symptoms of absence of ovaries (gonadal agenesis or dysgenesis) and short stature. The basic genetic defect is a missing sex chromosome, so that the total count is 45,X. There are several variants of this syndrome. For example, in some cases, the second X may, though present, be partially deleted. In others, the so-called mosaics, some cells of the body are 45,X, and some 46,XX. Treatment includes administration of female sex hormone at the age of puberty to induce adult appearance and menstruation. Girls with Turner's syndrome are almost invariably sterile.

ultraertia: in erotic/sexual usage ultraertia is an excess of either intensity or multiplicity of responsiveness or arousal at the proceptive phase. It may or may not continue into the acceptive phase. It is experienced subjectively as strength, urgency, or incessancy of desire or drive. Manifested as girl-watching, it is an obligatory component of the macho stereotype. *Antonym,* **inertia.**

undinism (*adjective,* **undinist**): urophilia; derived from undine (*German*) or ondine (*French*), a fabled female water spirit; *see* **urophilia.**

urethra: the canal through which urine is discharged, extending from the neck of the urinary bladder to the external opening or meatus.

urophilia (*adjective,* **urophilic**): the condition of being responsive to or dependent on the smell or taste of urine, or the sight and sound of someone urinating, in order to obtain erotic arousal and facilitate or achieve orgasm; *see* **undinism.**

vagina: in the female, the canal that opens into the vulva and, internally, connects with the cervix or mouth of the womb. It encloses the penis in sexual intercourse.

vaginal dryness: in women, insufficient lubrication of the vagina, or its premature loss of lubrication, during the proceptive or the acceptive phase of an erotic/sexual episode.

vaginismus: recurrent premature contraction of the musculature of the vagina before or at the acceptive phase of an erotic/sexual episode, so that it is too tight and too dry to receive the penis.

voyeurism (*noun,* **voyeur**): the condition of being responsive to, or dependent on, the risk of being apprehended while illicitly peering at an individual (usually female) or a couple undressing or engaged in sexual activity, in order to obtain one's erotic arousal and facilitate or achieve orgasm. A voyeur is also known as a peeping Tom. The actual event may be replayed in a masturbation or coital fantasy.

vulva (*adjective,* **vulvar**): the external female genitalia; *see also* **vagina.**

wet dream: a dream with erotic/sexual content that ends in sexual orgasm and occurs with greatest frequency in pubertal and adolescent boys. In some instances, the content of the dream is lost, and the ejaculate is the sole sign of the occurrence.

wolffian ducts: the embryonic structures that develop into the internal reproductive anatomy of the male, attached to the testicles; named for Kaspar F. Wolff, German embryologist (1733–94); *see also* **mullerian ducts.**

zoophilia (*adjective,* **zoophilic**): the condition of being responsive to, or depending on, sexual activity with an animal in order to obtain erotic arousal and facilitate orgasm; also known as bestiality. Sexual contact (oral or genital) with an animal may occur sporadically in the course of human development without leading to long-term zoophilia. *Synonym;* **bestiality.**

Sources by Chapter

Chapter 1
Harris, G. W., 1964
Jørgensen, C. B., 1971
Jost, A., 1972, 1974
Keller, K., and Tandler, J., 1916
Lillie, F. R., 1916, 1917
McClung, C. E., 1902
Money, J., 1968, 1979
Ohno, S., 1978
Price, D., 1972
Wachtel, S. S., 1978
Young, W. C., 1961

Chapter 2
Averill, J. R., 1976
Money, J., 1955, 1957, 1973, 1975

Chapter 3
Abramovich, D. R., and Rowe, P., 1973
Dan, A. J., 1976
Dantchakoff, V., 1938
Ehrhardt, A. A., 1978
Forest, M. G., et al. 1973, 1974
Frank, R. T., 1931
Goldfoot, D. A., 1977
Gorski, R. A., 1973
Goy, R. W., and Resko, J. A., 1972
Goy, R. W., et al. 1974
Grumbach, M. M., et al. 1974
Harris, G. W., 1964
Marx, J. L., 1979
May, R. R., 1976
Meyer-Bahlburg, H. F. L., 1978
Money, J., 1970, 1975, 1977, 1979
Money, J., and Ehrhardt, A. A., 1972

Money, J., and Mazur, T., 1977
Money, J., and Ogunro, C., 1974
O'Connor, J. F., et al. 1974
Phoenix, C. H., 1974
Reinisch, J. M., and Karow, W. G., 1977
Root, A. W., 1973
Rossi, A. S., and Rossi, P. E., 1977
Tanner, J. M., 1975
Visser, H. K. A., 1973
Young, W. C., 1961

Chapter 4
Beach, F. A., 1976, 1977
Calderone, M. S., 1967, 1973
Calhoun, A. W., 1960
Christhilf, S. M., 1977
Ford, C. S., and Beach, F. A., 1951
Freud, S., 1953
Galenson, E., 1975
Goldfoot, D. A., 1977
Halverson, H. M., 1940
Hertoft, P., 1977
Kinsey, A. C., et al., 1953
Marshall, D. S., and Suggs, R. C., 1971
Martinson, F., 1973
Michael, R. P., and Zumpe, D., 1978
Miller, H. L., and Siegel, P. S., 1972
Money, J., 1965
Money, J., and Clopper, R. R., Jr., 1975
Money, K. E., 1978
Murstein, B. I., 1971, 1974
Myers, L., and Leggitt, H., 1975
Phoenix, C. H., 1973
Shepher, J., 1971
Sherwin, R. V., 1969

Sutton-Smith, B., and Abrams, D. M., 1978
Tennov, D., 1979
Wikman, K. R. V., 1937

Chapter 5
Baum, M. J., et al. 1977
Beach, F. A., 1976
Benjamin, H., 1966
Commission on Obscenity and Pornography, 1970
Gessa, G. L., et al. 1978
Goodwin, M., et al. 1979
Green, R., and Money, J., 1969
Kaplan, H. S., 1974
Kinsey, A. C., et al. 1948, 1953
Laschet, U., 1973
MacLean, P. D., 1973
Masters, W. H., and Johnson, V. E., 1966, 1970
Money, J., 1970
Money, J., and Athanasiou, R., 1973
Money, J., et al. 1976
Nadler, R. D., 1977
Nickerson, M., et al. 1979
Phoenix, C. H., 1974
Richards, R. N., 1974
Rosenzweig, S., 1973
Roth vs. United States, 1957
Schwarz, G. A., 1967
Segraves, R. T., 1977
Shorey, H. H., 1976
Story, N. L., 1974

Chapter 6
Barlow, D. H., et al. 1974
Baum, M. J., et al. 1977
Benedek, T., and Rubenstein, B. B., 1939a, 1939b
Birk, L. et al. 1973
Brecher, E., 1969
Brodie, H. K. H., et al. 1974
Bulbrook, R. D., et al. 1973
Bullough, V. L., 1976
Coppen, A., and Kessel, N., 1963
Cullberg, J., 1972
Dalton, K., 1959, 1964
Davis, K. B., 1929
Dickinson, R. L., 1949
Doerr, P., et al. 1973, 1976
Dörner, G., 1976

Dörner, G., et al. 1975
Eisdorfer, C., and Raskind, M., 1975
Ellis, H., 1944, undated
Evans, R. B., 1972
Frölich, M., et al. 1976
Glass, G. S., et al. 1971
Gottschalk, L. A., et al. 1962
Griffiths, P. D., et al. 1974
Hamburg, D. A., et al. 1968
Hart, R. A., 1960
Hartman, M. S., 1977
Henderson, M. E., 1976
Hoenig, J., 1977
Hopson, J. L., 1979
Ivey, M. E., and Bardwick, J. M., 1968
James, W. H., 1971, 1971
Janiger, O., et al. 1972
Janowsky, D. S., et al. 1969
Kane, F. J., et al. 1967, 1969
Kinsey, A. C., et al. 1948, 1953
Kolodny, R. C., et al. 1971, 1972
Krafft-Ebing, R. von, 1969
Lamb, W. M., et al. 1953
Loraine, J. A., et al. 1971, 1970
Luschen, M. E., and Pierce, D. M., 1972
MacKinnon, I. L., et al. 1959
MacLean, P. D., 1973
Mandell, A. J., and Mandell, M. P., 1967
Marañón, G., 1929
Margolese, M. S., 1970
Markowitz, H., and Brender, W., 1977
Martin, C. E., 1975, 1977
Masters, W. H., and Johnson, V. E., 1966, 1970
May, R. R., 1976
McCance, R. A., et al. 1937
McCauley, E., and Ehrhardt, A. A., 1976
McClintock, M. K., 1971
Meyer-Bahlburg, H. F. L., 1977, 1979
Michael, R. P., 1972
Moll, A., 1912
Money, J., 1970
Moos, R. H., 1968
Moos, R. H., et al. 1969
Morris, N. M., and Udry, J. R., 1978
Morton, J. H., et al. 1953
O'Connor, J. F., et al. 1974
Parks, G. A., et al. 1974
Persky, H., et al. 1977, 1978
Pfeiffer, E., et al. 1968, 1969
Pillard, R. C., et al. 1974

Robbins, M. B., and Jensen, G. D., 1978
Rose, R. M., 1972
Rossi, A. S., and Rossi, P. E., 1977
Seyler, L. E., Jr., et al. 1978
Shainess, N., 1961
Smith, S. L., and Sauder, C., 1969
Spitz, C. J., et al. 1975
Stenn, P. G., and Klinge, V., 1972
Taylor, G. R., 1970
Tissot, S-A., 1781
Tourney, G., et al. 1975
Udry, J. R., and Morris, N. M., 1968,
   1970
Udry, J. R., et al. 1973
Vermeulen, A., et al. 1972
Verwoerdt, A., et al. 1969, 1969
Wetzel, R. D., et al. 1971
Zelnik, M., and Kantner, J. F., 1977

Chapter 7
Burns, R. K., 1961
Chan, S. T. H., 1970
Christhilf, S. M., 1977
Clopper, R. R., Jr., et al. 1976
Goffman, E., 1976
Gowen, J. W., 1961
Green, R., and Money, J., 1960
Hosken, F. P., 1978
Jones, H. W., Jr., and Scott, W. W., 1971
Key, M. R., 1975
Money, J., 1968, 1979
Money, J., and Clopper, R. R., Jr., 1975
Money, J., and Ehrhardt, A. A., 1972
Money, J., and Russo, A. J., 1979
Richards, M. P. M., et al. 1976
Ringler, N. M., et al. 1975
Robertson, D. R., 1972, 1973
Schlegel, R. J., and Gardner, L. I., 1975
Tanner, J. M., 1962
Thoman, E. B., and Gaulin-Kremer, E.,
   1977
Van Wyk, J. J., and Grumbach, M. M.,
   1974
Waxman, S., 1976

Chapter 8
Baum, M. J., et al. 1977
Broverman, D. M., et al. 1980
Durkin, J. J., 1971, 1980
Ehrhardt, A. A., and Baker, S. W., 1974
Meyer-Bahlburg, H. F. L., et al. 1974

Money, J., 1961
Money, J., and Ehrhardt, A. A., 1972
Money J., and Schwartz., 1976
Money, J., et al. 1974
Murken, J-D., 1973
Rose, R. M., 1975
Shorey, H. H., 1976
Shuster, R. H., 1976
Willson, J. R., et al. 1971
Wolfgang, M. E., 1961

Chapter 9
Aveling, J. H., 1977
Bradley, R. A., 1974
Dick-Read, G., 1970
Lamaze, F., 1958
Leboyer, F., 1975
Mitchell, G., 1977
Money, J., 1977
Money, J., and Hosta, G., 1968
Neumann, F., 1971–72
Rosenblatt, J. S., 1977
Trause, M. A., et al. 1977
Vellay, P., 1960
Williams, G., and Money, J., 1980

Chapter 10
Broverman, D. M., et al. 1980
Durkin, J. J., 1971, 1980
Ernest, J., 1976
Everett, H. C., 1964
Hardy, K. R., 1974
Hughes, R., 1977
Koranyi, L., and Lissak, K., 1974
Koranyi, L., et al. 1976
Lambert, H. H., 1978
Maccoby, E. E., and Jacklin, C. N., 1974
Money, J., 1962, 1966, 1968
Money, J., et al. 1955

Chapter 11
Beach, F. A., 1948
Benjamin, H., 1944, 1945
Bleuler, M., 1954
Brooks, C. McC., et al. 1948
de Wied, D., et al. 1976
Donovan, B. T., 1978
Gardner, L. I., 1975
Guillemin, R., 1978
Harlow, H. F., and Harlow, M. K., 1962
Harris, G. W., 1964

Jørgensen, C. B., 1971
Martini, L., and Besser, G. M., 1977
Money, J., 1970, 1977
Money, J., and Ogunro, C., 1974
Money, J., et al. 1978
Ohno, S., 1978
Olmsted, J. M. D., 1946
Pfeiffer, C. A., 1936
Sandler, M., and Gessa, G. L., 1975
Sara, V. R., et al. 1974
Schally, A. V., 1978
Schally, A. V., and Arimura, A., 1977
Silvers, W. K., and Wachtel, S. S., 1977
Snyder, S. H., 1974, 1976

Stone, C. P., 1939
Suomi, S. J., 1976
Vogel, W., et al. 1979
Wachtel, S. S., 1978
Yalow, R. S., 1978
Young, W. C., 1961

Chapter 12
Commission on Obscenity and
    Pornography, 1970
Gibson, E. L., 1978
Miller vs. California, 1973
Roth vs. United States, 1957
Sexual Law Reporter, 1978

Bibliography

Abramovich, D. R., and Rowe, P. Foetal plasma testosterone levels at mid-pregnancy and at term: relationship to foetal sex. *Journal of Endocrinology* 56:621–622, 1973.

Aveling J. H. *The Chamberlens and the Midwifery Forceps.* London, J. and A. Churchill, 1882 and 1977.

Averill, J. R. *Patterns of Psychological Thought.* Washington, Hemisphere, 1976.

Barlow, D. H., Abel, G. G., Blanchard, E. B., and Maviffakalian, M. Plasma testosterone levels and male homosexuality: a failure to replicate. *Archives of Sexual Behavior* 3:571–575, 1974.

Baron, R. A. *Human Aggression.* New York, Plenum, 1977.

Baum, M. J., Everitt, B. J., Herbert, J., and Keverne, E. B. Hormonal basis of proceptivity and receptivity in female primates. *Archives of Sexual Behavior* 6:173–192, 1977.

Beach, F. A. *Hormones and Behavior: A Survey of Interrelationships between Endocrine Secretion and Patterns of Overt Response.* New York, Hoeber, 1948.

Beach, F. A. Cross-species comparisons and the human heritage. *Archives of Sexual Behavior* 5:469–485, 1976.

Beach, F. A. Sexual attractivity, proceptivity, and receptivity in female mammals. *Hormones and Behavior* 7:105–138, 1976.

Beach, F. A. *Human Sexuality in Four Perspectives.* Baltimore, Johns Hopkins University Press, 1977.

Benedek, T., and Rubenstein, B. B. The correlations between ovarian activity and psychodynamic processes: I. The ovulative phase. *Psychosomatic Medicine* 1:245–270, 1939a.

Benedek, T., and Rubenstein, B. B. The correlations between ovarian activity and psychodynamic processes: II. The menstrual phase. *Psychosomatic Medicine* 1:461–485, 1939b.

Benjamin, H. Eugen Steinach—a tribute. *Proceedings of the Rudolph Virchow Medical Society* 3:88–92, 1944.

Benjamin, H. Eugen Steinach, 1861–1944: a life of research. *Scientific Monthly* 61:427–442, 1945.

Benjamin, H. *The Transexual Phenomenon.* New York, Julian Press, 1966.

Birk, L., Williams, E. H., Chasin, M., and Rose, L. I. Serum testosterone levels in homosexual men. *New England Journal of Medicine* 289:1236–1238, 1973.

Bleuler, M. *Endokrinologische Psychiatrie.* Stuttgart, Georg Thieme Verlag, 1954.

Bradley, R. A. *Husband-Coached Childbirth.* New York, Harper and Row, 1974.

Brecher, E., *The Sex Researchers.* Boston, Little, Brown, 1969.

Brodie, H. K. H., Gartrell, N., Doering, C., and Rhue, T. Plasma testosterone levels in heterosexual and homosexual men. *American Journal of Psychiatry* 131:82–83, 1974.

Brooks, C. McC., Gilbert, J. L., Levey, H. A., and Curtis, D. R. *Humors, Hormones, and Neurosecretions.* New York, State University of New York, 1948.

Broverman, D. M., Klaiber, E. L., and Vogel, W. Gonadal hormones and cognitive functioning. In *The Psychobiology of Sex Differences and Sex Roles* (J. Parsons, ed.). Washington, D.C., Hemisphere, 1980. In press.

Bulbrook, R. D., Hayward, J. C., Herian, M., Swain, H. C., Tong, D., and Wang, D. Y. Effects of steroidal contraceptives on levels of plasma androgens, sulphates and cortisol. *Lancet* 1:628–631, 1973.

Bullough, V. L. *Sexual Variance in Society and History.* New York, Wiley, 1976.

Burns, R. K. Role of hormones in the differentiation of sex. In *Sex and Internal Secretions.* 3rd ed., vol. 1 (W. C. Young, ed.). Baltimore, Williams and Wilkins, 1961.

Calderone, M. S. Sex, religion, and mental health. *Journal of Religion and Health* 6:195–203, 1967.

Calderone, M. S. *Human Sexuality and the Quaker Conscience: 1973 Rufus Jones Lecture.* Philadelphia, Friends General Conference (1520 Race Street, 1912), 1973.

Calderone, M. S. Historical perspectives on the human sexuality movement: hindsights, insights, foresights. In *Sex Education for the Health Professional: A Curriculum Guide* (N. Rosenzweig and F. P. Pearsall, eds.). New York, Grune and Stratton, 1978.

Calhoun, A. W. *A Social History of the American Family from Colonial Times to the Present.* New York, Barnes and Noble, 1960.

Chan, S. T. H. Natural sex reversal in vertebrates. *Philosophical Transactions Royal Society London* B.259:59–71, 1970.

Christhilf, S. M. Health care. In *Anne Arundel County, Maryland: A Bicentennial History, 1649–1977* (J. C. Bradford, ed.). Annapolis, Anne Arundel Co. Bicentennial Committee (St. Johns College), 1977.

Clopper, R. R., Jr., Adelson, J. M., and Money, J. Postpubertal psychosexual function in male hypopituitarism without hypogonadotropinism after growth hormone therapy. *Journal of Sex Research* 12:14–32, 1976.

Comfort, A. (ed.). *The Joy of Sex.* New York, Crown Publishers, 1972.

Comfort, A. (ed.). *More Joy.* New York, Crown Publishers, 1974.

Commission on Obscenity and Pornography. *Report of the Commission on Obscenity and Pornography* and *Technical Report of the Commission on Obscenity and Pornography.* vols. 1–9. Washington, D. C., U. S. Government Printing Office, 1970.

Coppen, A., and Kessel, N. Menstruation and personality. *British Journal of Psychiatry* 109:711–721, 1963.

Cullberg, J. Mood changes and menstrual symptoms with different gestagen/estrogen combinations: a double blind comparison with a placebo. *Acta Psychiatrica Scandinavica, Supplementum 236.* Copenhagen, Munksgaard, 1972.

Dalton, K. Menstruation and acute psychiatric illness. *British Medical Journal* 1:148–149, 1959.

Dalton, K. *The Premenstrual Syndrome.* Springfield, Ill., Charles C Thomas, 1964.

Dan, A. J. Behavioral variability and the menstrual cycle. Type-script, American Psychological Association Annual Convention, Washington, D.C., 1976.

Dantchakoff, V. Sur les effets de l'hormone male dans une jeune cobaye femelle traité depuis un stade embryonnaire (inversions sexuelles). *Comptes rendues de la Societé Biologique* 127:1255–1258, 1938.

Davis, K. B. *Factors in the Sex Life of 2,200 Women.* New York, Harper and Row, 1929.

de Wied, D., Bohus, B., Gispen, W. H., Urban, I., and van Wimersma Greidanus, Tj. B. Hormonal influences on motivational, learning, and memory processes. In *Hormones, Behavior and Psychopathology* (E. J. Sachar, ed.). New York, Raven Press, 1976.

Dickinson, R. L. *Human Sexual Anatomy.* 2nd ed. Baltimore, Williams and Wilkins, 1949.

Dick-Read,G.*Childbirth without Fear: The Principles and Practice of Natural Childbirth.* 2nd rev. ed., paperback. New York, Harper and Row, 1970.

Doerr, P., Kockott, G., Vogt, H. J., Pirke, K. M., and Dittmar, F. Plasma testosterone, estradiol, and semen analysis in male homosexuals. *Archives of General Psychiatry* 29:829–833, 1973.

Doerr, P., Pirke, K. M., Kockott, G., and Dittmar, F. Further studies on sex hormones in the male homosexual. *Archives of General Psychiatry* 33:611–614, 1976.

Donovan, B. T. The behavioural actions of the hypothalamic peptides: a review. *Psychological Medicine* 8:305–316, 1978.

Dörner, G. *Hormones and Brain Differentiation.* New York, Elsevier, 1976.

Dörner, G., Rohde, W., Stahl, F., Krell, L., and Masius, W. -G. A neuroendocrine predisposition for homosexuality in men. *Archives of Sexual Behavior* 4:1–8, 1975.

Durkin, J. J. The potential of women. *Bulletin #87*, The Johnson O'Connor Research Foundation, Washington, D.C., 1971 (4 pp. typescript).

Durkin, J. J. Male and female differences and similarities in aptitude testing. In *Medical Sexology: The Published Proceedings of the Third International Congress, Rome, 1978* (R. Forleo and W. Pasini, eds.). Littleton, Mass., PSG Publishing Co., 1980.

Ehrhardt, A. A. Behavioral effects of estrogen in the human female. *Pediatrics* 62 (Supplement):1166–1170, 1978.

Ehrhardt, A. A., and Baker, S. W. Fetal androgens, human central nervous system differentiation, and behavior sex differences. In *Sex Differences in Behavior* (R. C. Friedman, R. M. Richart, and R. L. Vande Wiele, eds.). New York, Wiley, 1974.

Eisdorfer, C., and Raskind, M. Aging, hormones and human behavior. In *Hormonal Correlates of Behavior.* Vol. 1 (B. E. Eleftheriou and R. L. Sprott, eds.). New York, Plenum, 1975.

Ellis, H. *Psychology of Sex.* London, Heinemann, 1944.

Ellis, H. *Studies in the Psychology of Sex.* 2 vols. New York, Random House, undated.

Ernest, J. Mathematics and sex. *American Mathematical Monthly* 83:595–614, 1976.

Evans, R. B. Physical and biochemical characteristics of homosexual men. *Journal of Consulting and Clinical Psychology* 39:140–147, 1972.

Everett, H. C. Sneezing in response to light. *Neurology* 14:483–490, 1964.

Ford, C. S., and Beach, F. A. *Patterns of Sexual Behavior.* New York, Harper and Row, 1951.

Forest, M. G., Cathiard, A. M., and Bertrand, J. A. Evidence of testicular activity in early infancy. *Journal of Clinical Endocrinology and Metabolism* 37:148–150, 1973.

Forest, M. G., Sizonenko, P. C., Cathiard, A. M., and Bertrand, J. Hypophyso-gonadal function in humans during the first year of life: I. Evidence for testicular activity in early infancy. *Journal of Clinical Investigation* 53:819–828, 1974.

Frank, R. T. The hormonal causes of premenstrual tension. *Archives of Neurology and Psychiatry* 26:1053–1057, 1931.

Freud, S. *Three Essays on Sexuality.* Standard ed. vol. VII. London, Hogarth Press, 1953.

Frölich, M., Brand, E. C., and van Hall, E. V. Serum levels of unconjugated aetiocholanolone, androstenedione, testosterone, dihydroepiandrosterone, aldosterone, progesterone and oestrogens during the normal menstrual cycle. *Acta Endocrinologica* 81:548–562, 1976.

Galenson, E. Discussion (Early sexual differences and development, P. B. Neubauer). In *Sexuality and Psychoanalysis* (E. T. Adelson, ed.). New York, Brunner/Mazel, 1975.

Gardner, L. I. (ed.). *Endocrine and Genetic Diseases of Childhood and Adolescence.* 2nd ed. Philadelphia, Saunders, 1975.

Gessa, G. L., Paglietti, E., and Quarantotti, B. P. The role of serotonin, dopamine and enkephalins in the regulation of sexual behavior in male rats. Paper read to the III International Congress of Medical Sexology, Rome, 1978.

Gessa, G. L., Paglietti, E., and Quarantotti, B. P. Induction of copulatory behavior in sexually inactive rats by naloxone. *Science* 204:203–205, 1979.

Gibson, E. L. *Get Off My Ship. Ensign Berg vs. the U. S. Navy.* New York, Avon Books, 1978.

Glass, G. S., Heninger, G. R., Lansky, M., and Talen, K. Psychiatric emergency related to the menstrual cycle. *American Journal of Psychiatry* 128:705–711, 1971.

Goffman, E. *Gender Adverstisements* (Studies in the Anthropology of Visual Communication, vol. 3, #2). Washington, D.C., SAVICOM (1703 New Hampshire Ave., N.W., 20009), 1976.

Goldfoot, D. A. Sociosexual behaviors of nonhuman primates during development and maturity: social and hormonal relationships. In *Behavioral Primatology, Advances in Research and Theory.* Vol. 1 (A. M. Schrier, ed.). Hillsdale, N. J., Lawrence Erlbaum, 1977.

Goldfoot, D. A., and Wallen, K. Development of gender role behaviors in heterosexual and isosexual groups of infant rhesus monkeys. In *Recent Advances in Primatology.* Vol. 1, *Behaviour* (D. J. Chivers and J. Herbert, eds.). London, Academic Press, 1978.

Goodwin, M., Gooding, K. M., and Regnier, F. Sex pheromone in the dog. *Science* 203:559–561, 1979.

Gorski, R. A. Perinatal effects of sex steroids on brain development and function. In *Progress in Brain Research.* Vol. 39 (E. Zimmerman, W. H. Gispen, B. H. Marks, and D. de Weid, eds.). New York, Elsevier, 1973.

Gottschalk, L. A., Kaplan, S. M., Gleser, G. C., and Winget, C. M. Variations in magnitude of emotion: a method applied to anxiety and hostility during phases of the menstrual cycle. *Psychosomatic Medicine* 24:300–311, 1962.

Gowen, J. W. Genetic and cytologic foundations for sex. In *Sex and Internal Secretions.* 3rd ed., vol. 1 (W. C. Young, ed.). Baltimore, Williams and Wilkins, 1961.

Goy, R. W. Development of play and mounting behaviour in female rhesus virilized prenatally with esters of testosterone or dihydrotestosterone. In *Recent Advances in Primatology.* Vol. 1, *Behaviour* (D. J. Chivers and J. Herbert, eds.). London, Academic Press, 1978.

Goy, R. W., and Resko, J. A. Gonadal hormones and behavior of normal and pseudohermaphroditic nonhuman female primates. *Recent Progress in Hormone Research* 38:707–733, 1972.

Goy, R. W., Wallen, K., and Goldfoot, D. A. Social factors affecting the development of mounting behavior in male rhesus monkeys. In *Reproductive Behavior* (W. Montagna and W. A. Sadler, eds.). New York, Plenum, 1974.

Green, R., and Money, J. Incongruous gender role: nongenital manifestations in prepubertal boys. *Journal of Nervous and Mental Disease* 130:160–168, 1960.

Green, R., and Money, J. *Transexualism and Sex Reassignment.* Baltimore, Johns Hopkins Press, 1969.

Griffiths, P. D., Merry, J., Browning, M. C. K., Eisinger, A. J., Huntsman, R. G., Lord, E. J. A., Polani, P. E., Tanner, J. M., and Whitehouse, R. H. Homosexual women: an endocrine and psychological study. *Journal of Endocrinology* 63:549–556, 1974.

Grumbach, M. M., Grave, G. D., and Mayer, F. E. (eds.). *Control of the Onset of Puberty.* New York, Wiley, 1974.

Guillemin, R. Peptides in the brain: The new endocrinology of the neuron. *Science* 202:390–402, 1978.

Halbreich, U., Segal, S., Chowers, I. Day-to-day variations in serum levels of follicle-stimulating hormone and luteinizing hormone in homosexual males. *Biological Psychiatry* 13:541–549, 1978.

Halverson, H. M. Genital and sphincter behavior of the male infant. *Journal of Genetic Psychology* 56:95–136, 1940.

Hamburg, D. A., Moos, R. H., and Yalom, I. D. Studies of distress in the menstrual cycle and the postpartum period. In *Endocrinology and Human Behavior* (R. P. Michael, ed.). New York, Oxford University Press, 1968.

Hardy, K. R. Social origins of American scientists and scholars. *Science* 185:497–506, 1974.

Harlow H. F., and Harlow, M. K. Social deprivation in monkeys. *Scientific American* 473:1–11, 1962.

Harris, G. W. Sex Hormones, brain development and brain function. *Endocrinology* 75:627–648, 1964.

Hart, R. A. Monthly rhythm of libido in married women. *British Medical Journal* 1:1023–1024, 1960.

Hartman, M. S. *Victorian Murderesses.* New York, Schocken, 1977.

Hatcher, R. A., Stewart, G. K., Stewart, F., Guest, F., Stratton, P., and Wright, A. H. *Contraceptive Technology 1978–1979.* 9th rev. ed. New York, Irvington Publishers, 1978.

Henderson, M. E. Evidence for a male menstrual temperature cycle and synchrony with the female menstrual cycle. *New Zealand Medical Journal* 84:164, 1976 (abstract).

Hertoft, P. Nordic traditions of marriage: The betrothal system. In *Handbook of Sexology* (J. Money and H. Musaph, eds.). New York, Excerpta Medica, 1977.

Hoenig, J. Dramatis personae: Selected biographical sketches of 19th century pioneers in sexology. In *Handbook of Sexology* (J. Money and H. Musaph, eds.). New York, Excerpta Medica, 1977.

Hopson, J. L. Scent and human behavior: olfaction or fiction? *Science News* 115:282–283, 1979.

Hosken, F. P. The epidemiology of female genital mutilations. *Tropical Doctor* 8:150–156, 1978.

Hughes, R. Rediscovered—women painters. *Time,* January 10, 1977, pp. 60–63.

Ivey, M. E., and Bardwick, J. M. Patterns of affective fluctuation in the menstrual cycle. *Psychosomatic Medicine* 30:336–345, 1968.

James, W. H. Coital rates and the pill. *Nature* 234:555–556, 1971.

James, W. H. The distribution of coitus within the human intermenstruum. *Journal of Biological Science* 3:159–171, 1971.

Janiger, O., Riffenburgh, R., and Kersh, R. Cross cultural study of premenstrual symptoms. *Psychosomatics* 13:226–235, 1972.

Janowsky, D. S., Gorney, R., Castelnuovo-Tedesco, P., and Stone, C. B. Premenstrual-menstrual increases in psychiatric hospital admission rates. *American Journal of Obstetrics and Gynecology* 103:189–191, 1969.

Johnson, D. F., and Phoenix, C. H. Hormonal control of female sexual attractiveness, proceptivity, and receptivity in rhesus monkeys. *Journal of Comparative and Physiological Psychology* 90:473–483, 1976.

Jones, H. W., Jr., and Scott, W. W. *Hermaphroditism, Genital Anomalies and Related Endocrine Disorders.* 2nd ed. Baltimore, Williams and Wilkins, 1971.

Jørgensen, C. B. *John Hunter, A. A. Berthold, and the Origins of Endocrinology.* Odense, Odense University Press, 1971.

Jost, A. A new look at the mechanisms controlling sex differentiation in mammals. *Johns Hopkins Medical Journal* 130:38–53, 1972.

Jost, A. Mechanisms of normal and abnormal sex differentiation in the fetus. In *Birth Defects and Fetal Development: Endocrine and Metabolic Factors* (K. S. Moghissi, ed.). Springfield, Ill., Charles C Thomas, 1974.

Kane, F. J., Jr., Daly, R. J., Ewing, J. A., and Keeler, M. H. Mood and behavioral changes with progestational agents. *British Journal of Psychiatry* 113:265–268, 1967.

Kane, F. J., Jr., Lipton, M. A., and Ewing, J. A. Hormonal influences in female sexual response. *Archives of General Psychiatry* 20:202–209, 1969.

Kaplan, H. S. *The New Sex Therapy: Active Treatment of Sexual Dysfunctions.* New York, Brunner/Mazel, 1974.

Keller, K., and Tandler, J. Über des Verhalten der Eihäute bei der Zwillingsstrachtigkeit des Rindes. Untersuchungen über die Enstehungsursache der geschlechtlichen Unterentwicklung von weiblichen Zwillingskälbern, welche neben einem männlichen Kalbe zur Entwicklung gelangen. *Wien Tierärztl. Wehnschr.* 3:513, 1916.

Key, M. R. *Male/Female Language.* Metuchen, N. J., Scarecrow Press, 1975.

Kinsey, A. C., Pomeroy, W. B., and Martin, C. E. *Sexual Behavior in the Human Male.* Philadephia, Saunders, 1948.

Kinsey, A. C., Pomeroy, W. B., Martin C. E., and Gebhard, P. H. *Sexual Behavior in the Human Female.* Philadelphia, Saunders, 1953.

Kolodny, R. C., Jacobs, L. S., Masters, W. H., Toro, G., and Daughaday, W. H. Plasma gonadotrophins and prolactin in male homosexuals. *Lancet* 2:18-20, 1972.

Kolodny, R. C., Masters, W. H., Hendryx, J., and Toro, G. Plasma testosterone and semen analysis in male homosexuals. *New England Journal of Medicine* 285:1170-1174, 1971.

Koranyi, L., and Lissak, K. Multiple units and responsiveness to sensory stimuli during maternal behavior. *Pavlovian Journal of Biological Science* 9:178, 1974 (abstract).

Koranyi, L., Lissak, K., Tamasy, V., and Kamaras, L. Behavioral and electrophysiological attempts to elucidate central nervous system mechanisms responsible for maternal behavior. *Archives of Sexual Behavior* 5:503-510, 1976.

Krafft-Ebing, R. von. *Psychopathia Sexualis.* Paperback (DM 4374). New York, Bantam Books, 1969.

Lamaze, F. *Painless Childbirth: Psychoprophylactic Method.* London, Burke, 1958.

Lamb, W. M., Ulett, G. A., Masters, W. H., and Robinson, D. W. Premenstrual tension: EEG, hormonal and psychiatric evaluation. *American Journal of Psychiatry* 109:840-848, 1953.

Lambert, H. H. Biology and equality: a perspective on sex differences. *Signs: Journal of Women in Culture and Society* 4:97-117, 1978.

Laschet, U. Antiandrogen in the treatment of sex offenders: mode of action and therapeutic outcome. In *Contemporary Sexual Behavior: Critical Issues in the 1970s* (J. Zubin and J. Money, eds.). Baltimore, Johns Hopkins University Press, 1973.

Leboyer, F. *Birth without Violence.* New York, Knopf, 1975.

Levi, L. *Society, Stress, and Disease.* Vol. 3, *The Productive and Reproductive Age—Male/Female Roles and Relationships.* New York, Oxford University Press, 1978.

Lillie, F. R. The theory of the freemartin. *Science* 43:611-613, 1916.

Lillie, F. R. The freemartin: a study of the action of sex hormones in the fetal life of cattle. *Journal of Experimental Zoology* 23:371-452, 1917.

Llewellyn-Jones, D. *Everywoman: A Gynecological Guide for Life.* 2nd ed., paperback. London and Boston, Faber and Faber, 1978.

Loraine, J. A., Adamopoulos, D. A., Kirkham, K. E., Ismail, A. A. A., and Dove, G. A. Patterns of hormone excretion in male and female homosexuals. *Nature* 234:552-555, 1971.

Loraine, J. A., Ismail, A. A. A., Adamopoulos, D. A., and Dove, G. A. Endocrine function in male and female homosexuals. *British Medical Journal* 4:406-408, 1970.

Luschen, M. E., and Pierce, D. M. Effect of the menstrual cycle on mood and sexual arousability. *Journal of Sex Research* 8:41-47, 1972.

Maccoby, E. L., and Jacklin, C. N. *The Psychology of Sex Differences.* Stanford, Stanford University Press, 1974.

MacKinnon, I. L., MacKinnon, P. C. B., and Thomsen, A. D. Lethal hazards of the luteal phase of the menstrual cycle. *British Medical Journal* 1:1015-1017, 1959.

MacLean, P. D. *A Triune Concept of the Brain and Behavior: The Clarence M. Hincks Memorial Lectures.* Toronto, Toronto Universiy Press, 1973.

Malinowksi, B. *The Sexual Life of Savages in North-Western Melanesia.* New York, Halcyon House, 1929.

Mandell, A. J., and Mandell, M. P. Suicide and the menstrual cycle. *Journal of the American Medical Association* 200:792-793, 1967.

Marañón, G. *The Climacteric.* St. Louis, Mosby, 1929.

Margolese, M. S. Homosexuality: a new endocrine correlate. *Hormones and Behavior* 1:151-155, 1970.

Markowitz, H., and Brender, W. Patterns of sexual responsiveness during the menstrual cycle. In *Progress in Sexology: Selected Papers from the Proceedings of the 1976 International Congress of Sexology* (R. Gemme and C. C. Wheeler, eds.). New York, Plenum, 1977.

Marshall, D. S., and Suggs, R. C. (eds.). *Human Sexual Behavior—Variations in the Ethnographic Spectrum.* New York, Basic Books, 1971.

Martin, C. E. Marital and sexual factors in relation to age, disease, and longevity. In *Life History Research in Psychopathology.* Vol. 4 (R. D. Wirt, G. Winokur, and M. Roff, eds.). Minneapolis, University of Minnesota Press, 1975.

Martin, C. E. Sexual activity in the ageing male. In *Handbook of Sexology* (J. Money and H. Musaph, eds.). New York, Excerpta Medica, 1977.

Martini, L., and Besser, G. M. (eds.). *Clinical Neuroendocrinology.* New York, Academic Press, 1977.

Martinson, F. *Infant and Child Sexuality: A Sociological Perspective.* St. Peter, Minn., Gustavus Adolphus College, 1973.

Marx, J. L. Dysmenorrhea: basic research leads to a rational therapy. *Science* 205:175-176, 1979.

Masters, W. H., and Johnson, V. E. *Human Sexual Response.* Boston, Little, Brown, 1966.

Masters, W. H., and Johnson, V. E. *Human Sexual Inadequacy.* Boston, Little, Brown, 1970.

May, R. R. Mood shifts and the menstrual cycle. *Journal of Psychosomatic Research* 20:125-30, 1976.

McCance, R. A., Luff, W. L. and Widdowson, E. E. Physical and emotional periodicity in women. *Journal of Hygiene* 37:571-611, 1937.

McCauley, E., and Ehrhardt, A. A. Female sexual response: hormonal and behavioral interactions. *Primary Care* 3:455-476, 1976.

McClintock, M. K. Menstrual synchrony and suppression. *Nature* 229:244-245, 1971.

McClung, C. E. The accessory chromosome—sex determinant? *Biological Bulletin* 3:43-84, 1902.

Meyer-Bahlburg, H. F. L. Sex hormones and male homosexuality in comparative perspective. *Archives of Sexual Behavior* 6:297-325, 1977.

Meyer-Bahlburg, H. F. L. Behavioral effects of estrogen treatment in human males. *Pediatrics* 62 (Supplement):1171-1177, 1978.

Meyer-Bahlburg, H. F. L. Sex hormones and female homosexuality: a documentation. *Archives of Sexual Behavior* 8:101-119, 1979.

Meyer-Bahlburg, H. F. L., Boon, D. A., Sharma, M., and Edwards, J. A. Aggressiveness and testosterone measures in man. *Psychosomatic Medicine* 36:269-274, 1974.

Michael, R. P. Determinants of primate reproductive behavior. *Acta Endocrinologica, Supplementum* 166:322-361, 1972.

Michael, R. P., and Zumpe, D. Potency in male rhesus monkeys: effects of continuously receptive females. *Science* 200:451-453, 1978.

Miller vs. California. 413 U.S. 15(1973).

Miller, H. L., and Siegel, P. S. *Loving: A Psychological Approach.* New York, Wiley, 1972.

Mitchell, G. Parental behavior in nonhuman primates. In *Handbook of Sexology* (J. Money and H. Musaph, eds.). New York, Excerpta Medica, 1977.

Moll, A. *The Sexual Life of the Child.* New York, Macmillan, 1912.

Money, J. Linguistic resources and psychodynamic theory. *British Journal of Medical Psychology* 28:264-266, 1955.

Money, J. *The Psychologic Study of Man.* Springfield, Ill., Charles C Thomas, 1957.

Money J. Phantom orgasm in the dreams of paraplegic men and women. *Archives of General Psychiatry* 3:373–382, 1960.

Money, J. Sex hormones and other variables in human eroticism. In *Sex and Internal Secretions.* 3rd ed., vol. 2 (W. C. Young, ed.). Baltimore, Williams and Wilkins, 1961.

Money, J. (ed.). *Reading Disability: Progress and Research Needs in Dyslexia.* Baltimore, Johns Hopkins Press, 1962.

Money, J. Negro illegitimacy: an antebellum legacy in obstetrical sociology. *Pacific Medicine and Surgery* 73:349–352, 1965.

Money, J. (ed.). *The Disabled Reader: Education of the Dyslexic Child.* Baltimore, Johns Hopkins Press, 1966.

Money, J. *Sex Errors of the Body: Dilemmas, Education, Counseling.* Baltimore, Johns Hopkins Press, 1968.

Money, J. Matched pairs of hermaphrodites: behavioral biology of sexual differentiation from chromosomes to gender identity. *Engineering and Science* (California Institute of Technology) 33:34–39, 1970.

Money, J. Sexual dimorphism and homosexual gender identity. *Psychological Bulletin* 74:425–440, 1970.

Money, J. Use of an androgen-depleting hormone in the treatment of male sex offenders. *Journal of Sex Research* 6:165–172, 1970.

Money, J. Gender role, gender identity, core gender identity: usage and definition of terms. *Journal American Academy of Psychoanalysis* 1:397–403, 1973.

Money, J. Nativism versus culturalism in gender-identity differentiation. In *Sexuality and Psychoanalysis* (E. Adelson, ed.). New York, Brunner/Mazel, 1975.

Money, J. Psychologic counseling: hermaphroditism. In *Endocrine and Genetic Diseases of Childhood.* 2nd ed. (L. I. Gardner, ed.). Philadelphia, Saunders, 1975.

Money, J. The syndrome of abuse dwarfism (psychosocial dwarfism or reversible hyposomatotropinism). *American Journal of Diseases of Children* 131:508–513, 1977.

Money, J. Hermaphroditism and pseudohermaphroditism. In *Gynecologic Endocrinology.* 3rd. ed. (J. J. Gold and J. B. Josimovich, eds.). Hagerstown, Md., Harper and Row, 1980.

Money, J., Annecillo, C., Van Orman, B., and Borgaonkar, D. S. Cytogenetics, hormones and behavior disability: comparison of XYY and XXY syndromes. *Clinical Genetics* 6:370–382, 1974.

Money, J., and Athenasiou, R. Pornography: review and bibliographic annotations. *American Journal of Obstetrics and Gynecology* 115:130–146, 1973.

Money, J., Clarke, F. C., and Beck, J. Congenital hypothyroidism and IQ increase: a quarter century follow-up. *Journal of Pediatrics* 93:432–434, 1978.

Money, J., and Clopper, R. R., Jr. Postpubertal psychosexual function in postsurgical male hypopituitarism. *Journal of Sex Research* 11:25–38, 1975.

Money, J., and Ehrhardt, A. A. *Man and Woman, Boy and Girl: The Differentiation and Dimorphism of Gender Identity from Conception to Maturity.* Baltimore, Johns Hopkins University Press, 1972.

Money, J., Hampson, J. G., and Hampson, J. L. An examination of some basic sexual concepts: the evidence of human hermaphroditism. *Bulletin of the Johns Hopkins Hospital* 97:301–319, 1955.

Money, J., and Hosta, G. Negro folklore of male pregnancy. *Journal of Sex Research* 4:34–50, 1968.

Money, J., and Mazur, T. Endocrine abnormalities and sexual behavior in man. In *Handbook of Sexology* (J. Money and H. Musaph, eds.). New York, Excerpta Medica, 1977.

Money, J., and Musaph, H. (eds.). *Handbook of Sexology.* New York, Excerpta Medica, 1977.

Money, J., and Musaph, H. (eds.). *Handbook of Sexology.* 5 vols., paperback. New York, Elsevier, 1978.

Money, J., and Ogunro, C. Behavioral sexology: ten cases of genetic male intersexuality with impaired prenatal and pubertal androgenization. *Archives of Sexual Behavior* 3:181-205, 1974.

Money, J., and Russo, A. J. Homosexual outcome of discordant gender identity/role in childhood: longitudinal follow-up. *Journal of Pediatric Psychology* 4:29-41, 1979.

Money, J., and Schwartz, M. Fetal androgens in the early treated adrenogenital syndrome of 46,XX hermaphroditism: influence on assertive and aggressive types of behavior. *Aggressive Behavior* 2:19-30, 1976.

Money, J., and Tucker, P. *Sexual Signatures: On Being a Man or a Woman.* Boston, Little, Brown, 1975.

Money, J., Wiedeking, C., Walker, P., and Gain, D. Combined antiandrogenic and counseling program for the treatment of 46,XY and 47,XYY sex offenders. In *Hormones, Behavior and Psychopathology* (E. J. Sachar, ed.). New York, Raven Press, 1976.

Money, J., and Wolff, G. Late puberty, retarded growth and reversible hyposomatotropinism (psychosocial dwarfism). *Adolescence* 9:121-134, 1974.

Money, K. E. Physical damage caused by sexual deprivation in girls. *Medical Hypotheses* 4:141-148, 1978.

Moos, R. H. The development of a menstrual distress questionnaire. *Psychosomatic Medicine* 30:853-867, 1968.

Moos, R. H., Kopell, B. S., Melges, F. T., Yalom, I. D., Lunde, D. T., Clayton, R. B., and Hamburg, D. A. Fluctuations in symptoms and moods during the menstrual cycle. *Journal of Psychosomatic Research* 13:37-44, 1969.

Morris, N. M., and Udry, J. R. Pheromonal influences on human sexual behavior: an experimental search. *Journal of Biosocial Sciences* 10:147-157, 1978.

Morton, J. H., Additon, H., Addison, R. G., Hunt, L., and Sullivan, J. J. A clinical study of premenstrual tension. *American Journal of Obstetrics and Gynecology* 65:1182-1191, 1953.

Murken, J-D. *The XYY-Syndrome and Klinefelter's Syndrome: Investigations into Epidemiology, Clinical Picture, Psychology, Behavior and Genetics.* Stuttgart, Georg Thieme, 1973.

Murstein, B. I. (ed.). *Theories of Attraction and Love.* New York, Springer, 1971.

Murstein, B. I. *Love, Sex, and Marriage through the Ages.* New York, Springer, 1974.

Myers, L., and Leggitt, H. *Adultery and Other Private Matters.* Chicago, Nelson-Hall, 1975.

Nadler, R. D. Sexual behavior of the chimpanzee in relation to the gorilla and orang-utan. In *Progress in Ape Research* (G. H. Bourne, ed.). New York, Academic Press, 1977.

Neumann, F. Use of cyproterone acetate in animal and clinical trials. *Gynecologic Investigation* 2:150-179, 1971-72.

Nickerson, M., Parker, J. O., Lowry, T. P., and Swenson, E. W. *Isobutyl Nitrite and Related Compounds.* San Francisco, Pharmex, 1979.

O'Connor, J. F., Shelley, E. M., and Stern, L. O. Behavioral rhythms related to the menstrual cycle. In *Biorhythms and Human Reproduction* (M. Ferin, F. Halberg, R. M. Richart, and R. L. Vande Wiele, eds.). New York, Wiley, 1974.

Ohno, S. The role of H-Y antigen in primary sex determination. *Journal of the American Medical Association* 239:217-220, 1978.

Olmsted, J. M. D. *Charles-Édouard Brown-Séquard: A Nineteenth Century Neurologist and Endocrinologist.* Baltimore, Johns Hopkins Press, 1946.

Parks, G. A., Korth-Schutz, S., Penny, R., Hilding, R. F., Dumars, K. W., Frasier, S. D., and New, M. I. Variation in pituitary-gonadal function in adolescent male homosexuals and heterosexuals. *Journal of Clinical Endocrinology and Metabolism* 39:796-801, 1974.

Peele, S., and Brodsky, A. *Love and Addiction.* New York, New American Library, 1976.

Persky, H., Charney, N., Lief, H. I., O'Brien, C. P., Miller, W. R., and Strauss, D. The relationship of plasma estradiol level to sexual behavior in young women. *Psychosomatic Medicine* 40:523-535, 1978.

Persky, H., Lief, H. I., O'Brien, C. P., Strauss, D., and Miller, W. Reproductive hormone levels and sexual behavior of young couples during the menstrual cycle. In *Progress in Sexology: Selected Papers from the Proceedings of the 1976 International Congress of Sexology* (R. Gemme and C. C. Wheeler, eds.). New York, Plenum, 1977.

Pfeiffer, C. A. Sexual differences of the hypophyses and their determination by the gonads. *American Journal of Anatomy* 58:195-226, 1936.

Pfeiffer, E., Verwoerdt, A., and Wang, H. S. Sexual behavior in aged men and women: I. Observations on 254 community volunteers. *Archives of General Psychiatry* 19:753-758, 1968.

Pfeiffer, E., Verwoerdt, A., and Wang, H. S. The natural history of sexual behavior in a biologically advantaged group of aged individuals. *Journal of Gerontology* 24:193-198, 1969.

Phoenix, C. H. Ejaculation by male rhesus as a function of the female partner. *Hormones and Behavior* 4:365-370, 1973.

Phoenix, C. H. Prenatal testosterone in the nonhuman primate and its consequences for behavior. In *Sex Differences in Behavior* (R. C. Friedman, R. M. Richart, and R. L. Vande Wiele, eds.). New York, Wiley, 1974.

Pillard, R. C., Rose, R. M., and Sherwood, M. Plasma testosterone levels in homosexual men. *Archives of Sexual Behavior* 3:453-458, 1974.

Price, D. Mammalian conception, sex differentiation, and hermaphroditism as viewed in historical perspective. *American Zoologist* 12:179-191, 1972.

Reinisch, J. M., and Karow, W. G. Prenatal exposure to synthetic progestins, and estrogen: effects on human behavioral development. *Archives of Sexual Behavior* 6:257-288, 1977.

Richards, M. P. M., Bernal, J. F., and Brackbill, Y. Early behavioral differences: gender or circumcision. *Developmental Psychobiology* 9:89-95, 1976.

Richards, R. N. *Venereal Diseases and Their Avoidance*. New York, Holt, Rinehart and Winston, 1974.

Ringler, N. M., Kennell, J. H., Jarvella, R., Navojosky, B., and Klaus, M. H. Mother-to-child speech at 2 years—effects of early postnatal contact. *Behavioral Pediatrics* 86:141-144, 1975.

Robbins, M. B. and Jensen, G. D. Multiple orgasm in males. *The Journal of Sex Research* 14:21-26, 1978.

Robertson, D. R. Social control of sex reversal in a coral reef fish. *Science* 177:1007-1009, 1972.

Robertson, D. R. Sex change under the waves. *New Scientist*, pp. 538-540, May 31, 1973.

Root, A. W. Endocrinology of puberty: I. Normal sexual maturation. *Journal of Pediatrics* 83:1-19, 1973.

Rose, R. M. The psychological effects of androgens and estrogens. In *Psychiatric Complications of Medical Drugs* (R. I. Shader, ed.). New York, Raven Press, 1972.

Rose, R. M. Testosterone, aggression, and homosexuality: a review of the literature and implications for future research. In *Topics in Psychoendocrinology* (E. J. Sachar, ed.). New York, Grune and Stratton, 1975.

Rosenblatt, J. S. Parental behavior in nonprimate mammals. In *Handbook of Sexology* (J. Money and H. Musaph, eds.). New York, Excerpta Medica, 1977.

Rosenzweig, S. Human sexual autonomy as an evolutionary attainment, anticipating proceptive sex choice and idiodynamic bisexuality. In *Contemporary Sexual Behavior: Critical Issues in the 1970s* (J. Zubin and J. Money, eds.). Baltimore, Johns Hopkins University Press, 1973.

Rossi, A. S., and Rossi, P. E. Body time and social time: mood patterns by menstrual cycle phase and day of week. *Social Science Research* 6:273-308, 1977.

Roth vs. United States. 354 U.S. 476 (1957).

Sandler, M., and Gessa, G. L. (eds.). *Sexual Behavior: Pharmacology and Biochemistry.* New York, Raven Press, 1975.

Sara, V. R., Lazarus, L., Stuart, M. C., and King, T. Fetal brain growth: selective action by growth hormone. *Science* 186:446–447, 1974.

Schally, A. V. Aspects of hypothalamic regulation of the pituitary gland: Its implications for the control of reproductive processes. *Science* 202:18–28, 1978.

Schally, A. V., and Arimura, A. Physiology and nature of hypothalamic regulatory hormones. In *Clinical Neuroendocrinology* (L. Martini and G. M. Besser, eds.). New York, Academic Press, 1977.

Schlegel, R. J., and Gardner, L. I. Ambiguous and abnormal genitalia. In *Endocrine and Genetic Diseases of Childhood and Adolescence.* 2nd ed. (L. I. Gardner, ed.). Philadelphia, Saunders, 1975.

Schwarz, G. A. The orthostatic hypotension syndrome of Shy-Drager. *Archives of Neurology* 16:123–139, 1967.

Scott, J. P. Social genetics. *Behavior Genetics* 7:327–346, 1977.

Segraves, R. T. Pharmacological agents causing sexual dysfunction. *Journal of Sex and Marital Therapy* 3:157–176, 1977.

Sevely, J. L., and Bennett, J. W. Concerning female ejaculation and the female prostate. *Journal of Sex Research* 14:1–20, 1978.

Sexual Law Reporter. Amnesty International includes homosexuals as prisoners of conscience. *Sexual Law Reporter* 4:30, 1978.

Seyler, L. E., Jr., Canalis, E., Spare, S., and Reichlin, S. Abnormal gonadotropin secretory responses to LRH in transexual women after diethylstilbestrol priming. *Journal of Clinical Endocrinology and Metabolism* 47:176–183, 1978.

Shainess, N. A re-evaluation of some aspects of femininity through a study of menstruation: a preliminary report. *Comprehensive Psychiatry* 2:20–26, 1961.

Shepher, J. Mate selection among second generation Kibbutz adolescents and adults: incest avoidance and negative imprinting. *Archives of Sexual Behavior* 1:293–307, 1971.

Sherwin, R. V. *Compatible Divorce.* New York, Crown Publishers, 1969.

Shorey, H. H. *Animal Communication by Pheromones.* New York, Academic Press, 1976.

Shuster, R. H. Lekking behavior in Kafue lechwe. *Science* 192:1240–1242, 1976.

Silvers, W. K., and Wachtel, S. S. H-Y antigen: behavior and function. *Science* 195:956–960, 1977.

Silverstein, C., and White, E. *The Joy of Gay Sex.* New York, Crown Publishers, 1977.

Sisley, E., and Harris, B. *The Joy of Lesbian Sex.* New York, Crown Publishers, 1977.

Slob, A. K., Wiegand, S. J., Goy, R. W., and Robinson, J. A. Heterosexual interactions in laboratory-housed stumptail macaques (Macaca arctoides): observations during the menstrual cycle and after ovariectomy. *Hormones and Behavior* 10:193–211, 1978.

Smith, S. L., and Sauder, C. Food cravings, depression, and premenstrual problems. *Psychosomatic Medicine* 31:281–287, 1969.

Snyder, S. H. *Madness and the Brain.* New York, McGraw-Hill, 1974.

Snyder, S. H. Catecholamines, serotonin and histamine. In *Basic Neurochemistry* (G. J. Siegel, R. W. Albers, R. Katzman, and B. W. Agranoff, eds.). Boston, Little, Brown, 1976.

Spitz, C. J., Gold, A. R., and Adams, D. B. Cognitive and hormonal factors affecting coital frequency. *Archives of Sexual Behavior* 4:249–264, 1975.

Stenn, P. G., and Klinge, V. Relationship between the menstrual cycle and bodily activity in humans. *Hormones and Behavior* 3:297–305, 1972.

Stone, C. P. Sex drive. In *Sex and Internal Secretions.* 2nd ed. (E. Allen, C. H. Danforth and E. A. Doisy, eds.). Baltimore, Williams and Wilkins, 1939.

Story, N. L. Sexual dysfunction resulting from drug side effects. *Journal of Sex Research* 10:132-149, 1974.

Suomi, S. J. Factors affecting responses to social separation in rhesus monkeys. In *Animal Models in Human Psychobiology* (G. Serban and A. Kling, eds.). New York, Plenum, 1976.

Sutton-Smith, B., and Abrams, D. M. Psychosexual material in the stories told by children: the fucker. *Archives of Sexual Behavior* 7:521-543, 1978.

Tanner, J. M. *Growth at Adolescence*. 2nd ed. Oxford, Blackwell, 1962.

Tanner, J. M. Growth and endocrinology of the adolescent. In *Endocrine and Genetic Diseases of Childhood and Adolescence*. 2nd ed. (L. I. Gardner, ed.). Philadelphia, Saunders, 1975.

Taylor, G. R. *Sex in History: The Story of Society's Changing Attitudes to Sex Throughout the Ages*. New York, Harper Torchbooks, 1970.

Tennov, D. *Love and Limerence—The Experience of Being in Love*. New York, Stein and Day, 1979.

Thoman, E. B., and Gaulin-Kremer, E. Correlates of human parental behavior: a review. In *Handbook of Sexology* (J. Money and H. Musaph, eds.). New York, Excerpta Medica, 1977.

Tissot, S-A. *L'Onanisme, Dissertation sur les Maladies Productes par la Masturbation*. 7th ed. Lausanne, Franç. Grosset, 1781.

Tourney, G., Petrilli, A. J., and Hatfield, L. M. Hormonal relationships in homosexual men. *American Journal of Psychiatry* 132:288-290, 1975.

Trause, M. A., Kennell, J., and Klaus, M. Parental attachment behavior. In *Handbook of Sexology* (J. Money and H. Musaph, eds.). New York, Excerpta Medica, 1977.

Udry, J. R., and Morris, N. M. Distribution of coitus in the menstrual cycle. *Nature* 220:593-596, 1968.

Udry, J. R., and Morris, N. M. Effect of contraceptive pills on the distribution of sexual activity in the menstrual cycle. *Nature* 227:502-503, 1970.

Udry, J. R., Morris, N. M., and Waller, L. Effect of contraceptive pills on sexual activity in the luteal phase of the human menstrual cycle. *Archives of Sexual Behavior* 2:205-214, 1973.

Van Wyk, J. J., and Grumbach, M. M. Disorders of sex differentiation. In *Textbook of Endocrinology*. 5th ed. (R. H. Williams, ed.). Philadelphia, Saunders, 1974.

Vellay, P. *Childbirth without Pain*. New York, E. P. Dutton, 1960.

Vermeulen, A., Rubens, R., and Verdonck, L. Testosterone secretion and metabolism in male senescence. *Journal of Clinical Endocrinology and Metabolism* 34:730-735, 1972.

Verwoerdt, A., Pfeiffer, E., and Wang, H. S. Sexual behavior in senescence: I. Changes in sexual activity and interest in aging men and women. *Journal of Geriatric Psychiatry* 2:163-180, 1969.

Verwoerdt, A., Pfeiffer, E., and Wang, H. S. Sexual behavior in senescence: II. Patterns of sexual activity and interest. *Geriatrics* 24:137-154, 1969.

Visser, H. K. A. Some physiological and clinical aspects of puberty. *Archives of Disease in Childhood* 48:169-182, 1973.

Vogel, W., Klaiber, E. L., and Broverman, D. M. Roles of the gonadal steroid hormones in psychiatric depression in men and women. In *Progress in Neuropsychopharmacology, 1978*. New York, Pergamon, 1979. In press.

Wachtel, S. S. Genes and gender. *The Sciences*, pp. 16-17, 32-33, May/June, 1978.

Walster, E., and Walster, G. W. *A New Look at Love*. Reading, Mass., Addison-Wesley, 1978.

Waxman, S. *What Is a Girl? What Is a Boy?* Culver City, Calif., Peace Press, 1976.

Wetzel, R. D., Reich, T., and McClure, J. N., Jr. Phase of the menstrual cycle and self-referrals to a suicide prevention service. *British Journal of Psychiatry* 119:523-524, 1971.

Wikman, K. R. V. Die Einleitung der Ehe. *Acta Academiae Aboensis, Humaniora XI*, 1–384. Åbo, Åbo Akademi, 1937.

Williams, G., and Money, J. (eds.). *Traumatic Abuse and Neglect of Children at Home.* Baltimore, Johns Hopkins University Press, 1980.

Willson, J. R., Beecham, C. T., and Carrington, E. R. *Obstetrics and Gynecology.* 4th ed. St. Louis, C. V. Mosby, 1971.

Wolfgang, M. E. Pioneers in criminology: Cesare Lombroso (1835–1900). *Journal of Criminal Law, Criminology and Police Science* 52:361–391, 1961.

Yalow, R. S. Radioimmunoassay: a probe for the fine structure of biologic systems. *Science* 200:1236–1245, 1978.

Young, W. C. (ed.). *Sex and Internal Secretions.* 3rd ed., 2 vols. Baltimore, Williams and Wilkins, 1961.

Zelnik, M., and Kantner, J. F. Sexual and contraceptive experience of young unmarried women in the United States, 1976 and 1971. *Family Planning Perspectives* 9:55–71, 1977.

Zubin, J., and Money, J. (eds.). *Contemporary Sexual Behavior: Critical Issues in the 1970s.* Baltimore, Johns Hopkins University Press, 1973.

Name Index

243

Subject Index

Refer to the Table of Contents and the tables in the text as supplements to this index, also the Glossary and Bibliography.